The Brotherhood of Believers

An Ancient Tale
for the
Modern Truth-Seeker

Lisa
I am gratefull
for your friendship
consider my self lucky
to be your sister and
in Christ
love
Deb

Curt Simmons

The Brotherhood of Believers

An Ancient Tale
for the
Modern Truth-Seeker

Illumination Publishers International
ipi

The Brotherhood of Believers
Copyright © 2007 by Curt Simmons
ISBN: 0-9797886-2-5

Cover and Interior Design: Toney Mulhollan

Printed in the United States of America
09   08   07   1   2   3

Illumination Publishers International
www.ipibooks.com

ipi

Dedication

To my amazing wife, Patty.
Thanks for your heart, your humility,
your humor, your hard work
and always holding true to the sacred vows
you made to me twenty-five years ago.
If a monetary value could be placed upon
how blessed I have been to be married to you,
all the gold ever discovered in the world
would only be a poor beginning.

Contents

Introduction

My mother often reminds me that I had quite a vivid imagination as a child, and that I regularly entertained visitors to our home with one tall tale after another. While that imagination got me into plenty of trouble during the days of my youth and beyond, for the past 26 years since making a decision to follow Jesus, I've tried to use that cranial creativity for noble purposes and make the Scriptures come alive in my preaching, teaching and writing.

In 1995, in my first book, *The Unveiling*, I used that gift to help me dig deeper in exploring the nature of God. Ten years later, I put it to use again in *The Revealer*, trying my best to capture what it might have been like to be in the presence of Jesus as he walked the Earth in the first century. And I'm happy to say that I'm at it again! In my final installment of what I'm calling *The Trilogy of Testimony* (how God has made himself known throughout the ages), I've taken this tool of imagination to an entirely new level. In *The Brotherhood of Believers*, I have created an imaginary character, given him a name, a history, a family, a myriad of life experiences and challenges, a number of interactions with biblical figures, a pre- and post-salvation story and even a time of death. But while the main character, his family and their mingling with historical people are completely imaginary, the setting in which I have allowed them to live and breathe is anything but—the dawning of Christianity and the incredibly exciting times of spiritual revival and renewal described in great detail in the book of Acts.

I'm quite confident individuals like my imaginary friend really existed in the first century and would have quite the stories to tell if given the opportunity. This book is an example of what I believe one of those stories would entail, and an opportunity for you, the reader, to get a better sense of what day-to-day Christianity might have been like back then when disciples of Jesus were being used by God to saturate their world with the truths of the gospel.

I completely understand the potential dangers in writing a book like this. And I'm also very aware of the clear warnings about adding to or subtracting from the truths of God found in the Bible. So to counter those dangers, everything you're about to read is built upon a totally safe scriptural foundation. And in keeping with the desire to be completely biblical in my approach, I have included hundreds of scriptures for you to ponder, and these can be located at the very end of the book.

As I do with all my students and readers, I urge you to dig deep into these and other passages to see if what I am saying is indeed true. Better yet, if you desire greater evidence for my insights into first-century Christianity, let me encourage you to carefully study the Scriptures, beginning in the Gospel of Matthew and reading all the way to the closing admonitions found in the book of Revelation, and watch the story unfold for yourself. No, you won't discover my imaginary friend and his family if you choose to take that route. But I'm certain you will locate proof as to the strong possibility for the existence of people who were very much like them. And you would discover that what these fictional characters experienced is nothing far-fetched or hyper-spiritual compared to what other members of the first-century church lived out as well.

I have decided not to include any references to these passages throughout this presentation, because I thought it might take away from the flow of the story. But whatever you do with this book, please don't ignore the verses I've left for you to consider. Read them, contemplate them carefully and ready yourself to put them into practice in the same way my imaginary friend did some two thousand years ago.

While I urge you to remember that "this is a story, this is only a story", I'm also of the firm belief that it will inspire you to cling to the greatest non-fiction story ever told—the story of God coming to visit mankind in the person of Jesus, giving each of us the opportunity to experience salvation in his blood and setting up a one-of-a-kind kingdom that would never end, the Brotherhood of Believers. My fervent prayer is that my imagination will lead you to a deeper appreciation and admiration for God, the one who can give every last one of us far more than we could ever ask or imagine. And I truly hope it will do for you, while reading it, exactly what it did for me while writing it—provide a sober examination of your life and doctrine and an opportunity to change anything that might be keeping you from pleasing God in either area.

Special thanks to my publisher, Toney Mulhollan, for his willingness to take on yet another of my projects, and for his ongoing commitment to my writing ministry. I'm grateful as well for Elizabeth Thompson, who did a fantastic job of editing this book, not just in a grammatical sense, but even more so with her great insights and comments about staying true to both the historical setting and biblical text. And my heartfelt thanks to so many of you who, through the years, have given me the encouragement to keep on writing and the help I needed to stay faithful to serving God with all of my heart, soul, mind and strength.

– Curt Simmons
Lisle, Illinois
Email: curt@curtsbooks.com
csimmons@chnts.net

Chapter One:
Welcome to Paradise

Greetings! Welcome to Paradise. My name is Jacob, and I'm humbled and honored to have this opportunity to tell you my story. From among the many residents in my community, I've been selected to pass along some vital information to you, spiritual truths which are essential for you to grasp.

You're probably aware that we Paradise residents aren't able to leave the premises here and come visit your neck of the woods. I admit most of us have felt that we could do some good on your turf should we be allowed to spend a little bit of time there. However, we realize that the good angels have done a fine job of assisting humans up to this point, and we certainly understand we couldn't match their efforts. And even if one of us did come back from the dead to appear to your generation, our great leader has often remarked that this wouldn't change the heart of anyone who didn't already have the desire to serve and honor him. Besides, those who possess that inner longing for God don't feel the need for further proof from the great beyond. They believe without seeing, and nothing brings a bigger smile to our leader's face than watching them act out their faith in this manner.

I hope you're one of those unique people. If so, the time you spend hearing my story will likely serve to bolster the convictions you already possess. If not, then it is the hope of the entire Paradise population that you will allow my testimony to cause you to reexamine your spiritual life. May it be an opportunity for you to straighten out any crooked thinking you might have in regard to what living a life for God entails, and may it inspire you in your efforts to serve him to the best of your ability.

You've entered what's called the Testimony Center, a favorite location of many of my fellow residents and the place we often congregate to share the amazing stories of how we came to salvation and how we spent our time as followers of Christ. Of all the places to gather in Paradise, it's perhaps the most encouraging, though the other spots we visit regularly are awe-inspiring as well.

To give you a better idea of what I'm talking about, here's a sampling of some of the places where we spend our time—luxurious, open-air fellowship centers where the redeemed have opportunities to meet with their fellow keepers of the faith.

The Gratitude Center is where we spend time thanking the people who helped us in our spiritual walk on Earth. First-time visitors to this room are always caught a bit off-guard when they realize just how many people God used in a collective effort to keep them on the straight and narrow.

The Laughter Center is where we reminisce about the many moments on Earth when it looked as though Satan had gotten the best of us, only to see God prevail in the end. The man best known to most people as "the thief on the cross" spends the greatest amount of time there, sharing more humbly and joyfully than anyone about his understanding and appreciation of that subject matter.

In the Praise Center, we spend time singing hymns and spiritual songs and sharing with each other just how amazing God was and still is in our lives. And best of all, there's no choir practice required! Perfect harmony is something we experience in Paradise in more ways than just our relationships with each other.

The Replay Center is where, on a screen the size of Mount Rushmore, we're able to view everything from the creation of the world to the crumbling of the walls of Jericho; from the sun standing still at Gibeon to the Son standing steady at Golgotha.

On entering the Heroes Center, we meet biblical figures like Moses, Meshach and Mary; Esther, Elijah and Ezra; and Noah, Nathan and Nehemiah. All of them feel extremely humbled that a room has been dedicated in their honor, and they constantly remind us that anyone who stays true to God until death is a real hero, regardless of whether or not their name appears in the pages of Scripture.

In the Relaxation Center, we simply kick back and soak in the wonderful reality of life in a perfect place like Paradise. It's such a popular spot that the average length of visit there is a little more than a year.

And the Jesus Center is where we have the unbelievable opportunity to spend time alone with the Lord, letting him know just how we feel about him and listening to him share how he feels about us.

All these fellowship centers are usually packed around the clock, and some even require reservations to enter, but no one minds waiting, since time isn't an issue around here. Any time spent waiting in Paradise is just another opportunity to meet someone new and develop another eternal relationship. None of us can really decide which of these situations is more encouraging—the actual time spent in the various fellowship centers or the magnificent moments we enjoy before and after our visits to each!

The trips we make between visits to the various fellowship centers are always astounding as we take in more of the indescribable beauty of our new home. The beaches in Paradise make the pristine beaches of Hawaii and Aruba look like nothing more than backyard, above-ground swimming pools! The countless trees we marvel at each day are greater than anything you could ever imagine, making your California Redwoods seem like well-worn toothpicks. The stunning mountain views cause every human here who ever conquered Mt. Everest to wonder if their six-mile journey up the earthly slope was merely a waste of time. The crystalline streams running through Paradise are soothing to the eyes and ears, more peaceful than any earthly getaway of the grandest proportion. And the skies display a softer, yet deeper blue than any hue seen on Earth, a tint that crayon makers will never be able to reproduce.

I could continue with my description, but I believe you get the point by now. Paradise is beyond postcard-perfect, and should you have the privilege of coming here after your time on Earth, you'll spend the first few weeks just shaking your head at the amazing wonders of God.

Now look what I've done: I got so caught up in the grandeur and glory of Paradise that I almost forgot to finish my description of the Testimony Center! But I hope you enjoyed my digression nonetheless.

Here in the Testimony Center, we relive the stories of how God saved us during our days on Earth. We celebrate the ways we all came to be a part God's family, and marvel at the complex plans he designed in order to win each of our hearts. This fellowship center usually boasts an overflowing crowd, as people just can't seem to get enough of hearing about all God did to get his children to Paradise. If one of us spends a full day there, we might hear a dozen or so stories—and just one of these stories is more than enough to convince anyone that God is all about love and all about giving every person the best possible chance of arriving here safely.

But for the next little while, the crowds will clear and the Testimony Center will be empty—except for me and you. And even though residents here are a bit bummed that the salvation storytelling will be put on temporary hold, they all agree that having you around for a brief while to listen to my story is well worth the wait before it reopens for regular business. We all believe that telling you my story will help you get here someday so that we can hear you tell yours!

I wish I could tell you that you'll be given a little vision of Paradise while we're together in the Testimony Center, something similar to what a few privileged human beings were granted in the past. But I'm afraid you'll be hearing a whole lot more than you'll be seeing. Actually, you won't even get a glimpse of the beautiful setting here, but I hope what you're about to hear will bring you one step closer to seeing Paradise for yourself one day.

Feel free to stay here with me for as long as you want. I have plenty of energy to tell you the entire story at one setting, but I do understand your need for things like sleep and showing up for work. However, your time in the Testimony Center will be concluded when you hear the final words of my story. I'm confident that every second, every minute and every hour you devote to hearing my story will be time well spent. But as of right now, you're not welcome to stay for good. Not that we wouldn't want you to stay, it's just that only God can decide as to if and when you'll be welcomed back here permanently. Oh, he wants you here desperately—that point has never been in question. The determining factor is your willingness to answer his calling for your life.

Although I hope my story will serve as a major inspiration in your life, it's really nothing special or out of the ordinary. Actually, anybody here in Paradise could have been chosen for this honor, as all of our stories possess a similar theme and tone. Only the names, dates and locations are different. That's because we all followed the same leader and we all knew the same expectations he had called us to embrace. So what you're about to hear isn't the tale of some superhuman member of God's redeemed people through the years, someone who somehow managed to reach the upper echelons of spirituality. That's definitely not why I've been asked to share my story with you. No, I was just one of the gang. That's how we saw it back then, and that's definitely how we still see it here in Paradise.

As usual, the decision that allowed for me to share my story with you was made without issue. You see, where I live, things like envy, jealousy and selfish ambition are all things of the past. Everyone in my community gladly put their personal desires on hold in order for me to be selected. In fact, they wouldn't have it any other way, and each of them is thrilled that I was granted the opportunity to fulfill this crucial role.

Personal desires haven't been an issue for quite some time for me and the others in my community, because now we have everything we've always hoped for or wanted. Actually, we have immeasurably more than we ever imagined we'd have, and at times, we simply have to remind ourselves and each other that this is real and we're not just dreaming.

While we're excited about our present position in life, everyone in my community is also somewhat sobered and saddened, as we've become more aware of the situation that you and your fellow Earth-dwellers find yourself in at the present time—though our sadness hasn't resulted in tears. Our decision to open up the Testimony Center to the general public is a first, and we've been told that it will probably never happen again. You might think that this one-shot challenge would make me a bit nervous, but we're all certain that we'll accomplish our goal. And somehow the pressure to succeed doesn't bother me at all. As a matter of fact, nothing really bothers me any more, and that's what makes living in my community such an absolute blast! And as far as this mission being successful or not—well, from our perspective, everything that originates from here is a complete success, no matter how it's viewed by those on the outside.

I must say it's been a very long time since I've had the chance to chat with someone in your community. I haven't been keeping very close track, but one of my friends tells me that I've been here for about two thousand years. My first response when I heard that figure was to tell him that he must be pulling my leg, because I thought it was probably much closer to five hundred or a thousand. But you know what they say—time flies when you're having fun!

Since we're separated by so many years, I've asked our most honorable leader to help me be as relatable as possible and to give me just the right words to say. He said not to worry because, even though it's been a long time in human terms, and though technology and modes of travel are so very far advanced beyond our humble, first-century standards, humans really haven't changed that much since I walked the planet. They still have the same problems, insecurities and gaping holes in their hearts, not to mention the same sins, and they still need him and his solutions to rectify their inadequacies.

The Brotherhood of Believers

While I suppose you could say that I'm not one of you, I was definitely a full-fledged member of your earthly community at one time. Even more importantly, I was a member of the Brotherhood of Believers in its early years. And the term "Brotherhood of Believers" was a most appropriate one for what I experienced. Even though a number of my blood relatives never became members of the Brotherhood, my time in the first-century church was truly a family experience. We were as close as any earthly family could have been, often even closer. We laughed together, cried together, worked together, ate together, prayed together, fasted together, shared our faith together, played together, grew together, worshiped together and, yes, even suffered together. That's a lot more "togetherness" than most physical families shared in my day, and I'm guessing you could say the same thing about most families in the twenty-first century.

Not that we were down on our physical families or didn't desire spending any time with them. Quite the contrary! Many of us developed much closer bonds with our families after we became disciples, both with those who eventually became our spiritual brothers and sisters in

Christ, and even with those who didn't. But it was always especially encouraging and exciting whenever a member of someone's physical family also became a Christian. We called that a double-dip of pleasure, bringing nearly as much excitement to the family member witnessing the baptism as the one being baptized. But for those believers whose families rejected their faith, and for those who were disowned by the members of their physical family, the Brotherhood was an amazing place of refuge and a special gift of God. Without the incredible bond from the relationships in the Brotherhood, many of those same people would have never gone the distance in keeping their faith.

The term believer also was an appropriate word for who we were in the first century. But what we clung to was much more than mere mental assent about a few spiritual truths. We really believed who we followed, and we really believed in the cause he had called us to embrace. We believed in the total humanity and total divinity of Jesus, regardless of the difficulty we sometimes felt in understanding it completely ourselves or in explaining it to an unbeliever. We believed in his perfect record of righteousness and his powerful resurrection from the dead. We believed only two options existed for life after death: A literal heaven and hell, where people would receive their final punishment or reward. We believed in the absolute truth of the Scriptures and that we would be judged by our response to the commandments of God and his Son Jesus Christ. We believed that people had to make a personal response to Jesus in order to be saved, and that no individual could rely upon their religious heritage or their popularity among their fellow man to enjoy that special privilege. We believed that we were called to work for God and to work with God at the prodding of his Spirit to give every human being on the planet an opportunity to come to Christ. We believed that we were called to be deeply involved in each other's lives and that we really were our brother's keeper. And we believed that we needed each other's encouragement and admonition to be our best for God.

Yes, the Brotherhood of Believers was quite a place to call home in the first century, and my hope is that by the end of my presentation, you will long to be a part of it and do everything you can to find the kind of faith and fellowship that I enjoyed for so many years.

More Than I Ever Imagined

But while the Brotherhood of Believers was the best place to be on Earth, it was and still is a mere drop in the eternal bucket of blessings that God has in store for you. Yes, as I have already tried to tell you, right now I'm in a much better place than you could ever imagine. I've been enjoying Paradise and its glorious perks now for nearly two millennia, but there was a time when I faced some of the exact same trials and tribulations that you're being called to endure today. It's not easy, is it? But believe me—it's totally worth it to keep on fighting. I wish I could adequately explain to you how much it's worth it to remain faithful to God, but our distinguished leader says I'm not allowed to give too much away in that area. (What I already told you was about the limit of what can be described concerning the pleasures of Paradise.) He reminds us quite often that it's every individual's personal responsibility to trust that the Bible's revelations of the next life are indeed true.

During my time in the Brotherhood, a number of us tried to get Lazarus to offer up some "inside information" about the afterlife. And while he was willing to oblige us on a few occasions, he was also incredibly tongue-tied whenever he tried to paint a picture for us about just how incredible his four-day stint was in Paradise. Back then, I didn't fully appreciate what he was doing his best to describe, but I sure do now! And the apostle Paul wasn't even permitted to elaborate about the time God allowed him to temporarily check out Paradise. But we knew it had to be great! He always said that even just the sounds of Paradise were enough to motivate him to make sure he got there permanently, and also enough for God to humble him with a thorn in his flesh so he wouldn't become prideful about his temporary visit. When I first heard of Paul's vision, I remember thinking that, if the sounds were that amazing in Paradise, I could only imagine what the sights must be like! Well, now I can tell you that those thoughts were right on target, and I'm so glad I brought them to mind on a regular basis while I was living in your community. You, too, would do well to think in this manner.

Time Is of the Essence

You're probably wondering why we believe that now is the ideal time to allow earthly visitors to enter the Testimony Center. It's simple, really. Some recent move-ins to our community convinced us that this effort is absolutely necessary if there's any chance of a population explosion here. Billions of people on Earth feel confident they're coming to join our jubilant celebration, but most of them are deceived. The concerned newcomers to Paradise said that the state of the world is worse than it's ever been, and our leader (who we're pretty convinced had the original idea all along) has decided to go ahead and see how this effort will be received.

Those of us here want nothing more than to see the population of Paradise dramatically increase! The more the better! These newcomers' passion for you and the others in your community has been amazing, and our leader was quite moved to allow their request to become a reality. That's one of the traits of our leader that has most impressed me since I arrived here—he cares so deeply about people and will do anything to make those of us here and those of you there as happy as possible. Of course, for the most part, I knew that was true back when I lived in your community. It's just that now I see how little I really understood then about his unconditional love and selfless nature.

I want you to know that I'm thrilled to spend this time with you, and to move in to your space (your heart and mind) for a while and talk to you about what I can remember. I hope it will help you to better know where you need to go in your spiritual life. Although I now reside in a much better place than you do at the moment, I hope you never lose sight of the fact that I know where you're coming from completely. And because of that truth, I think the two of us should get along just fine.

One of the Originals

Yes, I was there when it all started. I saw God's church get built from the ground floor up, and it rested upon the most solid foundation ever known. I was privileged to be one of the first three thousand souls to have our names recorded in the Lamb's Book of Life under the new covenant, just a few short hours after Peter challenged and inspired us with his heart-cutting sermon about two thousand years ago. And for the next number of years, I experienced what you would have to call "history in the making."

Though you can't read about me anywhere in the biblical text, I was there. You might say I was a "behind-the-scenes" guy, but I was an active member of God's church in century number one. I'm here simply to tell you what I remember about those days and to encourage you to honestly compare what you're involved in right now to what I experienced back then. No, I'm not here to judge you! As a matter of fact, I don't know anything about you other than the fact you're alive and that you have a heart that's inclined to seek out spiritual truths because you've made it this far in listening to my story. And besides, a "less information, less judging" approach by me was our leader's plan all along. He's always been a whole lot more into saving people than judging them, so he expects nothing less than that from those in our community. My job is to relay the undeniable facts of first-century Christianity, not to put you on the defensive. I hope that you'll evaluate your present lifestyle and your church community and make any necessary changes to fit the pattern presented to you by those of us who were privileged to be first-century lovers of God.

Strategies

Before going any further, however, I need to let you know how important it will be for you to answer a few questions while listening to my story. As a matter of fact, asking questions throughout my entire presentation will be one of my main ways of helping you to evaluate your current walk with God. (We'll talk about some of the reasons for that in just a little while.)

As you listen to my story, take some time to answer these tough questions: If you call yourself a Christian, is the life you're experiencing right now similar to what I experienced in the beginning days of Christianity? Is the church you're a member of today following in the footsteps of the one I was blessed to be a member of in the first century? I would also humbly ask you to put away any pride, fear or defensiveness that might well up in your heart at times so that you may answer those two questions honestly. Do it just as if your eternal destiny depended on it and you weren't concerned about how your friends, your family or your fellowship of believers might respond to similar questions.

Due to where I live, it won't be necessary for you to question my honesty. You see, it's impossible for me to tell a lie. But if you still doubt my presentation and desire to double-check its veracity, my good friend Luke wrote a couple of great books that are at your disposal and those would undoubtedly be the best places to start. Besides being a participant in about half of the world-changing events he recorded in his second book, Luke also spent many a long day interviewing people from the Brotherhood of Believers in order to accurately record the events he didn't witness firsthand.

So after we spend a brief amount of time talking about why I'm about to ask you more questions than you've probably been asked in quite some time, join me on a most exciting journey back in time, to the time when God shook the foundations of the world, establishing a powerful kingdom that would never be destroyed—the Brotherhood of Believers.

Chapter Two:
Questions and Answers

As I stated in my introduction, I don't have any personal information about you or the church you may call home. I do, however, know that answering some probing questions will change your life, if you're willing to answer them honestly. And I also know that interrogations of a spiritual nature have been one of God's greatest methods for reaching into the hearts of men and women throughout the centuries. So before I share my story about the Brotherhood of Believers, and before I ask you a myriad of questions about your personal life and church family, let's do a little overview of how questions were used in the Scriptures to bring people to a deeper awareness of God and his calling.

Old Testament Interrogations

Let's begin with the books you refer to as the Old Testament. (In my day, there was no *Old* Testament, because the *New* Testament was still being written!) The first question God ever asked of man was quite simple, and one to which God no doubt already knew the answer. Yet he still asked it, not for his benefit, but for that of Adam and Eve: *"Where are you?"* It was a question that encouraged openness. It was a question designed to bring Adam and Eve to God and to stop their steady and dangerous move away from him. It forced them to deal with the biggest issues at hand—their sin and seduction by the serpent's schemes. It set them up for an ultimate confession session, one they desperately needed in order to experience the amazing grace of God and to be better equipped to resist the clever and cunning enemy who was still lurking nearby.

And God asks a similar question of you today: *"Where are you?"* What is going on in your life at the moment? Have you moved away from God instead of closer to him, and, if so, why? Is there something you need to be open and honest about right now? Yes, God's question is a tough one. But if you answer it sincerely and honestly, it's a question that will usher you into the glorious grace of God and help you to more fully appreciate how much he loves you and wants to be the guiding force in your life, despite the sins you may have committed against him.

The second question in the Scriptures is one that deals with our attitudes, and especially with our uncanny ability to blame God or the guy next to us for what we don't have that we think we should have, or what we do have that we think we shouldn't: *"Why are you angry? Why is your face downcast?"* It was a crucial question posed to an upset and unsettled Cain, one that gave him a golden opportunity to avoid the evil deed that Satan had already planted in his heart—harming his brother Abel. As you probably know, the ending of Cain's story wasn't so good. But that wasn't God's fault. With that challenging question, God tried to get Cain to deal with the blame-shifting and bellyaching going on in his heart before they led to violent behavior.

And God is asking you a very similar question today about your state of mind, your relationships and your feelings about the things which have transpired throughout your life. If you're angry about something or angry with someone, why do you suppose that's the case? If you're downcast about something, how do you suppose you arrived at that saddened state?

So if I should ask you any similar questions during my presentation, please realize that, through me, God is simply doing what he can to ward off the evil that Satan no doubt wants to plant in your heart. And he wants to give you the best possible chance of staying out of trouble during your remaining days.

I find it interesting that, in just the first four chapters of the Bible, we see God asking two of the most important questions man has ever or will ever be asked. And that's because God deeply cares about our lives. He uses these questions to give us the greatest shot at getting it right. But the questions don't stop there. He continues to probe the hearts of men and women throughout the Old Testament, calling his people to deal with their hearts and their biggest challenges through his interrogations.

Here are just a few more examples:

To help ninety-nine-year-old Abraham and ninety-year-old Sarah believe that he could enable them to bring a baby boy into the world at their outrageous ages, God said, *"Is anything too hard for the Lord?"*

To expose the lack of obedience a prideful King Saul had just displayed in his half-hearted efforts to annihilate an evil nation, God introduced truth to him through the prophet Samuel by saying, *"What then is this bleating of sheep in my ears?"*

To drive home the need for a wimpy and way-too-accommodating King Ahab to get some guts and take a stand for truth, God asked him, through the prophet Elijah, *"How long will you waver between two opinions?"*

To help Job realize his steady decline of righteous thinking, God came on the scene and posed a few questions that Job knew he had no business answering:

"Where were you when I laid the earth's foundation?"
"Who has the wisdom to count the clouds?"
"Who has a claim against me that I must pay?"

These were just three of the dozens of questions God asked of Job, all designed to bring him to a point of deep repentance where he could accept God's sovereignty in all situations. Job did repent shortly thereafter, an intelligent move that paved the way for many wonderful days during his remaining time on Earth.

David posed a crucial question to himself (and ultimately to his readers) about a vital part of our spiritual lives—a question that you would do well to ask yourself on a daily basis before you meander into a world full of sexual impropriety and deviation: *"How can a young man keep his way pure?"* He asked himself another important question that reminded him how to view monumental victories and resist the temptation to think he could win future battles without divine intervention, saying, *"Where does my help come from?"*

Solomon spoke the words of God to all mankind, warning us to consider the rocky bottom of sin before diving in head first, asking, *"Can a man scoop fire into his lap without his clothes being burned?"*

Many well-known and lesser-known prophets also did their part to ask the questions God wanted his people to answer, and as always, the questions were designed to get people moving in the right direction:

"And what does the Lord require of you?" This was a great question posed by Micah for those who felt as though they were walking on the correct road and closing in on their ultimate destination, when in actuality they had strayed from the intended path many miles earlier.

"Is it a time for you yourselves to be living in paneled houses, while this house remains in ruins?" This pointed question was designed to drive out the materialism, complacency and worldliness in every listener's heart, and a question that you should ask yourself about your role in building up the Brotherhood of Believers.

Questions Jesus Asked

But the questions didn't stop with the Old Testament Scriptures. Jesus was the master of asking the most appropriate questions at the best possible times. His questions, too, were designed to give people the greatest chance of doing what was right, thereby either gaining or securing their relationship with God.

To help his disciples tackle their tendency to fret and be faithless, he asked them an insightful question after describing the importance of every single sparrow on the planet: *"Are you not much more valuable than they?"* And to close his thoughts concerning the dreaded diseases of worry and why me?, he asked another simple but sensational question: *"Who of you by worrying can add a single hour to his life?"* Wouldn't those be great questions to ask yourself and your fellow believers?

To help the legalistic Pharisees come to grips with how far they, as God's sheep, had fallen into a spiritual pit, Jesus challenged their heartless interpretation of Scripture with this question: *"If any of you has a sheep and it falls into a pit on the Sabbath, will you not take hold of it and lift it out?"*

To show his twelve apostles that they needed to grow in their faith, Jesus often asked these two questions: *"Why did you doubt?"* and *"Do you still not understand?"*

And to indicate that a personal faith was needed rather than a popular one, Jesus asked, *"But what about you? Who do you say I am?"*

Jesus often posed questions to his detractors, doing all he could to show them that the most obvious and sensible solutions to their problems with him and his "strange" teachings were right at their fingertips:

"Why are you thinking these things?"

"Have you never read in the Scriptures....?"

"What is written in the Law? How do you read it?"

"John's baptism—where did it come from? Was it from heaven, or from men?"

To help his disciples deal with their most recent conflict with one another, an issue that no doubt would have continued without this line of questioning, Jesus boldly interrupted their secret competition by asking, *"What were you arguing about on the road?"*

To help people appreciate the deepest levels of God's love and his constant work on their behalf, Jesus asked, *"Which of you fathers, if your son asks for a fish, will give him a snake instead?"*

To make sure his disciples really understood the significance of the foot-washing they had just received from him, Jesus asked, *"Do you understand what I have done for you?"*

And perhaps most probing of all his interrogations, Jesus asked Peter an important question, one that you also must be asked in regard to your level of commitment to the Lord: *"Simon son of John, do you truly love me?"*

I realize that hearing these questions all at once can be a bit overwhelming. And if probing questions like these were asked of you constantly, it would likely hurt your faith rather than help it. But if these questions were asked at the appropriate times, and if you decided to answer them honestly, think about how much you could strengthen your faith and your relationship with God. So take some time to go back and review Jesus' questions, and see if they don't take you to a greater level of spirituality when you answer them in a truthful manner.

Questions for the Brotherhood

But the questions didn't stop with Jesus. His followers rightly reasoned that if Jesus used questions as an important part of his ministry, then they should employ the same strategy with the Brotherhood of Believers, as well as with those who were thinking about possible membership.

The greatest question a non-believer could ever ask is recorded in the book of Acts: *"What must I do to be saved?"* But this is only a good question if a person is willing to accept the answers that God and his leaders gave in the first century.

And the questions asked by the writers of the New Testament letters were all used by God to urge disciples to deal with their struggles or sins in a proper manner.

The letter to the Romans posed numerous challenging questions. And for centuries, God has used Paul's thought-provoking queries to refine the hearts of Christians around the world: *"You who say that people should not commit adultery, do you commit adultery?"* That question sure forces a disciple of Christ to spend a whole lot more time working on their own weaknesses than pointing them out in others.

"Shall we go on sinning so that grace may increase?" That question is great to ask someone in the Brotherhood who you sense might be abusing the grace of God or not appreciating it as they should, or whenever your own conscience begins to dull.

Paul also asked this all-important question of his Roman readers: *"If God is for us, who can be against us?"* That would be a tremendous scripture to cite whenever you're faced with personal persecution or tempted to throw your own pity-party in honor of the seemingly negative situations in your life.

Paul continued his questioning strategy in his other letters. He asked the Corinthian church a number of important questions, as they were often tempted to conform to the worldly environment in which they lived and worked. *"Is Christ divided? Was Paul crucified for you? Were you baptized into the name of Paul?"* With these powerful opening questions, Paul attacked the worldly wisdom of members there who were siding with their favorite preachers (all of whom were completely unified) based on things such as speaking ability, style of leadership and scholastic background, and even creating divisions over those preferences. After all, when has the eloquence of a presentation ever been more important to God than the ears of those hearing it? And where in the Scriptures do we discover that less-educated men of God typically offered up less valuable points to ponder than those with a scholastic pedigree?

"Why not rather be wronged? Why not rather be cheated?" Both of these excellent questions addressed those who dared to sue a fellow member of the Brotherhood. As if those actions would produce any confidence in a lost person's mind about how joining the Brotherhood would be a welcomed relief from life in the typical dog-eat-dog world. As if that would bring honor and glory to the God who commanded his subjects to keep their focus on forgiveness and find ways to reach peaceful solutions at all cost.

"Are all apostles? Are all prophets? Are all teachers? Do all work miracles?" What terrific questions for those in Corinth who were arrogantly thinking "my gift's better than your gift." And what great questions for anyone who struggles to believe that they have an important role in building God's kingdom, be they a baker of the communion bread, a regular babysitter for the married couple who needs a night out or the brother who cleans the sanctuary and fellowship hall after a Sunday morning worship service.

Do you see how useful questions are in bringing about a righteous life? Do you see why my leader has directed me to make sure I give you a number of them to chew on throughout my presentation? I could continue to tell you about the questions Peter, James and John asked in their epistles, but I trust you've gotten the point by now—

questions are extremly useful in your pursuit of a strong spiritual life.

Personal Interrogations

I was asked lots of questions during my time in the Brother-hood of Believers, a few of which made me somewhat uncomfortable or highly uncomfortable on occasion. And you will do well to be asked (and also to ask others) some of the same questions. Here's a small sampling:

How are you feeling about your walk with God lately? How is everything going with your marriage and kids? How has your battle against lustful thoughts been going this week? Is there anything you need to be open about before I leave? Do you have any pressing needs that I can help you with at this time? Is there anybody in the church you need to talk with in order to stay unified in your heart with them? How are things going at work? How is your faith? How is it going in your outreach to the lost? How are your times of prayer and reading the Scriptures going? Would you like to get together and pray sometime soon? Do you understand what God is expecting you to do? How are your efforts going in responding to the needs of the poor? Are you feeling discouraged about anything lately, and if so, how can I help you find encouragement? Do you feel any bitterness or resentment about anything that's happened recently? How do you see Satan attacking you lately?

These were just some of the questions I was asked during my time in the Brotherhood, and I can't tell you how grateful I am for the people who asked them of me, despite the various levels of discomfort I experienced. I'm here in Paradise today as a direct result of those meaningful interrogations. And I pray that my questions will be used by God in the very same way with you, and that one day we can reminisce about them together in Paradise.

So with that in mind, and with the understanding that I would like you to especially slow down when you come to the question sections of my presentation, let's begin. Let me tell you my story, a story that will help to answer some of the most important questions of all: Does God really love me? What does he expect of me? Is he really working on my behalf? And will he go to any and all lengths to give me the very best possible chance to make it to heaven?

Chapter Three:
The Worst Day of My Life

It really was the worst day of my life. The day my father passed away was probably the saddest day of my life, and my mother's passing a few months later was similar in the emotional despair it wrought. But this day brought about the deepest emotions of every kind and painfully put my life in front of a full-length, squeaky-clean mirror that showed me a clear reflection of my pitiful spiritual condition.

I decided to get up a bit earlier than usual that morning. We had a few relatives staying with us from out of town for the Passover Feast, and we were a little short on a few of the essentials that would keep all of our stomachs satisfied for the duration of the busy holiday weekend. So about an hour after sunrise, I ventured out to get what I thought would be a head start on most of the other shoppers in Jerusalem that day, hoping to get to the marketplace before it became a human rat race as it usually did during the Passover celebrations. My beautiful wife, Rachel (yes, I guess you could say we were destined to be together with names like Jacob and Rachel!), and my three children—Joseph, who was six, Miriam, who was five, and Benjamin, the youngest at three—were all still in bed. My older sister, Deborah, her husband, Ethan, and their two children were asleep as well. They were all pretty exhausted after making their yearly trek to our great city from their hometown of Joppa to participate in the holiday that many of my fellow Israelites considered the most significant of our nation's three annual celebrations.

Much to my surprise, the streets weren't anywhere near desolate. As a matter of fact, they were busier than ever for that time of the day. I was curious as to what was leading to all the commotion, so I asked someone if they knew what had caused so many people to get out of bed at such an early hour, and with so much energy. It was then that I heard that Jesus had finally been arrested and would likely be brought to trial and executed soon thereafter, perhaps even that very same day.

The Jesus I Had Come to Hate

I knew a little bit about Jesus, and most of what I knew didn't do much to endear him to me. Personally, I didn't have much respect for the man on a secular level. You see, I, too, was the son of a carpenter, the grandson of a carpenter, even the great-grandson of a carpenter. And while I had hoped that I could find a way out of being the next son to "gladly" and "gratefully" take over the family business, I had given up on that dream long before I could become bold enough to think about pressing the issue with my father. My father took deep pride in his role as the son of a carpenter, so I knew he would fight against my wishes with every fiber of his being until he had won. So from the time I was about twelve years old, I was there in the carpentry shop. Throughout most of every working day, I labored alongside my father, learning the tricks of the trade. And at the age of seventeen, I was thrust into the owner and management role when my father became ill and passed away about three months later.

I knew from other people that Jesus had chosen not to follow in the footsteps of his carpenter father, and I had assumed that his decision was all about taking the easier and more selfish path in order to realize his own desires and dreams. And, I was told, he even had the audacity to justify his dismissal from that important responsibility by saying he had to be about his father's business—meaning that God had somehow personally delivered him the message that it was okay to become an itinerant preacher instead. Yet wasn't this the same God who penned the fifth commandment and expected his followers to show honor to their fathers? No wonder Jesus was going to end up having his life cut short, I thought. How could he let his father down like that? And how could he force his three younger brothers to feel even greater pressure to help out the family while he went out to do his own thing? I hadn't put my younger brother in that predicament. And why did he get to do what he really wanted to do, while I was forced to adhere to the societal standards of our day and learn the trade of my father?

While those were a few of my personal issues with Jesus, I (along with countless other Jews) had many other problems with his personal life and his ministry approach as a so-called preacher of the truths of God. The few times he had visited Jerusalem, he always seemed to cause an incredible stir—whether it was with his terrible temple-tantrums that cost the local merchants a bundle of potential profits and caused the Jewish leaders to seethe with anger, or by always making the leaders of our religion so upset and nervous about his apparent intentions to alter our sacred laws, overthrow the Roman government and establish his own kingdom. Most of my countrymen thought it was best for him to die before he got too out of hand and the Romans started coming down hard on the rest of us as they had done in the recent past when a few radical zealots employed a similar takeover strategy.

So on that early morning, hearing news of Jesus' upcoming trial, and especially the possibility of his imminent death, was no huge deal to me. It was a good thing, I concluded. I didn't realize at the time how little actual truth I knew about the man, nor did I know that I would come face to face with him in only a matter of hours.

Like the majority of my people, I thought Jesus was way off-base, to say the least. Sure, a small number of Jews had become his disciples in the three years since he had begun his new kingdom campaign, but it seemed like most of them were people who didn't have a good education, or lacked a thorough understanding of our sacred laws and traditions, or had nowhere to go in life—and some of his followers fell into all three categories! And those of us in Jerusalem were pretty familiar with the few nut cases who had tried in the recent past to gather followers and take on our religious leaders or the ruling body of Rome. Some even had the audacity to claim that they were the promised Messiah who was prophesied in the Holy Scriptures, the one we had been anxiously awaiting for hundreds of years. But none of those seriously misguided individuals were still around to pose a threat. They were either in jail or dead, and none of their followers—the same people who were so fired up to join them during their attempted rise to power—were anywhere to be found after their leaders were locked up or laid to rest. I just assumed that Jesus and his insignificant band of ruffians would end up the same way. Much to my shame, that was just one of the hundreds of misconceptions about Jesus I would come to regret during the next few weeks.

I never had actually heard any of the sermons Jesus had preached. I always said I didn't have the time, as I was too busy with my religious life, keeping up with the demands of operating my own business and doing my best to keep my family on the right track. I was content with where I was at spiritually, and I didn't like it when I heard about some of the things Jesus said concerning the overall state of our Jewish religion. Of course, if Jesus declared that the Jewish religion wasn't up to speed, and if I was a lifetime member of that religion and grooming my children to follow in my footsteps, it was pretty easy to deduct what Jesus must think about me. And for someone to attack our religious way of life, a proven and workable system of beliefs that had been around for more than fifteen hundred years since the days of Moses (not to mention that we Jews were the only group on the planet who still believed in the one and only God, Jehovah), well that seemed pretty arrogant and unappreciative. After all, we believed we were all working hard to keep our faith alive! Of course, I never really took the time to find out exactly what it was about our beliefs or lifestyle that Jesus was challenging. I just didn't like the idea of being attacked, period. So to see this man get arrested and possibly be put to death—that, for the most part, was good news to me and to many others in the Jewish faith.

Wrong on Many Counts

If you don't mind, please allow me to dive into my first digression during our time together. There will be many more of these to come while I recount the first-century history of the Brotherhood, all in the hope that you will examine your heart and life. I'd like to address the way that religious people tend to quickly dismiss anything new or different that's brought to their attention by other religious people. I should know, because I was one of the biggest offenders in my day.

My main problem was that I had made up my mind about Jesus long before I had even heard a single word of what he actually said. Oh sure, I had heard a few sketchy versions of what he had said, but every last one of those accounts was shared by people whom I knew didn't like him in the least. But as I mentioned a moment ago, I had never actually been present to hear one of his entire sermons, or even a small portion of one of his sermons. I had never spoken to any of his followers, let alone the twelve men we called apostles, who followed him day-in and day-out for three years—the individuals who, no doubt, could have helped me resolve the hang-ups I had about him. And I definitely had never talked to Jesus himself in order to find out what he was really like, what he really had said, what he really had meant by what he said or what he really thought applied to me specifically. No, unfortunately, I was content with my religious beliefs and my knowledge of the Scriptures—an amount of knowledge that I thought was pretty thorough. I would later come to realize just how little I really knew about the Old Testament, and just how prejudiced I was when it came to deciding what the Messiah figure should look like, act like and preach like.

You see, I thought Jesus was harsh and insensitive. Turns out he was merely hard-line and actually the most sensitive man to ever walk the planet.

Because he had never married, I thought his masculinity was in question and that he was a bit wimpy for any woman to find him attractive. Turns out he was more a "man's man" than even King David—and David was the greatest leader in our nation's storied history.

I thought he was loose on matters of the Law, both when it came to obeying it himself and expecting it to be obeyed by others. Turns out he obeyed it better than anyone ever had or ever will—to perfection—and his seeming failure to uphold the Law was actually a refusal on his part to bow to man-made traditions. As I understood later on, we Israelites had come to hold human traditions as equal to—and sometimes superior to—God's Law that had been delivered to Moses on Mount Sinai.

I thought Jesus was too quick to forgive and forget. Turns out he just loved to see people live guilt-free lives. His compassion gave him an incredible knack for transforming some of the most sinful members of society into the greatest saints of their time.

I thought he didn't care enough about our people reacquiring their rights to the Promised Land from the Roman rulers. Turns out he just had his mind on a much better piece of property, one that the rest of us weren't very focused on at the time.

I thought he didn't care enough about getting ahead in life and other important money matters. Turns out he just didn't want people to get too entangled in one of the nastiest roots of all evil and thereby be disqualified from one day receiving the real riches.

To summarize, I thought Jesus was just another ordinary man. Turns out he was the extraordinary Son of God. Thankfully, my story ended well, as God had great mercy upon me and was incredibly patient with my pride and ignorance. Sadly, I fear that there are many people today whose stories won't have such a happy ending.

I fear some have been involved in their religion for so long that they believe everything they cling to spiritually is already one hundred percent accurate, and that they have nothing else to add to their faith. That could be true, but I doubt it! It's foolish not to consider that further truths may exist in the Scriptures, and to automatically dismiss any differing spiritual perspective. What is there to be afraid of anyway?

Let's use you for an example. If you hear another person share about their differing beliefs and, in so doing, discover that what they're presenting is indeed false, you haven't lost anything just by listening. At least you didn't shut them out completely. You never know—they could have had valuable information about how to join my community here in Paradise! And besides, if yours is truly a biblical position and their's isn't, then you'll know for sure exactly where that individual stands and why they're wrong. Even better, you will then be in a great position to help that misguided soul make a change in their spiritual life. And most importantly, if you hear them out and actually end up discovering that they really do have something important to say to you about spiritual matters, you will no doubt be eternally grateful you listened! And who knows? You might even discover that what they're teaching and what you're teaching are more similar than you thought they'd be. If so, perhaps you'll find some ways to work together in the future, instead of being completely isolated and independent like so many religious people and groups have become in the twenty-first century.

I only wish that more of my friends and family members had taken that course of action. Thankfully, some of them are here with me today because of God's mercy and their own willingness to finally get humble and learn what the Brotherhood of Believers had to offer. But many of those I was closest to on Earth aren't enjoying the privileges of Paradise as I am, and I'm sure they would do anything to be where I am today. As my good friend Luke shared in his Gospel, those very people, if it were possible, would do anything to warn you about the dangers of arrogance and pride and ending up where they did because of it. Unfortunately, that's not a possibility for them. But you still have the chance to avoid their mistakes so that your story can have a happy ending.

You don't have to let pride stand in your way of learning some new and valuable things from the Bible, information that will no doubt benefit your spiritual life. Open your heart again and see if you really understand the Bible the way God wants you to understand it. Read the Bible all over again with fresh perspective, and make sure that what you believe now is what you actually should believe. Study out those uncomfortable topics that deal with your personal salvation, and be humble enough to admit it if your beliefs aren't verifiable in the Scriptures— and do it regardless of how strong you feel your relationship with God already is, how involved you are with your church at the moment or how certain you feel that you're saved and on your way to heaven. If you're willing to humble yourself, then there's a great chance for you to be a part of the Brotherhood of Believers and an equally great chance for those you love to join that group as well. If you don't choose the higher ground of humility, then what chance is there for your loved ones to ever discover the truth if they happen to be in error?

Now, of course, I'm not talking about throwing all caution to the wind and easily buying into some of the strange teachings that are being spread in your community right now, or allowing people who don't stick to the context of Scriptures to deceive you with their flattery and the few verses they can find to bolster their shaky case. I can't tell you how many times I heard Paul, Peter and the other Brotherhood leaders warn us about doing that! There's plenty of false teaching to be swallowed in your world today, and you must be careful to eat only what God puts on your plate. But I am saying that you should be very willing to examine the Scriptures carefully and make sure you haven't formed the wrong ideas about who God is, who Jesus is and what you're expected to do to inherit salvation.

About fifteen years into my time with the Brotherhood of Believers, we became inspired to imitate the attitude of some special people we were being told about—a group of Bereans with an inquisitive and humble approach when it came to spiritual matters. As a matter of fact, one of my Berean friends here in Paradise wanted me to make sure that I included that part, as he was one of the fortunate ones who displayed a humble spirit when he first encountered Paul's presentation of Christianity. And, wow, is he ever thankful he did! After all, what else could be more important than making sure you're right with God? So many people in my day quickly dismissed Jesus as a kook, a fake or even a menace to society. And after his death and ascension to heaven, most people continued to have that same mind-set about the message and lifestyle of the Brotherhood of Believers. But they couldn't have been further from the truth!

Following the Lamb

Well, let's get back to the worst day of my life. I was told that some final proceedings were occurring near the governor's official residence, and that a decision would be made shortly about Jesus' fate. Wanting to satisfy my curiosity about the whole situation, I decided to go there and check it out for myself. I knew that I still had a little bit of time before my household would be stirring and in need of a hearty breakfast. So I decided to go to the governor's mansion, return to the marketplace after a few minutes, buy the necessary groceries and hurry on home. While my plan was a good one in my mind at the time, it never materialized the way I thought it would. And that turned out to be both good news and bad news.

I arrived at the governor's mansion just minutes before Pilate appeared on the upstairs balcony to address the crowd. I thought I would be able to make my way to the very front, quite certain that not very many people would actually be there for the proceedings. Wow, was I ever wrong! The word had spread quickly about Jesus and his possible fate, and hundreds, perhaps even somewhere around a thousand people, had gathered to hear the final verdict. Little did we all know that, in only a matter of minutes, we would become the jury!

I managed to find a spot in the crowd where I was positioned about fifty feet or so from the balcony, and it allowed me to see and hear what was happening without much of a problem. After some ceremonial proceedings introducing Pilate, the governor appeared, along with two other men, one on his right, the other on his left. Even though I had never actually seen Jesus, I had heard a general description of him. But I was surprised at what I saw that morning. He looked ordinary, and he seemed calm and unfazed by his surroundings or the imminent threat to his life. He was a bit bloody and swollen around his face, and it was apparent that the guards had roughed him up a bit prior to his appearance before Pilate.

The other man, however, I recognized in an instant. It was Barabbas. We all knew about him and, even more, we knew quite well of his terrible reputation. He was a thief, a rebel, and worst of all, a murderer. And the most frightening fact about the man was that he didn't feel bad about wearing any of those labels. The Romans had been looking to nab him for quite some time, but like most troublemakers and terrorists, he had a knack for disappearing at just the right time and avoiding arrest. But now they had him. He was one of Rome's most wanted, and no doubt all of us would have been greatly relieved and much better off without having to worry about what he would do next to disrupt the peace and quiet we all still enjoyed under Roman rule.

But Jesus was a wanted man as well. Our leaders had become increasingly wary of his supposed plans to take on the Romans and set up a brand new kingdom. He had even talked openly about this new kingdom and how it would be far superior to any kingdom man had ever established in the past, much greater than any kingdom that existed in the present and grander than any kingdom that would be established in the years to come. And they felt it was in the nation's best interest to get rid of him before anything too substantial was brought to Rome's attention, evidence which would perhaps encourage the Romans to crack down on our nation's comfortable way of life and the freedom they afforded us to worship without the threat of being censored or squelched.

As for what happened next, well, I think we all saw it coming. It was totally in line with what happened during almost every Passover I could remember. The leaders of Rome saw it as a token gesture—a small way of keeping the Jews content with them and their leadership over us, and a small way of honoring our Passover tradition. It was meant to be a poignant reminder of all the lambs that had been spared during the Feast, as well as all the unfortunate lambs that had been chosen for slaughter.

Then Pilate asked the question: "Which of the two do you want me to release to you? Barabbas, or Jesus?" I wasn't quite ready for it, but I guess it was inevitable. Pilate wasn't about to make the final decision concerning the two men's fate. He had a reputation for not having much of a backbone, and he was always looking for ways to become more popular with either the Israelites or his Roman countrymen. So it would be up to us that day to decide the destiny of both men. One would be set free, the other would die. I was guessing that the crowd would probably split fifty-fifty. After all, everybody I knew wanted Barabbas off the streets and off their minds. No doubt even some of the people there that day had been personally affected by his criminal activities through the years. As for me, I wasn't sure which direction to go. Actually, I was pretty set on leaving early in order to escape the dilemma, but it was virtually impossible to wiggle my way out of the ever-increasing mob. So I stayed. And that was the one of the worst things that could have happened to me. I definitely should have gone with my first instincts and bolted. But, as I discovered later, and as I see quite clearly now, staying there was actually one of the best things that ever happened to me during the worst day of my life.

Then the people in the crowd started to shout. I could see the chief priests and elders of our people working the crowds and doing their best to promote their agenda. Most of the people there that morning were like me. They didn't have a clear idea as to how they should answer the governor's question. But after hearing all the information about Jesus that the priests and elders were sharing with such passion and confidence, most of the people in the crowd shifted their thinking and, one by one, began to shout out, "Barabbas, Barabbas."

I didn't shout it right away. It took me about two or three minutes to get comfortable with the idea. But everybody else was doing it, and I couldn't risk looking like a sympathizer with a man who was obviously dead-set against our religion, especially during such an emotional time of year like the Passover. And after a few of the shouters started to stare at me, I figured I had better go along before some of their anger turned against me.

"Barabbas, Barabbas," I shouted—still with some hesitation.

But it wasn't long before I was shouting that notorious name with confidence and a clear conscience. There's just something about a mob crowd and its seismic pressure that makes you go along for the ride. But had you interviewed the people there that day who asked for Barabbas' release, no doubt a great many of them would have known about as much information on Jesus as I did—and perhaps some even a whole lot less. Nevertheless, we all kept on shouting.

From what I could see, Pilate wasn't very comfortable with our choice. Later I would come to understand why, but at the time, I just thought he was meandering and being milk-toast like he was purported to be when it came to making any important decision. He was noticeably nervous, even sweating from his forehead a bit. But pretty soon, as Pilate saw it, he had no choice in the matter. After asking those of us in the crowd one final question as to Jesus' ultimate punishment, and upon hearing our united response of "Crucify him, crucify him!" for the next five minutes, he surrendered to our will. Simultaneously, and without a single call for a mistrial or a single thought of escaping through miraculous means, Jesus surrendered to the will of God—a painful and humiliating death by crucifixion that would pave the way for me to be forgiven of my most dreadful decisions on that most dreadful day!

To satisfy his conscience and avoid accepting responsibility for Jesus' death, Pilate washed his hands in front of us just before heading back inside his mansion. His final words reminded us that the decision was ours and that any guilt we might feel about it later on—well, we couldn't say that he hadn't warned us! But by that time, I didn't care. My anger had gone from simmering to boiling during the twenty minutes or so that I was there, and I was sufficiently convinced that Jesus was the right choice on that day and that I had made the right decision by shouting out Barabbas' name along with the rest of the crowd. We all thought that what we were doing was right. We were certain it was right. We were so convinced we were right that we even risked losing our relationship with God over the decision if it turned out to be wrong. We were actually willing to stake our physical lives on being right. But we couldn't have been any more wrong than we were that day.

I have to tell you, however, that it wasn't easy to make that decision. Initially, I couldn't help but feel that the whole scene was a big mistake and that I was in the middle of an awful nightmare. Jesus didn't appear to be a threat. He didn't even say anything the whole time he was there in front of us. I knew Barabbas was guilty—I only thought Jesus was. And that bothered me deeply for a while—at least until my thoughts and feelings were obviously becoming a minority position. My guilt dissipated once I decided that it wasn't worth risking my physical safety, or even my reputation, by siding with a man about whom I knew so very little.

The other time my heart seemed to skip a few beats was when I stared for a brief moment at Jesus. He was looking down most of the time while he stood next to Pilate on the balcony, but occasionally he would lift his head and pan the crowd. His eyes looked more sad than angry. On one of those occasions, I was almost certain that he caught my eye. I couldn't say for sure then, but I did clear up the matter with him upon my arrival here. And it turned out that, yes, Jesus did indeed fasten his eyes upon me for a few moments. In those brief seconds, he forced me to reexamine my present behavior and gave me one last chance to recant my sinful position. But it wasn't a "you're-going-to-pay-for-this" look that Jesus gave me. It was more of an "I'm-disappointed-that-you're-taking-this-position" look. It felt so incredibly uncomfortable. But I quickly stuffed away those feelings of godly sorrow and the proddings of my conscience, hoping they would simply disappear in due time. Yet they never did. And I'm so very grateful they didn't!

The choice had been made. Barabbas was to be released instead of Jesus, and Jesus was to be crucified to pay for his awful "crimes" of blasphemy against God and sedition against the Roman Empire and its Caesar.

Going Against the Grain

At this juncture of the story, I would like to pause and discuss a very important matter. It involves how crucial it is to stand up for your personal convictions and to never allow a crowd to sway you in its deadly direction.

I'm not saying that it wasn't my fault for joining the crowd. But I do remember feeling wrong about what I was doing at first, only to be swept under by the powerful waves of peer pressure that crashed upon the shores of my heart, ultimately drowning me in the sea of popular thinking. I wish I had had more guts to listen to that voice of reason, the voice that was desperately trying to communicate with me in those early moments of the worst day of my life. But how could so many religious and well-meaning people be wrong? And why wasn't anybody there standing up for Jesus? Those two questions were very legitimate in my mind, so it didn't take long for that strong voice to fade into a mere whisper and then go totally mute. And once that voice was silenced, it was rather easy for me to follow the crowd and find comfort in doing so. Yet as I looked back upon that ordeal a few days later, all I had to do to gain conviction about my sin that day was to remember a few of my heroes in the sacred Scriptures.

Noah had always been one of my all-time favorites. I remember thinking often about how great a man he must have been to stand firm on his "rainy day" convictions while millions of others were no doubt mocking his back-yard building project. What an amazing man— someone who couldn't have cared less about the popular opinion polls; a man who followed his conscience and the commands of God, regardless of the difficulty and the daily torment he must have faced from the multitudes opposing him. That's who I should have imitated that morning. That's the man who should have come to mind, whose example should have pulled my heart in the proper direction.

Then there were Joshua and Caleb, two more mighty men of God whom I had always held in high esteem. God had called the Israelites to forge ahead by faith and courageously march their way into the Promised Land. After a brief twelve-man tour of the territory, Joshua and Caleb were the only two out of two million souls who said, "Let's fight!", while everybody else said, "Let's fold!" Those were two amazing guys! To put it in perspective, that would be like an American being one of only three hundred people in all of the United States standing firm on their convictions and going against the wishes of an entire nation. It's simple math—the odds were a million to one! But they did it, and I could have taken a similar stand for God as well. And the odds were much better for me, perhaps only a thousand to one. But I succumbed to the pressure and paid for it dearly with the worst day of my life.

Examine Yourself

Allow me a few moments to bring this important point to you on a personal level. How are you in the midst of an angry mob? How strongly do you stand for something you believe if the majority is moving in a different direction? How firm would you be about a biblical stand you were taking if almost everybody else in your church told you to mellow out? Would you be willing to go against the beliefs of your parents, your best friend or your spouse if the word of God was prompting you to do so? Are you willing to address the ungodly situations going on around you, even if it means you'll be labeled as a radical? In my community, I'm surrounded by people who endured much suffering and heartache in their Christian days, much of it because they refused to go along with the crowd. And each of them wanted me to make sure that I didn't hold back on really preaching this point.

I've also heard that words like "compromise" and "peace" are popular words in many religious communities today, and that catch-phrases like "Let's just agree to disagree" and "All roads lead to heaven anyway" are thriving in the murky waters of the religious world.

I'm also being told of a number of ministers who have strong personal convictions about the need for things like sacrifice, sharing the gospel worldwide and saying "no" to temptation and sin, but they're wimpy in private meetings and pulpit presentations because they fear losing members or losing a substantial amount of money from their congregation's weekly contribution.

These and other sinful trends, often the result of the trembling and fear brought on by the maddening crowds, must be dealt with decisively. And I hope you'll start standing out and sticking up for what is good and right in the eyes of God—whether that's in your church, on your high-school or college campus or in your workplace.

I sure wish I could tell you to imitate my example in this area; however, you'll have to settle for the phrase that many of us parents in the Brotherhood unfortunately were forced to utter to our children in regard to our pre-Christian days: "Do as I say, not as I did." But I do thank God for changing my heart after that dreadful day. Though I can't say I was perfect and that I never gave in to the temptation to "fit in" or "find common ground at all cost" after that awful moment in time, I can say that I worked hard to turn my terrible weakness into a strength. I actually became known in the Jerusalem church for my willingness to ruffle a few feathers to protect the truths of God and the integrity of the Brotherhood.

One of my biggest moments of boldness occurred when I challenged Barnabas to be more probing with the brothers when it came to addressing their temptations and sins. That was a big step for me, because Barnabas had such a great reputation (a much-deserved reputation, I might add) for being one of the most encouraging and inspiring brothers in the world. I just felt he needed to excel in that other important area as well. And, of course, he took my admonition very well. Actually, we were good friends for many years. I can't tell you how many times, when the world was stealing large sums from my positive self-esteem account, that Barnabas made me feel like a million bucks after I had spent a few minutes in his presence. And nobody could help me to find the right perspective about my personal pains better than Barnabas could. There's no doubt in my mind that he was one of the biggest reasons why I stayed in the spiritual ring those few times when I felt like totally tossing in the towel. And I'm convinced that unless you have access to some spiritual surgeons like Barnabas in your life, men and women who can perform similar salvation-saving operations, your chances of making it here to Paradise are slim. (By the way, Barnabas was happy to hear that I was going to include that little "iron-sharpening-iron" story, one of the few times when it became necessary for me—or any others for that matter—to cause the spiritual sparks to fly on his behalf.)

A Beaten and Bloodied Messiah

Upon turning Jesus over to be scourged and later crucified, the crowds quickly dispersed, and people went back to their daily routines. It was almost as if nothing major had happened, and people wanted to believe that their lives would neither be worse nor better for their time spent on jury duty in Jerusalem. I suppose I should have just headed back to the marketplace, returned home and gotten on with my life, but something was pulling me in a very different direction. I felt in my heart the need to follow this ordeal through to the very end. I was seriously hoping that I could rid myself of the guilt I was feeling at the time, or at least figure out why my heart was racing like it never had before. A few other people were following as well and came with me to the place where Jesus was scheduled to be scourged.

While on my way there, I couldn't get it out of my mind that I had actually made eye-contact with this man Jesus, and that in those few seconds, I had experienced a feeling in my heart unlike any other in my entire life. What was the real meaning of all of this? Was God speaking to me through that brief encounter, or was it merely a figment of my imagination and something that I'd soon forget?

I wasn't able to actually see the scourging of Jesus, but I did see the end result. I could not believe how horribly they had tortured this man. Suffice it to say, it wasn't anything like what many Hollywood directors have tried to portray through the years. And even though the most recent portrayal of His suffering on the big screen came much closer to reality than most have in the history of film-making, no camera can accurately depict how the terrible torture affected Jesus' body. The flogging was brutal to say the least. And the feelings of guilt in my heart kept multiplying. I couldn't move past the thought that I had just made the biggest mistake of my entire life, and that already, at such an early hour, this would have to be classified as one of the worst days of my life.

I walked about ten to fifteen yards behind the soldiers who were flanking Jesus on the road to his crucifixion. He was losing blood rapidly, and soon collapsed under the weight of the crossbeam. Unbelievably, he was being forced to carry his instrument of torture to Golgotha, the place where criminals—the worst of the worst—were put to death for their heinous crimes. And still, Jesus said nothing.

People along the route were constantly mocking him, calling him the most awful and derogatory names. Some were even throwing clods of dirt and small stones, while others were spitting on him, much of it landing on his face and neck. I was waiting for a few retaliatory barbs from Jesus to counter the cruel comments of the roadside bystanders, but they never came.

It was about an hour before noon by this time, and I should have been home enjoying the stuffed feeling from a fabulous breakfast and catching up on life with my relatives. Actually, by then, I had completely forgotten about my responsibilities that morning. Rachel, meanwhile, had grown extremely worried and had sent Ethan into the streets of Jerusalem to search for my whereabouts. He never found me.

Jesus finally collapsed from exhaustion, and the soldiers forced a visitor from Cyrene to carry his cross the remaining few hundred yards up the steep hill to the execution site. It was clearly apparent to me that the African man was quite resistant to the whole idea. But when the soldiers threatened him with a similar fate should he continue to refuse their commands, he quickly obliged and carried the crossbeam up to Golgotha, where it would soon become one with the flesh of Jesus.

After what seemed like an eternity, we finally arrived at the site where Jesus would meet his end. Roman soldiers always did their brutal best to teach one last lesson about wayward behavior to criminals who were assigned death by crucifixion, a lesson they gave through their rough handling of the condemned, just prior to the pain they would face while hanging there awaiting their final breath. And in virtually all cucifixions, the criminals also saw this moment as their last opportunity to spew any of the bitter venom remaining in their hearts toward the soldiers and any curious onlookers. Most of them would also do their best to make the soldiers' job of nailing their hands and feet to the cross as difficult as possible—kicking, spitting and scratching to the bitter end.

As predicted, the other two men who were scheduled to be crucified alongside Jesus that day took a number of parting shots at the soldiers and the bystanders, and they hopelessly fought their ultimate doom of being nailed to their crosses. But not Jesus. He said nothing to those who were mocking him and offered his hands and his feet to the soldiers without a fight, allowing them to do their job of methodically hammering three six-inch spikes into his flesh. And with each minute that passed during this awful ordeal, I couldn't help but think that I had participated in one of the biggest blunders in the history of crime and punishment. Though I didn't know very much about Jesus, I clearly saw that his execution was completely unjustified.

The Crucified Christ

They fastened Jesus' hands and feet to the wood, lifted him up on the cross and left him to die. I decided to stay around for just a few more minutes to see if Jesus would say anything that might clue me in to his mysterious actions throughout the most humiliating torture known to man. And to be totally honest, I wanted to wait long enough to see if he would finally act like I expected him to act—full of bitterness and hatred for the life he had lived and for the way he was being treated in his last hours. Surely, I thought, he would eventually succumb to human tendencies and tear into his accusers. But no hateful words ever came from his lips. I did hear his sincere prayer for forgiveness, offered on behalf of those who were executing him and gambling for his remaining garments. I did hear his genuine request for someone named John to look after his despondent mother. I did hear his promise of Paradise to one of the men dieing next to him. And I did hear his desperate cry to the heavens that communicated his feelings of being forsaken by God.

And then it all went black. Piercing darkness enveloped the land and I was left there for three long hours to think about my life. It was so dark that I couldn't even see my hands in front of my face. Thinking that the darkness would only be temporary, I remained there for a few minutes, waiting for my eyes to get adjusted to the dark so I could head on home. Three hours later, I finally left. And what I felt during those three hours changed the course of my life and was the first big step toward my entrance into the Brotherhood of Believers.

All I could manage to think about during those three hours was my past life and how many times I had broken my vows to God and dishonored his holy word. I had never had a time of self-examination like this. Always before, I had justified my sinful behavior by convincing myself that everybody else had similar struggles, and even worse, that my sins probably weren't as bad as the sins being committed by other people I knew. I had always thought that my errors of judgment were no huge deal to God, and that my lack of commitment to him at various times in my life was something he both understood and excused. But my whole perspective changed during those next three hours. Everything was coming to the surface, and I found myself talking to God in a way I had never talked to him before.

Gut-Level Honesty

I was being honest about things I had never verbalized to God prior to that day. Sure, no doubt he already knew all of it, but I had never had the humility or the guts to converse with him about any of it in a very specific way. And for the first time, I felt the massive weight of each of those sins upon my heavy heart, and I experienced deep sorrow for the fact that I had chosen those ungodly paths—the time I slapped Joseph in the face when he was three because he just wouldn't listen to me; the time I paid a day's wage to enjoy a few sexual favors from a prostitute while on a business trip, something I never told my wife about or anybody else, and a memory I had hoped would just eventually leave my mind; the few times I'd had too much to drink and embarrassed myself and my family members with my behavior; the times I deeply wished I hadn't been born a Jew so I wouldn't have to be involved in all the religious expectations that came along with my heritage; the times I overcharged a few customers for my services because I knew I would never get caught and that they would probably never feel the pinch of surrendering up some additional funds; the times I ignored my wife or made her feel like a second-class citizen in our household; the many times I gratified myself sexually in the privacy of my own home, viewing those moments as a necessary release from the pressures of life and a positive way to avoid any further episodes with the prostitutes I would likely encounter on future business trips. And for the first time in my life, I cried about my sin.

I didn't cry very often before I became a part of the Brotherhood of Believers. Granted, I had shed a few tears through the years, like on the days when my father and mother passed away, and when my three children were born. But I had never felt anywhere near this amount of sorrow over my ungodly behavior. So why did I suddenly feel it there in the darkness? Did it have anything to do with the man I had been following for the past few hours? And did the crucifixion I was witnessing play into that drama as well? Thankfully, I would discover the answer to all of these questions and a whole lot more about fifty days later.

Personal Inventory

Let's finish this section of my story with some important questions I would like to ask you. How does your personal sin affect you? Have you ever cried over how you've hurt God with your disobedience? Have you allowed all of your sin to come to the surface so you can be honest and humble about it with God and with people who can help you to change? Or are there things about you that nobody else knows, secrets that are plaguing your heart this very moment? Have you allowed yourself to confront just how devastating your sin is and the way it affects not only you but all of those around you? Have you felt the pain as I did for what Jesus endured that day? I was devastated by his suffering, and I didn't have very much understanding of what was happening at the time; I certainly didn't realize that Jesus was taking on the punishment for every last one of my sins. But you know all of that, don't you? Does it move you? Have you ever hurt deeply enough to cry over it? Do you still hurt over it? I've been told that too many religious people constantly distance themselves from their sin, and far too many of their preachers and leaders allow them to do it—probably because they're doing the same thing themselves.

This was not the case in the Brotherhood of Believers. We dealt decisively with our own sin and with each other's sin on an ongoing basis. I'll share quite a bit more about that later on in the story, but we got real on a regular basis! We had many much-needed times of confession and repentance. These times weren't scheduled, nor were they occasional events—repentance was simply a way of life for those of us in the first-century church.

Most of us who grew up in the Jewish faith weren't all that comfortable with the concept of confession, and I suppose you aren't, either. Even though the teaching was definitely a part of God's plan in the Old Testament, and even though there were numerous stories we could read that told of the dangers of hidden or continual sin, we had steadily moved away from any type of radical confrontation of sin in each other's lives. Sin was a personal thing, we concluded—something between us and God. And besides, once a year we could count on the all-important Day of Atonement ceremonies to wipe away our sin and guilt from the previous twelve months.

But I quickly came to understand the importance of regular honesty with God about my struggles and sins, along with an equal conviction about consistent openness with my brothers and sisters in Christ. And the reason we engaged in this practice was simple: We had heard enough warnings in sermons and other spiritual settings to know that we weren't fighting against a powerless or part-time foe. Satan was all about getting us to stop somewhere before the finish line, and we knew we couldn't completely relax until we had broken the tape. Whether we were struggling with sexual temptations and sins, or relationship conflicts, or financial matters, or pride, or even character weaknesses and quirks, nothing was off limits. We got in each other's lives and asked the tough, probing questions. There was never a "No Trespassing" sign hanging over anybody's heart because of their position in the Brotherhood or their past spiritual accomplishments. And if we sensed people weren't being honest and open, we pursued it until we either heard the truth or until we were assured that something other than sin was the major issue in their life. We didn't necessarily like it all of the time, but we knew we needed it to be our best for God.

Sure, there were a few times when we were insensitive while broaching the subject of sin with someone, or when we went too far in offering up a follow-up challenge upon someone's confession. And no doubt there were a few occasions when we didn't trust in one another's honesty as we should have. But we all had an agreement (a philosophy, you might say) that it was much better to err on the side of caution and concern than to simply assume that none of us were struggling with anything. We believed it was better to confront the powerful deceptions of the dark side than to give each other too much room to skirt the real issues and the devil too much room to dress up our bad behavior. And on occasion, we accidentally took our confrontations too far. If that happened, we quickly offered up forgiveness to one another and got back to the business of beating the devil and being our very best for God. And I'm of the firm belief that this godly practice is one of the biggest reasons why I'm enjoying the benefits of Paradise today.

Where would I have been without those brothers (and a few sisters, and even my wife and kids) who were gutsy enough to take me on in my pride or self-deception, saving me from my sinful path? Sure, I sinned a number of times during my days in your community, but because of the great encouragement and warnings I received for many years from the Brotherhood of Believers, I was able (with the help and strength of God) to overcome my sin.

Is that the type of religious group you're a part of at the moment? Do you have a few valiant friends who aren't afraid to wield their swords of correction in your direction? If not, I fear for your soul, and can only think that Satan has you exactly where he wants you.

It Is Finished/It Has Just Begun

Jesus finally took his last breath, much sooner than the other two men who were crucified that day. But I was so relieved about that. He didn't deserve his awful ending, and to see his pain and agony get cut at least a little bit short was very comforting to my soul. I walked home a few hours before sunset with a heavy heart, thinking about some huge hurdles that I needed to clear in order to make sense of the entire tragedy, the worst day of my life. And one by one, God enabled me to clear those seemingly insurmountable obstacles, setting me up for the most amazing day of my entire life.

Chapter Four:
A Long Seven Weeks

I made it back home about twenty minutes later and was greeted warmly by my family, all of them greatly relieved that I had returned safely. I was exhausted both physically and emotionally, and the encouragement from my family that afternoon helped to lessen the sting I was feeling from watching Jesus die. And the last thing I felt I needed at that moment was any form of correction for my late return. But in the privacy of our own bedroom, Rachel made it clear that she had been incredibly anxious and none too happy about my unscheduled disappearance for the past eight hours—not to mention that she felt embarrassed having to send Ethan to find me and pick up the needed groceries, just in case I failed to return at all. She said she didn't know whether I had been injured, had died or perhaps, for some strange reason, had decided to simply walk away from my family responsibilities. As usual, she was fairly respectful while she expressed her disappointment in me, but I could sense a definite edge in her tone that usually wasn't there. That edge didn't sit well with me at the time, and I was quick to let her know why. I reminded her that she was called by God to trust me in everything, even in trying moments, and that her first thoughts should have been those that led her to believe the best about my delay. And I was very upset that she seemed to have little or no concern about the heaviness in my heart that afternoon.

Sad to say, but things became much more intense after that. I raised my voice and put on my "I'm-your-leader-so-you-better-follow-me" look as best I knew how. For the next ten minutes, I methodically relayed the account of my morning and afternoon chaos and how the whole day seemed to get away from me. Of course, I paid little or no attention to Rachel's few rebuttals about how it would have been nice for me to at least make an effort to return home for a few minutes, just to make them aware of my changed plans, or even to send a message home explaining my delay. Or how this was another example of how I had made her feel unequal and unimportant through the years—that my plans and schedule were of top priority, while hers could easily be put on hold or changed altogether.

She didn't seem to get it. It was the worst day of my life, my heart was feeling things it never had felt before, I had just had the eeriest encounter of my life with an infamous stranger and all she seemed to care about was that my actions had changed our plans for breakfast and lunch and that my delay in returning had caused great angst to her and the rest of the family.

Unfortunately, I responded to her in much the same way I had for the previous seven years of our marriage. I got louder and even more aggressive. I threw accusations of selfishness at her, successfully shot down her feelings and said a number of things I never should have said. Unbelievably, hardly an hour had passed since I had watched an innocent man die in complete humility on a cross—yet there I stood, once again letting pride stand in the way of admitting my selfish and erring ways.

Rachel began to cry. My first thought was to simply walk away and wait for the whole thing to blow over, but thankfully that didn't happen. Somehow, my thoughts kept coming back to what I had just witnessed at Golgotha a few hours earlier and how I now needed to imitate Jesus' amazing display of humility in our argument. And I couldn't escape the idea that my pride in this current marital dispute had somehow played a role in his death as well.

A Lasting Image

Now it's important for you to understand that these were quite foreign thoughts for me at that time. Why couldn't I remove that picture of Jesus hanging on the cross from my mind, and why did I feel as though I couldn't walk out in anger and pride in the middle of our fight? So for the first time in quite some time in my married life, I shut my mouth and opened my heart to Rachel's pain. I walked over to the bed, sat down beside her, put my arm around her shoulder and apologized. Though I couldn't pinpoint why I was feeling that way, something was stirring in my heart, and I was fairly confident that much of it, if not all of it, was connected to the crucifixion of Jesus. I later came to find out that Rachel was shocked by the whole incident. She even said that when she saw me walk in her direction instead of walking away as I usually did, she feared that perhaps I had totally lost it and intended to physically harm her in some way. Wow, did that ever throw fuel onto my fires of repentance! It certainly helped me to get in touch with how much I had hurt Rachel through the years and what a poor example of humility I had been for her and our children.

I wish I could tell you that I never took a similar misstep in my marriage after that day, but I can't. Thankfully, both Rachel and I opened the door for other married couples to get involved in our lives and help us work through our disagreements and disappointments with one another. And we were happy to do the same for other couples in the Brotherhood, because we knew how much we had needed help. Of course, the sermons we heard about God's plan for marriage were always convicting, especially when the apostle Paul (a single man) came to town on occasion. I remember one particular admonition from him that husbands should treat their wives the same way Jesus treated the church and gave his life for her—that I was to be for Rachel and do for Rachel what I remember seeing in Jesus that awful day in Jerusalem. He would later be inspired to include that teaching in his letter to the church at Ephesus. That powerful reminder from Paul and others like it always put us husbands in our places and, more importantly, put our marriages back on the right track.

Marriage Habits

We talked about marriage a lot in the first century. Each wife was encouraged to be open with her husband, open with other wives in the Brotherhood and open with anyone who they felt could help them to rightly live out their God-given role as helpmate. Each husband was similarly honest with his wife and with others who could assist them in the daunting challenge of presenting their partners to God in a radiant manner. And on occasion, and when necessary, a few women came directly to me and expressed their concerns about the ways I was treating my wife. But that was okay with me, as I had told Rachel she could discuss our marriage (and my weaknesses specifically) with others in the Brotherhood, and that others, in turn, could address those concerns with me. Thankfully, it didn't happen often. Usually, Rachel's soft heart and silent righteousness broke my pride before outside intervention became necessary. At other times, Rachel simply let me know that we needed some face-to-face time with another couple to help straighten a few things out in our marriage, and I would always make sure we did so within a few days.

Why did we have these marital agreements and do what might be considered strange or overly radical by people outside of the Brotherhood? Well, first and foremost, we knew that our relationship with our spouse was a direct reflection of our relationship with God. We knew that God likely examined the marriage relationship more carefully and closely than any other relationship known to man. We also knew that we would be judged by how we had operated in our individual marriage roles. And we knew that our relationship would have a direct and profound effect on our children, regardless of whether or not they actually saw us disagreeing or were consciously aware of our marital struggles. But the biggest reason we did it was because it felt wonderful to be happily married, and we knew that achieving a state of wedded bliss was neither simple nor something we could concoct on our own.

Since we're on this subject, let me ask you some important questions: Assuming you're married, how much help do you get in your marriage? (If you're not married, simply apply these questions and suggestions to your other key relationships.) Who's helping you to "work it out" when the two of you just can't? If you're a husband, are you leading your wife or simply lording it over her? If you're a wife, are you submitting to your husband or setting yourself above him by your resistance to his directions? I can tell you from my experience in the Brotherhood of Believers that the condition of your relationship with your spouse must be a high priority or you won't have a godly marriage for long! And if you're not careful, it may not even be a marriage for long, even if the possibility of divorce seems unthinkable at this moment. My advice to you is to protect your marriage with all your might—much more carefully than you would protect a multi-million dollar lottery ticket on the way to claim your prize.

As the Scriptures indicate in numerous places, marriage is a relationship ordained by God, yet it's designed exclusively for your time on Earth. Rachel and I aren't married anymore, but we still have an amazing relationship here, and we always talk about how our time together as Christians and the many lessons we learned on marriage in the Brotherhood helped to solidify our places in Paradise.

More Weaknesses Exposed

Unfortunately, that argument with Rachel wasn't the only problem to be exposed in my heart during the next seven weeks. As much as I tried to change some of the other sinful patterns in my life, I always seemed to fall woefully short. Whether it was in avoiding lust, praying on a regular basis or just being nice to strangers—especially Gentiles—I seemed to fail on many fronts every single day. The harder I tried, the more I realized how little power I actually had to uphold any of God's standards or to overcome the sins and weaknesses I had accrued during the years of my involvement in careless and thoughtless religion. But the good thing about this realization was that, instead of getting frustrated and folding up my spiritual tent, I began longing for God to equip me with the necessary earthly camping supplies that could help me to live a better life—a life I could be proud of and that would ultimately be pleasing to him.

For so many years, I had wanted to make changes on my own. And I had decided in my mind that I didn't need help from God. If he told me to do something, I just needed to do it and somehow believe that I could. I also thought I didn't need much—if any—help from others. Through a scripture I had memorized from the book of Ecclesiastes (chapter 12 in your Bible), I was fully aware that I would give an account to God someday for my actions. But I also determined that I didn't need anybody else getting involved in my life and messing up my chances of making a good score on my final exam. (Unfortunately, I forgot to memorize the last portion of chapter 4 in the same book, which discusses the importance of spiritual friendships!) But my heart was changing and my mind was getting cleared of the cobwebs of misguided and macho thinking.

I soon came to the conviction that I couldn't be righteous without God's power and unless I got tons of help from other people. I couldn't be a good husband or father on my own. I couldn't be pure. I couldn't be completely honest. I couldn't keep my feet securely planted on spiritual paths. I needed help, and lots of it. I needed God. I needed people. And I would soon discover that I needed the indwelling of the Holy Spirit and fellowship with others who possessed that same amazing gift. But little did I know just how incredible that indwelling of God's presence actually would be in my day-to-day activities.

The Spirit of Power, Love and Self-Control

Upon receiving him (as I will relate to you in full detail shortly), the Holy Spirit began to constantly remind me of what was right and what was wrong. And during those times when I resisted the truth and quenched the Spirit, I was promptly convicted of my wrongdoing by that same powerful force. The Spirit brought me to new heights in the all-important areas of love, joy, peace, patience, kindness and gentleness, along with countless other qualities that I came to learn Jesus had exemplified throughout his entire life.

He (the Spirit) often reminded me not to bypass an opportunity to witness for Jesus, then moments later gave me just the right words to share with that same individual. He led me to apologize first, and more quickly than I normally would. He implored me to forgive and forget the offenses that had been committed against me, even those done by people who were looking to make my life as miserable as possible. On a number of occasions, he took my mind back to those six or seven hours I had spent with Jesus on his road to Calvary. He pricked my conscience regularly and warned me often of Satan's nearby location, urging me to flee from him or giving me the spiritual agility to avoid the fiery arrows he launched in my direction.

But the Holy Spirit wasn't living inside me during those seven long weeks. Oh, I'm certain he was all around me and doing his part to help me as much as an outsider could. But without the permanent indwelling of the Holy Spirit, I was simply spinning my spiritual wheels. At the time, I didn't realize what (or rather who) it was that I needed, but I knew I couldn't serve God the way I needed to in my current capacity. I knew I would eventually spin those wheels one too many times and become eternally stuck in the mud of my religiosity, or I'd give up trying altogether. It was only a matter of which damning condition would be first to overtake my heart.

Passover and Synagogue Struggles

We continued to participate in other Passover traditions that evening. This may sound a bit strange, but in some ways, I really enjoyed doing that. In other ways, it was absolutely horrendous. I enjoyed it, in part, because I knew the various Passover celebrations were powerful reminders of God's deliverance and protection of our Jewish nation, and that in observing them, I was letting God know that I still believed in him and wanted to honor his remembrance request. I was feeling more of a desire to do what was right in the eyes of God than I had for quite some time, and the evening spent focusing on God with my family and my sister's family was at least consistent with that.

But that evening brought some heavy discouragement as well. All night long, I couldn't help but think that this 1,500-year tradition, in which we killed an innocent lamb to help us remember our deliverance from slavery in Egypt, now had greater meaning. I began to wonder if Jesus' death might have some strange connection to the Passover. Just as our Passover lamb had been slaughtered the day before, my mind kept racing back to Jesus dying in pain on his cross. And it was becoming more and more apparent to me that I had just participated in the death of an innocent man. But even in realizing that, I couldn't come close to putting all the pieces of the new Passover puzzle together. You might say I had finished with the borders, but plenty of inside pieces still were waiting for a proper connection.

For the next seven Saturdays, synagogue services were a bit like that Passover. I kept attending as usual, but with each passing Saturday worship experience, I couldn't help but think that we as a nation—all of us supposedly doing our best to participate in sincere and personal worship of God while prompting the nations around us to do likewise—had seriously missed the boat. I would soon discover that had we been worshiping in Noah's day, we too would have been excluded from the ride to salvation, which only eight souls had been blessed to take. And had we been living in similar fashion during the days of the Babylonian invasion of Judah, we too would have faced certain defeat

I had always considered our synagogue services to be somewhat impersonal and, frankly, a bit boring. But, at the same time, I usually left those times feeling pretty good about myself—at least I had put in my time for God, unlike a great number of my fellow Jews, and unlike almost all of the Gentiles in Jerusalem. But I rarely heard a challenging lesson while I was there. I rarely was called to carefully examine my personal life or to do a much better job of working to affect the lives of others. The singing was usually a bit heartless and heavy, and most people (including me!) didn't really "get into it," as you might say. But the preaching and the singing weren't the only things that needed to be revived in our synagogue gatherings. Our heart to give was far from what it should have been as well. Sure, my fellow worshipers and I typically gave our tithe every Saturday, but few of us knew where the money was actually being spent. That reality, along with the fact that no one held us accountable for our materialism or greed, meant that most of us were giving far less than we could have and should have been giving, and with much less joy about the privilege of showing God our appreciation for his ongoing care in our lives. And at times, I even dipped slightly below the tithing standard, although every time I did I knew it was in direct violation of God's commands.

I will say, however, that I did try to sing louder than usual during those seven weeks. But after a few weeks of displaying my renewed zeal for God via my increased decibels during the singing, I grew increasingly uncomfortable when no one else imitated my enthusiasm. Little by little, I turned down my volume. And even though I remembered how badly I felt after bowing to the desire of the masses during Jesus' final hours, I still didn't have the guts to stand out in the synagogue setting, either.

A New Spirit of Worship

Of course, that would all change in the Brotherhood of Believers. We were all so fired up to be together that we sometimes couldn't contain ourselves. Honestly, you felt a bit awkward in our fellowship if you weren't singing loudly! And we loved to sing! Five thousand people or five, instruments or no instruments, harmony or no harmony—we just wanted another opportunity to let God know how much we appreciated all he had done to change our lives and save our souls. We often got together just to sing. And we always had a blast, no matter how many of us were included in that impromptu choir.

We had a huge songbook already at our disposal—the book of Psalms, the same book we often used in our synagogue services before I became a follower of Jesus. Most of those Psalms were rich with both old and new meanings for us as disciples. But we also had a number of Spirit-filled brothers and sisters who wrote and composed new songs and hymns for us to sing during our times together. Needless to say, their talent and training in the area of music led to many times of joy and many tears of gratitude while we sang praises to God.

But enough about me! Let's talk about your worship experiences. How's the singing during your times of worship? What's the overall atmosphere like while you and your fellow members are engaged in a chorus of "How Great Thou Art"? Even more importantly, how loudly do you sing, and what is the atmosphere and spiritual temperature within your own heart? How much love do you feel in your heart for God when voicing those amazing lyrics about your amazing God? How deep does the gratitude sink in your heart when you sing "Amazing Grace," and just how sweet is the sound? Have you ever said that you just don't want to sing a particular song anymore? If so, has the message of that song lost its meaning and significance? Do you clap with the clappers and snap with the snappers, or are you too dignified and worshipful for that? Are you more worried how your neighbor in the pew will feel about your volume, or about how God will feel about your voice being lifted up to him in praise? Do you exude the same (or even greater!) level of zeal during a song of praise to God than what you exhibit in the stadium or in your own living room while rooting on your favorite sports team?

In my day, when a hundred or more of us sang our loudest (keeping in mind that few of those hundred could actually sing on key, or anywhere near it!), somehow our combined effort still sounded almost angelic. That miracle mystifies me even now!

And although we were always careful not to judge one another unjustly, whenever we saw a brother or sister withholding their voice in praise, we asked them about it. Many times, we discovered that something was amiss in their hearts: A hidden sin; a huge disagreement with a spouse; a heart heavy from discouraging news; even a desire to hurry through that day's worship so "more important" matters could be attended to—these were some of the main reasons we occasionally gave less than our best while singing to God. But thankfully, we were all committed to making sure we didn't allow those trends to continue from week to week in our assemblies.

Let me encourage you to keep a watchful eye on each other during your times of singing. Not only will you have opportunities to help others in your number deal with whatever might be choking their joy, but you'll be honoring the direction our apostles used to give us on a regular basis—the admonition to look around at each other while we sang, offering smiles of encouragement, realizing that we were singing not only to God, but to one another as well. It may feel awkward at first, but believe me, the more you do it, the more inspiring the singing will become and the more that sweet-smelling incense of joyful noise will float up to the heavens in praise and honor to God.

Helplessly Hoping

I really did try to get as much as possible out of the synagogue services during those seven weeks, especially from the lessons that were being taught each Saturday. But I eventually grew complacent with that effort as well. And although I did engage in more honest and sincere contemplation of the Scriptures, both in public and in private, my study and application of God's Word was nowhere near the level it would reach during my days in the Brotherhood, when I believed that God was using every lesson given by our leaders to speak directly to me.

I prayed more regularly during that time as well, mostly for God to bring meaning to the events that had occurred on that dreadful day when I encountered Jesus for the very first time. I actually began confessing my sins to God every few days, but I didn't open my heart up to people. No one had any idea of the struggles I regularly faced as I tried to control my sinful nature.

Rachel and I began to pray together a few times a week, something we had done only a few times a year prior to that. I talked to her occasionally about everything I was feeling, but she couldn't totally understand it. Because she hadn't been there with me, she didn't feel like she could help me with anything I was feeling. And for the most part, she was right. So I kept most of my sobering thoughts to myself.

Although I felt myself slowly slipping away from the sorrow and shame I had felt the day Jesus died, I was doing everything I could possibly think of to not let those emotions leave my heart or my mind entirely. I just hoped that someday I would come to figure everything out and be blessed as a result. I did wonder about trying to locate some of the followers of Jesus during those seven weeks, as I assumed they could help me make more sense of how I was feeling. But I was afraid to be seen with any of them. I would later come to find out that even had I tried, I likely would have failed because most of them were in hiding. And like me, they, too, were trying to make sense of everything they had heard and seen in Jesus.

A few days after Jesus' death, word began to spread that the disciples of Jesus were claiming he had been resurrected from the dead, just as he had predicted. They claimed that they had actually touched him, talked with him and heard him teach. But nobody I knew had seen him. So I doubted. If Jesus had really risen from the dead, wouldn't he have come and shown himself to the unbelievers as well as to the believers? Didn't we need to see him in a resurrected state just as much, or perhaps even more, than they did? And as for me, although I did believe Jesus was an innocent victim and never should have been crucified, I wasn't about to proclaim him as the Chosen One and believe such an outlandish claim.

The popular response by our people to those resurrection claims was that his disciples had stolen the body and were simply making the whole thing up to perpetuate their lie. I must say that I bought into this perspective, too, although I would later realize just how ridiculous the popular viewpoint actually was—far more unbelievable than the claim that Jesus had been resurrected! Many of my regular customers at the carpentry shop asked me how I felt about all of the events surrounding Jesus during that Passover weekend, but I kept my true feelings pretty close to the vest. Showing any signs of sympathy for Jesus or his followers might mean losing my regular customers' business, and I definitely couldn't afford for that to happen.

I had many restless nights during the next seven weeks, a few intense dreams that brought me back to those hours at the cross and even some physical challenges of fatigue and nausea. Looking back on all of that, my physical dysfunction was mostly due to a lethal combination of guilt, gobs of stress, great uncertainty and getting too little sleep. But it was all being used by God to prepare me for what, very soon, would become the greatest day of my life.

Chapter Five:
The Greatest Day of My Life

I was getting more and more nervous, thinking that I would never be able to make sense of what I had begun to refer to as my "Passover Problem." The problem started with my participation in a jury decision that blew it big-time on two fronts: We let a guilty man go, and we sentenced an innocent man to die by crucifixion. And I knew enough about the Scriptures to realize that God was none too pleased with me or my fellow jurors for making those decisions that day. My problem was compounded when I followed the condemned man to his death and ended up feeling guilt and shame like I had never experienced in my life. The problem persisted because I couldn't discuss the matter with anybody besides the "just-blow-it-off-and-get-on-with-your-life" crew—people who were eager to offer me scandalous information about Jesus, the man I believed to be innocent. I was even beginning to think Jesus was more than (perhaps a whole lot more than) our people as a whole were saying he was. And the biggest problem I faced was that the feelings and convictions I'd gained since that fateful day had begun to wane—and I knew that unless I got a pretty good sign sometime soon about where I needed to turn next on my road to reason, I was in danger of returning to my old way of life—something I was desperately hoping to avoid. I had recently celebrated my twenty-sixth birthday, and I made a vow to God on that day that I would serve him like never before if he would just help me make sense of everything I was feeling.

A Hope for Pentecost

While the problem stared at me in the mirror every morning, I clung to one ray of hope that I thought might provide just the right opportunity to have some of my questions answered. The Feast of Pentecost (or Feast of Weeks) was approaching, and in a rare moment of spiritual intuition, I was thinking that perhaps God might choose this holiday, with all its powerful symbolism, as an opportunity to reveal himself again.

Pentecost had two primary meanings for our people, and I was wondering if God might be aiming to bring our nation's collective heart to a much deeper understanding of those two things as well. First, it was a time for all of us to thank God for how he had provided our daily physical necessities through the yearly harvesting of our crops. I was excited about letting God know, in a big way, how much I appreciated his care for my life and how grateful I was to have such generous daily provisions for myself and my family. But in the years prior to my birth, our people had also attached an equally important significance to the celebration, that of honoring God for his deliverance of the Law on Mount Sinai. Where would our people have been in the desert without those clear directions? How would we ever have known where to go, what to do or how to do it if God hadn't spelled it out clearly for us on that day? The Law was everything to our people, and to double up on this day of celebration and thank God for meeting both our physical and spiritual needs, well, that made for a very special time and a raucous celebration indeed. Maybe, just maybe, I thought, this Pentecost would be the time God would choose to deliver some additional spiritual guidance to his people. Not an entirely new code of living, but one that would help us take things deeper into our hearts. And maybe, just maybe, Jesus would have something to do with the whole process.

My business was closed for the holiday, but my plan for Pentecost was to wake up earlier than usual and still head into town. I awoke that morning more excited than ever, yet also quite a bit nervous about the possibility of getting shut out in the "increased-spiritual-awareness" department. I got cleaned up, had a hearty breakfast and headed out for a walk. My desire was to spend a few hours just focusing on God and asking him to continue leading me in the direction he would have me to go. I would then head back home to get my family ready for the afternoon Pentecost celebrations, which so many Jews from all around the world had come to enjoy.

The streets of Jerusalem were crowded, but nothing like they had been during Passover when the arrest and trial of Jesus had lured the previously uninterested out into the heart of the city. I was thoroughly enjoying my time of prayer and meditation, yet I was still wondering if my hopes had been misguided and would get deferred once again, making my heart sicker than it had ever been. But around nine that morning, a few people came running toward the temple square, where I was finishing up my time of prayer. They were telling those of us there something about a strong, mysterious wind that had been felt in only a small portion of the city, and a semblance of fire that had hovered over a house near the outskirts of town. People were gathering there to see what was happening, and I wasted no time in making sure I was a part of the action as well. My heart leapt for joy that something amazing might be right around the corner, and I ran faster than I ever had to get there before I missed anything else.

Another Crowded Encounter

Like that dreadful day of Passover just seven weeks earlier, a large crowd had assembled. There were people there that day from countless nations. And they were all focused on a group of about a hundred people or so, and of that hundred, about a dozen were in the spotlight. Although at first I didn't think I recognized any of them, one man started to look familiar. Where had I seen him before? Or had I seen him before?

My heart raced back to those few hours I had spent at the cross of Jesus, and it was there that this man's face came into clear focus. He was the same young man Jesus had implored to take care of his mother—John was his name. Yes, that was John. He was one of Jesus' closet followers, and now he was addressing a portion of the crowd—but not in the way any of those people expected him to speak. No, this was in their native tongue. And I knew that there was no way in the world an ordinary fisherman from Galilee should have been able to rattle off the truths of God in a language I was confident he had never spoken or studied. But John was really doing it, and doing it with great eloquence and ease. But John wasn't the only one speaking in this miraculous manner.

He and the other members of Jesus' inner circle were introducing themselves to the crowd—and more importantly, they were introducing the real Jesus to those of us who had so misunderstood him while he was among us. One after the other, they spoke to Jews and converts to Judaism from Judea, Mesopotomia, Cappadocia, Pontus, Egypt, Libya, Asia and Rome, just to name a few. Everyone in the crowd was able to hear about the wonders of God in their own native language. It was mind-boggling.

The miracle of speaking in tongues was amazing, but what we heard about Jesus, the Old Testament Scriptures and God's ultimate plan for the salvation of all mankind was even more amazing. And best of all, it was starting to make sense to me. The pieces of the puzzle were being added to the borders I had completed seven weeks earlier, and it was thrilling to see the picture fill in, piece by piece. But I still didn't have the puzzle finished and ready to be framed.

And then it happened again. Someone in the crowd threw out the accusation, "You're just drunk!", and it was both amazing and sad how many people believed it. But I thought it was ridiculous to charge these men with inebriation at such an early hour. Others in the crowd claimed that nothing was making sense to them. Still others were saying that the speakers had probably secretly studied languages with Jesus in order to perpetuate the lie after he was gone.

But I kept telling myself, "Don't go there again, don't go there again, do not go there again! Don't dig yourself into a deeper hole than the one you're already in because of your problems at the Passover. Stay sober in your thinking. Stay individual in your thinking. Don't go with the crowd—go with your own convictions. Don't worry about what people are thinking of you, worry about what God is saying to you! Don't go there! Don't go there! Do not go there!"

And praise God I didn't! I just kept on listening. And what I had reasoned in my mind, Peter soon addressed, as he put to rest the lame and unfounded accusation of drunkenness with a reminder of the morning hour. Then he proceeded to lay out the truth about Jesus and the wonderful plan of redemption, culminating his message with the offer of salvation in the name of Jesus to those of us who were willing to accept it.

Keys to the Kingdom

Peter was an incredibly confident man. No one would have thought this was the same man who weeks earlier had succumbed to peer pressure himself and refused to be known as someone closely associated with Jesus—claiming at the time that he didn't even know the man. But the Spirit had changed this ordinary fisherman into a new man, just the same way Peter said God would for me if I surrendered to him and his plan for my life.

To summarize, Peter stepped forward on behalf of the others, spoke to the crowd in the one common language we all could understand and performed for me the necessary eye surgery, in a spiritual sense, that I needed—giving me the improved vision that allowed me to spot the missing pieces of the Jesus puzzle and figure out exactly where they needed to be placed to complete it. Of course, he didn't just provide that information for me alone. It was heralded to thousands of us there who were given first access to experience a new and more fulfilling Pentecost—the law of Christ that God delivered through Peter in Jerusalem, our new Mount Sinai. I was overwhelmed with gratitude to God for allowing me to be a part of the first harvest of spiritual souls under the new covenant and the chance to be a full-fledged and fired-up member of the Brotherhood of Believers.

Sight Recovery and Second Chances

Before moving on with the best part of the story (my baptism), I have to tell you about something that gives me a lot of godly pride. As I stated earlier, I didn't give in to the crowd's claim of drunkenness. But even better than that, at the close of Peter's initial sermon, I was one of the first to stand up, cut heart and all, and ask the all-important question to the men there—"Brothers, what shall we do?" Of course, I used the term "brother" because of our shared Jewish heritage, not because I thought I was already a member of their saved fraternity. But I knew they were right, and the only thing left for me to do was to ask about specifics regarding how to right the wrong I had committed fifty days ago, and how to erase all the sins I had committed in my twenty-six years of living. I needed forgiveness. I needed assurance that all was right between me and God. I needed to do whatever was necessary to get that forgiveness and find out what power was available to keep me from returning to those sinful ways. Thankfully, Peter covered all of that and more. I can still hear him—his voice resounding with power and poise, allowing each of us to understand all about the keys to the kingdom that he had been handed a few years earlier:

"Repent and be baptized, every one of you, in the name of Jesus Christ for the forgiveness of your sins. And you will receive the gift of the Holy Spirit. The promise is for you and your children and for all who are far off—for all whom the Lord our God will call."

So simple! So straightforward! So sweet to the ears! The offer of salvation was upon me, and I wasn't about to pass it up. I was definitely feeling called by God, and—to use an analogy you can understand—I wasn't about to let the message go to voice mail, hang up on him or ignore the call altogether. I was going to answer the call and hang on to every single word he sent my way on that particular day, and from that day forward.

I was ready. I wanted to be baptized right then and there, but as I would come to learn during the next few hours, I needed to take things much deeper in my heart and count the cost concerning the decisions I was about to make—decisions that involved a commitment for the rest of my life. So I listened to the warnings. Peter shared most of them, but the other apostles chimed in as well. They described their best memories of Jesus' teachings about the lies of the world, and also the love of God that needed to reside in our hearts if we ever expected to overcome the power of Satan and his plans to lure us to the dark side. And I listened to their pleadings, even though I can honestly say that I didn't need them. I didn't need to be inspired or encouraged to jump on the Jesus bandwagon. I just needed for someone to help me up so I could begin my lifelong ride.

But others there needed to hear the apostles' pleas. Many in the crowd felt sure that the message was true and acknowledged their need to call Jesus both Lord and Christ, but they didn't share my confidence that they could change and make the grade of true religion. They were apprehensive about how their families might react to the news of their conversion. They felt unequipped to return to their homes and explain to their loved ones the things that seemed so very clear to them at the moment. I, on the other hand, was eager to return home and let Rachel in on the greatest secrets available to mankind. I was pretty confident she would react well, and that my time in the Brotherhood of Believers would be shared with the person on Earth I loved the most. So, amazingly, I was even used by God to put a little faith in some doubtful hearts that day, and I'm thankful He was willing to use me, even before I was officially added to the number.

Personal Cost-Counting

After Peter felt confident he had given us enough information to make an informed decision and not just an emotional one (because, believe me, there was a whole lot of emotion swimming in the spiritual stream that afternoon), he asked those of us who were willing to make a commitment to Jesus to break up into small groups for some final instructions before our baptism. We would be given an opportunity to ask any questions to clear up anything that was still somewhat fuzzy in our minds. We would also be given a chance to publicly confess our sins, and shortly thereafter make a public renouncement of them—a way of proving our seriousness to both God and those in our presence, and a sure sign that we wouldn't get caught up in people-pleasing, either. Of course, the best part of that confession was the relief I felt after opening up to other people in that way. I couldn't believe it! I had just taken that frightening first step into the land of total transparency, and yet I was better off for taking it, not worse! It was the first of many similar steps I would take during my time in the Brotherhood, each one providing an escape route from the stranglehold of Satan and healing for a hurting and heavy heart.

I joined up with a group of about forty people, and we were privileged to be with Thomas for our final time of instruction before baptism. He was so perfect for me that afternoon. Before he opened it up for us to share in the group, he told us about his personal weaknesses, and concluded by bringing to light his own episode of doubt after the resurrection of Jesus. He was still moved to tears when he shared his sin, and it made me realize even more just how much grace God had available for everyone who so desperately needed it.

I shared my major weaknesses and sins with the group (we obviously didn't have enough time to go into great detail about everybody's life, but we did capture the essence of our sinful nature in our time of sharing), and was growing more and more excited about getting those same sins off of my spiritual account and having my name added to the Book of Life. I wanted to be saved. Nothing was more important to me then, yet I knew I needed to be patient about when that would happen. After all, God had been patient with me for all my life, especially during the past fifty days since I had joined with those who were calling for his Son's crucifixion.

Baptized into Christ

But it only took another forty-five minutes or so before I was in the water up to my waist, confessing "Jesus is Lord" to the heavens and to those who could hear me on Earth. I had never said anything with more volume or certainty. Upon my confession, Thomas reminded me of what was about to take place, told me how thankful he was for me and how thankful God was for my decision, then lowered me into the water where I was immersed for the forgiveness of my sins. It all happened so fast, and I was up and out of the water in no time. Though the time spent in the salvation process was short, the effects were long—eternal, you might say. And although I couldn't physically point to my sins floating away in the water, or actually see the power of the Holy Spirit who was now living inside me, I knew they were both a done deal, because God never breaks a promise!

I dried off as best I could, but I knew I would be walking home a little damp. But it was the most comfortable I had ever felt—wet or dry. I spent a few minutes talking with Thomas and a few of the other original disciples of Jesus, thanking them and asking them for advice about how to best approach my wife with the news of my conversion, and determining how I could learn more truths about Jesus and stay strong in my newfound faith.

After attaining that information, I headed home, singing and praying the entire way, enjoying my leap from the lower clouds all the way up to number nine. Though I would be arriving home a few hours later than I had promised Rachel, this time I would be returning with humility and, even greater than that, a real solution to the problem I had brought back with me during Passover. It was the greatest day of my life. I had finally found what I was looking for—even though you could say I wasn't even looking for it. But God was looking for me, and I'm so grateful he found me and was willing to save me from my sins and the wicked generation of which I had been a member for so many years.

You may have noticed that I haven't engaged in any digressions during my conversion story. I didn't feel it would have been right to preach and teach things for your benefit while I was sharing about how God reached out to me and spared me in spite of my ignorance. Besides, the story is just too good to be told in parts. I can't tell you how many times I told the story while I was alive, but it numbered in the thousands. And I'm still telling my story. As I mentioned in my introduction, one of the things we love to do here in Paradise is have a regular time of salvation sharing. We love hearing everybody's individual stories, and all of them are quite remarkable. And every time a story is told, we look at our leader and smile, knowing it was all because of him and his sacrifice that each story was made possible.

Now that you know the account of the day I entered the Brotherhood of Believers, I would love to share a few more things with you in regard to *the rest of the story*. These extremely important spiritual matters will perhaps enlighten you as to how my experiences in the first century Brotherhood of Believers might be significantly different from what many in the religious world are calling true Christianity today. I hope you find my sharing to be both thought-provoking and helpful in your pursuit of knowing and obeying the truths of God.

Chapter Six:
The First Twenty-four Hours

The whole way home, between periods of praying and singing, I couldn't help but rehearse what I was going to say to Rachel. My homecoming would be a little later than I had anticipated, and I wanted to make sure that I didn't react the same way I had after my delayed return during Passover. And I wanted to present the truth to her in a way she could easily comprehend, much the same way it had been presented to me a few hours earlier. While I went back and forth, considering what would be the best plan for success in helping Rachel come to salvation, I finally found comfort in the words that Thomas had relayed to our group about the power of the Holy Spirit. He had brought to our attention Jesus' promise that the Holy Spirit would provide us with the right words at the right time, whenever we offered a defense for the truth. That was comforting to me, as I was getting all worked up about something that God wanted to have happen a whole lot more than I did! So I decided to let the worry-wart in me take a temporary leave of absence and just share with her from my heart. I stopped analyzing whether or not my words would be in the proper order or sound just right. I knew I loved God. I knew he loved me. And that powerful combination was promise enough to be confident that I could do a good job in passing on the truth to Rachel and my other family members.

Excited to Share the Truth

Not that I didn't care about giving a proper defense, because I did. But there's a fine line between trusting God and tearing your hair out to make sure your presentation will be as perfect as possible, and I wanted to make sure I didn't cross it. And if I happened to forget something critical during my very first explanation of the conversion process, I believed God would cause Rachel to ask me about it, or that it would be brought to my attention and hers at a more appropriate time. So I said some simple prayers to God, asking him to open my mouth with a message of grace and truth and to open Rachel's heart with a desire to do what was right. After all, in my opinion, she was much more spiritual by nature than I was, and she even knew the Scriptures as well as I did. So I was counting on those two godly traits to carry her quickly and safely toward the waters of salvation.

I tried to live in this manner throughout my Christian life whenever I had an opportunity to preach the Word to a lost soul. Oh, at times I worried myself into a Satanic corner—like the time I had my entire salvation speech outlined to share with my sister, Deborah. She was two years older than me and always did her matriarchal best to check up on me and make sure I was doing okay, especially after our parents died, and even after I had married Rachel. About three weeks into my time in the Brotherhood, I had sent her and Ethan a letter, letting them know about Rachel's and my decision to follow Jesus. When they heard about our changed lives, they wrote back to tell us they would be making the two-day journey to Jerusalem as soon as they could to express their concerns. But upon their arrival, I found out that, since the delivery of their letter, they had met some disciples from Jerusalem who had been doing business in Joppa, and they had gone from being concerned to being caught up in the desire to learn more about Jesus from me! So instead of coming to Jerusalem on the attack, they were coming on the hope of finding answers for their lives. Not only were they both baptized on that visit, but within the next few weeks, they moved their entire family to Jerusalem to be close to us and have daily access to the great events happening in the Brotherhood of Believers.

It's God, Not You

We were taught quite often in the Brotherhood that God was always at work in people's hearts, and that we shouldn't fret about a perfect presentation of the gospel, as if there were such a thing. We were often reminded that even our mistakes weren't much of a hurdle for God to overcome, and that good-hearted people would overlook any weakness on our part and focus instead on the power of God to persuade them to make a proper decision. Thats not to say we didn't always try to do our best in sharing the good news. We were prepared and, for the most part, we knew how to answer people's questions. But if we didn't have an answer, we never felt like we had to give one just for the sake of saving face. We believed that God would work just as much through our humility to admit that we didn't know the answer, or perhaps even more, than he would through our wisdom and wealth of knowledge. And we trusted a lot in prayer. We believed that prayer played much more of a role in someone's conversion than our presentation. And we often prayed in the middle of conversations with the lost. Sometimes we simply stopped talking with someone for a few minutes, just to ask God for his guidance in our discussion.

I think you would do well to imitate this mind-set. While God does admire the creativity some have implemented through various Bible study series to help the lost, those attractive tracts and brochures that attempt to spell out the plan of salvation and all the well-organized worship services that strive to touch the hearts of church visitors each Sunday, I must warn you not to rely too much on these man-made methods. I was often reminded that when we become too concerned with our strategy, we sometimes forget to have simple faith and to trust in God's amazing ability to work in lost people's lives.

Remember, you are merely a vessel. And a sinful one at that! But God loves using you regardless of your weaknesses and slowness of speech. Remember Moses and his mutterings about not being able to speak the truth to Pharaoh or the people of Israel? Remember David, his single slingshot and the five smooth stones at his disposal, and how his simple faith in the power of God brought Goliath to his knees and the Philistines to their surrender? Remember fearful Esther approaching the Persian throne, and how God moved the heart of the mighty king to grant her unbelievably bold request? Remember Paul and his own admission of fear and speech tremors, but how God used him to build dynamic churches throughout the Gentile world? All these God-fearing people were either outnumbered, outclassed or out to lunch, you might say. Yet God came through for all of them because of their simple faith in him. Moses eventually found the right words, David was dead-on with his very first launch at the giant enemy, Esther spoke boldly and saved an entire nation and Paul did a pretty fine job of leading thousands and thousands of Gentiles to Christ.

How freely do you admit your weaknesses to God when it comes to sharing the gospel? How open are you with him about your fears? How much do you trust that the Holy Spirit is moving ahead of you in each and every gospel encounter? How much time do you devote to prayer about your evangelism, asking God to put the words in your mouth, compared to the time you spend outlining your speech or plan of attack? How much do you believe that gentleness, graciousness and a good personal example are just as important as giving a grand presentation about the purpose of Christ and the plan of salvation? How much do you believe that God has been working overtime in a lost person's life to set them up for an opportunity to talk with you about his Son? How much do you pray before, during and after your time with the lost—prayers for guidance and the spiritual gift of gab?

The older I grew as a Christian, the more I understood that evangelism was a lot more about God and a lot less about me. But even knowing that, I always tried to do my best when telling someone about Jesus. The combination of trusting God and taking pains to present the gospel to the best of my ability always proved to be a winning one. Not that everyone I talked to or studied with became a Christian. Far from it! But I always knew that whether someone listened and obeyed or laughed and walked away, I had partnered with God to give them the best shot at the best life possible on Earth, and a much better one beyond the grave.

Bringing the Gospel Home

I wish I could say I totally depended on God as I shared with Rachel that afternoon, but a few times in our conversation I did what most new disciples do and put a little bit too much emphasis on my role in the matter. But praise God that he knew my heart and my sincere desire to give her a good shot at hearing the truth in an understandable way. And God came through in a big way, as he always does. For the most part, I was able to communicate things in a very concise manner, and I remained calm throughout the entire three hours we talked. And although she was very open to what I was sharing with her and never became defensive about her need to get right with God, Rachel still wasn't completely convinced I had found the truth.

Thankfully, Thomas had told me not to worry if she didn't come around right away. He said that he hadn't always grabbed hold of the truth in an instant, and yet God still stuck on his heart until the next golden opportunity to believe came his way. And I knew that there were plenty of other people in the Brotherhood of Believers whom Rachel could meet in the future, and that the apostles had offered to help those with searching hearts to turn a difficult corner.

Rachel thanked me for sharing my story, leaned over and kissed my cheek and then said she felt like it was time for her to get some rest. We went to bed earlier than usual that night, and it was a glorious night of rest for me. My sins were forgiven. I had found the truth. I had been rescued from a corrupt generation. I was part of a dynamic group of people that I knew could help me stay strong in my newfound faith. My wife was open to hearing more. My kids now had a great shot of learning the truth. And best of all, my conscience was clear about my rotten past and my personal relationship with God! It sure is a whole lot easier to fall asleep and stay asleep when you've dealt with your conscience. And it all began with my encounter with Jesus during Passover, and ended with me embracing the gospel message on the day of Pentecost.

Some Thorns in My Bed of Roses

That first day was amazing, a day that I will never forget. And while day-two was wonderful as well, it didn't end without a few challenges along the way. I was still very happy about my decision to become a disciple of Jesus, and my conscience was still clear regarding my sinful past. But things didn't go quite the way I had hoped they would that day. Rachel busied herself with early-morning baking and caring for the children's needs, and she didn't seem as interested in a follow-up gospel presentation. I had hoped to share a few more gospel details with her before heading off to work that morning, and I had to fight off some major discouragement about that. But I left a few minutes later and decided to give her the space I felt she wanted. Then, one of my part-time employees at the carpentry shop didn't show up, leaving me to attend to his duties and keeping me from a few of the projects I had planned to finalize that day. After work, I even tripped over a small pebble in the street on the way home and skinned my knee up pretty bad. At first, I couldn't help but think, "God, what are you doing here? I became a Christian, I'm sharing my faith with others, I'm being nice to people, and look what I'm getting in return!"

After a few minutes of bathing in self-pity and what I would later come to classify as pathetic Christian living, I remembered another thing Thomas had warned us about after our baptisms. He said not to be surprised at all if things didn't go great all the time, especially in those first few days. He had shared a number of challenging things that had happened to him in the first few weeks after he had made the most radical of all decisions—to begin following Christ as one of his twelve disciples. Thomas also reminded us of the words Jesus had spoken to him and the other disciples just prior to His death: *"In this world you will have trouble. But take heart! I have overcome the world."* And he was quick to point out that Satan was none to happy about our decision to leave his camp and side with the Savior. He told us that it wouldn't surprise him a bit if Satan and his demons had a large target on all three thousand of us who had just been baptized—planning to do whatever they could to discourage us in those first few days, tempting us to believe that God wasn't coming through for us as he had promised.

I'm so thankful Thomas told me about what might happen to me as a young Christian. He had warned me before my baptism about the challenges of the faith, and he had adequately equipped me after my baptism for what I might encounter during those first few weeks of Christianity. In spite of my "trio of tragedies" that first day, I was able to quickly repent of my frustration with God and my doubts about whether he loved me or not. And I decided to use the day's difficulties as opportunities to glorify God rather than get mad at him. I didn't push Rachel to talk when she wasn't ready. Later, she told me how much she appreciated my patience, and how it provided her with further evidence of just how much I had changed. I also went by my employee's home that afternoon and brought him his regular wage, just in case something bad had happened. As it turned out, he'd had a pretty high fever the night before, and although it had come down some during the past few hours, he wasn't quite ready to put in a full day's work. He was so grateful for the money I brought him, and said he had just spent his last bit of cash on treatment to reduce the fever. And as for my knee, well, I can't really say that I saw anything positive come from that, other than the victory I had by not silently cursing when it happened—more proof that I really was different and that more changes were bound to come in the days ahead.

The Offer of Salvation

Sharing all these personal experiences with you leads me to address some concerns with you about how the gospel message is being shared today on many religious fronts. I've been told that many eager people are being offered salvation without any cost-counting, clear warnings or awareness of future challenges. For example, I've been told about certain scenarios like the following one:

Someone comes to a church service or revival meeting and hears a rousing sermon about salvation and the promise of eternal life in heaven. With a new understanding of their wrong behavior, and in their excitement to turn their lives around, this individual leaps into making a commitment to Christ, but without ever really knowing what's involved.

While that might seem okay on the surface, that would be a bit like a firearm's instructor giving a quick lesson of "Ready, fire, aim!" to a first-time student before sending him out on a hunting expedition.

That student's chances would be much greater of shooting himself or another human being than bagging his game of choice. Sadly, many people who are converted in this shotgun fashion end up leaving the Lord a short time later, often because they were never completely informed about the life and commitment of true disciples or the dangers that lie ahead for young Christians.

But that's not the way the apostles remembered Jesus inviting people to follow him. Whenever people expressed an interest in following him, they were told about the various costs involved. They were warned about the strong reactions they would likely receive from family members and other unbelievers. They were admonished about their past life of sin and implored to make specific changes before they could even consider joining his band of disciples. They were challenged on their sins and weaknesses and called to deal with them decisively. They were warned about Satan and his power of influence in the world and encouraged never to take him lightly. They were told of their need to give up everything, to take up their cross daily and to love Jesus far more than any other relationship they had. They were taught that their commitment to Jesus was until death, not until they found it too difficult to continue or discovered another way to feed their spiritual hunger. And they were told how much they would need to rely upon God and other people if they expected to finish their spiritual race.

Yes, it was an all-or-nothing proposition with Jesus, and that's exactly what I had heard from Peter and Thomas on the day of my salvation. We were told of the importance of prayer and being very acquainted with the Scriptures; of learning about Jesus from the apostles on a regular basis; of breaking bread consistently and engaging in daily fellowship. We were told to count the cost and make sure we were ready for this kind of serious commitment. We weren't just changing religions; we were radically changing our lives!

Is this the way you were taught to become a Christian? Did someone show you what was involved and ask you to make a decision based upon that? Or did you just meander into a meeting and make a decision after a thirty-minute, positive presentation about the love of God and how great heaven is going to be? Now I'm quite sure that even if you experienced that kind of "conversion," your heart was probably in a good spot. But that doesn't mean you did it correctly. That's not the way Jesus did it with the people he invited to follow him. That's not the way the gospel was communicated to me. And that's not what I taught others during my time in the Brotherhood of Believers.

People heard the truth: Challenges, commitment, costs and a clear plan for discipleship. People were asked to make a well-thought out decision based upon reason and commitment, not just emotion and excitement. People were expected to say "Jesus is Lord" before their baptism, a declaration that helped to drive home the point of who would run the show in their daily lives from that point forward. And people were talked to at length after their baptism, not left to think or fend for themselves. They were warned about Satan's evil response to their loving response. They were challenged to stay close to the members of the Brotherhood. They were called to acts of giving, sacrificing and serving; to use their money, time and talents to bless the kingdom first and foremost, not their personal interests. This was my experience, and I believe it was necessary for me to know all of this in order to remain faithful to the Lord all those years. I knew what I was getting into when I got baptized. There were no surprises in a large sense. Sure, I encountered many smaller surprises throughout the years, but when unexpected challenges came my way, I knew that either Satan was attacking me and accusing me, or God was allowing me to be tested so I could grow stronger and prove my undying loyalty to him.

Family Matters

I arrived home that evening to a wonderful dinner. It was a feast of feasts. We hadn't eaten like that for quite some time, and I was grateful for it, to say the least. God was moving in Rachel's heart, and I could not only see it in her, I could feel it in my stomach! After dinner, we spent some time with the children and I was able to share a little with them about the decision I had made and how I was going to work on being the best father and husband they had ever seen. It was the first of many conversations we would have as a family about God and his plans and expectations for our lives—conversations that kept us together and tight.

Rachel was pretty quiet for most of the evening, but she was willing to allow me to lead us in a prayer and was quite interested in hearing about my workday challenges. I shared with her how I had managed to work through each of my momentary lapses, trying my best not to brag about how I had responded—yet also trying to show her how the Spirit of God, who was now living in me, had given me the power to make the right choices. She asked a few questions, but nothing too deep. And from her response, it seemed to me that, although I could tell God had been moving in her heart during the past twenty-four hours, it still was going to take a little time for her to open her heart totally to the message of salvation.

We talked about some other things for the next few minutes, and then she fell asleep, long before I did. I guess I was just too excited to let this first full day of Christianity come to an end. I prayed silently for a few minutes, but mostly my mind just kept racing, thinking about all the events that had transpired during the past few months. I couldn't believe all that had happened, and that I was one of the first privileged few to gain membership in the Brotherhood of Believers. And I couldn't imagine what lie ahead for me and all of my brothers and sisters in Christ.

My final words before falling asleep were a simple "thank you" to the God who had spared me from the empty way of life passed on to me by my forefathers, the same God who had spurred me on to become what he had always planned for me to be from the moment he started knitting me in my mother's womb.

Chapter Seven:
The First Few Months

That first week in the Brotherhood of Believers was a whirlwind. Actually, my whole time in the Brotherhood could be described in that same way—it just seemed like the beginning was a bit more intense because I was living a completely new lifestyle. Everything was changing so fast. Not that that was bad—far from it! But there were so many things for me to learn, with the most important being the teachings of Jesus that were etched indelibly on the hearts and minds of the 120 original members of the Brotherhood, and especially the twelve apostles who had logged so much time with him during the previous three years. And I couldn't get enough of it! Every day, for at least a short while, I was with the brothers and sisters, putting myself in position to be taught and trained in how to be the best I could possibly be for God. That had truly become my all-consuming passion. What had once been a do-enough-to-just-get-by mind-set had transformed into a desire to please God on every front and to give my very best in every aspect of my life as a follower of Jesus Christ.

But it wasn't always easy to make this happen. I still had to keep busy with my work as a carpenter so that I would have enough income to support my family. I still had to spend time developing my relationship with Rachel and our three children. And I especially had to make room for a new hobby of mine—using my time and God-given opportunities to teach others what I had come to know about God, Jesus and the Brotherhood of Believers to which I now belonged.

While I was engaged in a number of discussions with the lost during those first few months, my focus was mostly on learning. When I did find someone interested in hearing about my newfound convictions, I told them what I knew, but then brought them to those who had spent large quantities of time with Jesus—brothers and sisters who were much more equipped to finish the presentation. And even though finding out more about Jesus and learning how he was the fulfillment of Scriptures took up a lot of my free time, I still needed to practice a great deal of sensitivity toward Rachel. I couldn't just be out and about with the people in the Brotherhood and sitting at the feet of the apostles all the time. I didn't want her to feel abandoned, and I wanted to spend as much time with her as possible so she could see the changes God was making in my life.

But none of those time constraints or worries about Rachel developing an attitude toward the Brotherhood was an acceptable excuse for not learning at an accelerated rate in those early days. Several days a week, I either closed up my shop or stopped my work on a building project an hour or two early and spent that time with my brothers and sisters in Christ. We often met in various homes for regular discipleship sessions and lessons from the apostles about the amazing truths and teachings of Jesus. I also was able to spend a few hours each week in the apostles' presence simply by staying up later than usual or getting up earlier than normal and devoting that time to learning. I guess you could say that I just couldn't get enough of what I concluded wasn't just a good thing, but a very good thing!

Weekend Activities

Saturdays were the biggest opportunities for me to learn, and I took every chance I could to spend time with someone who could fill in a few of the gaps on the life and teachings of Jesus. Sometimes we met as a group, sometimes one-on-one; either way, we were told that we were in no way violating the Sabbath laws and regulations, laws that I still wanted to obey as a member of the Jewish community. We also met on Sundays for what was called a resurrection celebration. Since Sunday was the day Jesus had risen from the dead, the apostles felt it made a lot of sense to spend time together focusing on that great event by singing, praying, learning and encouraging one another. Remembering Jesus' resurrection inspired us to be our best for God and to become more confident and focused on our own resurrection someday, when we would live for eternity in our glorious home in heaven.

While Rachel didn't come with me to any of those learning session during that first week, I was able to persuade her to come along (as well as bring the three children) that first Sunday for our first official time of public worship. Man, was I ever nervous about that! But I was confident as well. I had already figured out which people I wanted her to meet the most, and I knew she would be completely blown away by the love she would feel in their presence. I wasn't quite sure what would actually take place during the period of worship, as this would be my first official time as well. But I knew that it would have to be inspiring, organized and full of truth. I came to realize that the apostles always made sure of that. While our times of worship were Spirit-led, allowing for some needed spontaneity, they were always conducted in a very orderly environment, making sure everybody, members and visitors alike, had every opportunity to have their spiritual needs met and leave with a strong sense that God had been among us.

Most Sundays, the apostles invited someone to share their testimony. And that first Sunday was no different. Actually, two people had been chosen for that purpose, and they were asked to talk about the impact Jesus had made on their lives. But I had no idea of the effect they would have on Rachel's heart.

After some powerful singing and a few prayers that were led by the apostle John and his brother, James, Peter addressed the crowd again as he had the day I was baptized. He gave an overview of that first day for the first-time visitors, and I was thankful for that. He was able to fill in some of the pieces I had failed to properly explain to Rachel. Then he spent about forty-five minutes or so sharing about the first few weeks of his time with Jesus. He felt that was the best thing to share with most of us in attendance, because that's the point where most of us were at in our lives. This was week number one for three thousand of us, and we were about to enter into our second week of doing our best to imitate Jesus.

In addition to those of us who had been baptized that very first day, Peter shared that God had been moving powerfully during the past six days, and that about 250 others had been baptized as well. I had heard about some of the conversions, and one afternoon, when I had left work early to get more spiritual instruction from the apostles, I had witnessed five people receive the forgiveness of their sins.

Peter's sharing was intensely personal, and plenty loud enough for all of us to hear, even amid some of the distractions the hundreds of children were causing, although most of them (including mine) had been well-trained to stay quiet and show respect for the Lord during times of public worship. He was poised in his demeanor, but powerful in his delivery. He also shared personally about how the early miracles and teachings of Jesus had solidified his initial decision to become one of his followers, but that he had still been "worldly-minded"—confused and unaware of the complete picture and plan for the Messiah. It was so refreshing to hear that from Peter. I had experienced my fair share of doubts about my decision in that first week, and I, too, wasn't fully aware of the deeper meanings of the kingdom of God and my important place in the Brotherhood of Believers.

Just Like Us

But that's one thing we usually experienced whenever we heard lessons from our leaders. While they certainly were never afraid to challenge us and call us out of any lukewarm stupor we might have been wallowing in at the time, they were equally humble and willing to share their weaknesses—their struggles in the past and, more importantly, their struggles of the present. We never felt like they were talking down to us. We always felt like they were just one of us. They said they had learned that quality from Jesus, who was God in the flesh and never experienced a moment of sin in his entire life, yet was still just one of the guys. Peter said that Jesus never made them feel as though they were less than him—if anything, he treated them as better than himself!

Let me ask you at this point in the story if that's what you experience on a regular basis from your leaders. Better yet, if you're a leader, a preacher, a pastor, an evangelist or a teacher, is that your regular approach during sermons you deliver to your partners in Christ? How much do your people know the real you? Are you afraid to be totally honest with them, thinking they'll lose respect for you if you do? Or do you see the value of being open about your struggles and sins, believing that you need it for your own humility and that the people listening to you need it just as much for their encouragement? After all, nobody likes to feel preached at, do they? Rather, it's much better to make sure people feel *spoken to* and *communicated with* whenever you're opening up the word of God and making it available to them! Are you willing to admit your challenges at home? Do you readily reveal your times of cowardice in evangelism and how much you need God's help and their help if you're going to change and be what God needs you to be? Are you open about your struggles with impurity, complacency and pride?

From my experience, the more Peter and the other leaders got open about their sins and struggles, the more I felt the burden and the need to get open about mine. And I'm confident that this is how it will work in your congregation today. If you put aside your pride and your desire to be revered and respected, and if you simply focus on sharing who you really are—your sins and weaknesses, what has really happened in your life recently and how much you really need their help to be your best as a disciple—then I'm confident you'll find a supportive and submissive congregation of Christians to lead.

Now, if you're not in a leadership role or in an official leadership position within your church, just because your minister may not welcome you into his life and tell you about his moments of weakness and sin, that doesn't let you off the hook! The New Testament writers left ample warnings about the dangers of hiding sin or not letting other people explore your heart and life for recent deeds of darkness. What I learned in the first few months was that the more I got open with my life, the better I did spiritually and the better my chances were for keeping the devil at a distance. And the more people who knew about my struggles and sins, the better chance I had for not allowing those sins to make a return visit.

The Tax Collector's Testimony

When Peter was finished, he introduced the first of the two individuals who would share their testimonies that morning. A man by the name of Zacchaeus was called to take center stage. He was a short man, and one of the brothers brought a pedestal for him to stand on so he could be seen above the pulpit. While Zacchaeus was short, nothing in his heart was small of size. Wow, was he ever amazing, and he was someone whom I considered to be one of my first spiritual heroes. He didn't speak for long, but it was plenty long enough for me to recognize that my heart had a long way to go in forming the proper attitude about money and material wealth. Zacchaeus shared about the day he met Jesus and how quickly his heart had made a radical change when Jesus invited himself over to his house. He said something about the way Jesus carried himself and made him feel loved exposed the first cracks in his greedy foundation for a happy life.

Zacchaeus was open about his life of deceit and thievery as a tax collector for Rome, and also shared how his riches had brought him more grief than good. But he said that, for the longest time, he felt that there was no way of escaping the trap of wealth, and that he gradually and begrudgingly resigned himself to life as a tax collector for as long as his body would allow him to work. But all that changed when Jesus happened by Jericho one day. He was amazed that Jesus would even give him the time of day, since nearly everyone else Zacchaeus came in contact with (besides his fellow tax-collectors) wanted absolutely nothing to do with him. That, he said, started his heart moving. And when he realized that Jesus not only wanted to spend a few minutes talking with him, but rather to spend the entire day with him, that was the turning-point, the moment that moved his heart to break.

Zacchaeus described his on-the-spot decision of repentance—to pay back all the clients he had ripped off over the years and, on top of that, to give half of his many possessions to the poor. In your modern-day terms, Zacchaeus went from upper-class in society to barely being at middle-class. And while he continued working as an honest tax-collector (an oxymoron in my day) for the next few months, he finally felt that the temptation to return to his old ways was too strong for him to remain in that position. Before he left, however, he was able to inspire a few of his co-workers to change their evil ways of doing business. He even developed great relationships with some of the Jewish folks who had previously hated him, friendships that began when he fulfilled his vow and repaid the money he had stolen from them. We all laughed to hear Zacchaeus describe their shocked expressions when he not only returned the money he had stolen, but gave back four times the amount!

Here was a happy man indeed, and, amazingly, his happiness came from his descent in the material world, not his elevation in it! And although the main goal of Zacchaeus' message was to remind us that money and material possessions don't guarantee happiness in life, and to recount his awesome encounter with Jesus, he also issued a challenge to the Christians to use our possessions to meet a pressing need.

A Monumental Challenge

There were about 3,300 new members of the Brotherhood of Believers by this time. Quite a few of them had been visitors to Jerusalem during the recent feast of Pentecost. The leaders had encouraged every last one of them, if at all possible, to remain in Jerusalem for an extended period of time before returning home, just to make sure their faith was solid and that they had embraced the elementary truths of the gospel. As you might guess, this posed quite a large logistical problem. Where were these people going to live? How were they going to be fed during that time? Granted, a few of the outsiders had skills that enabled them to secure some type of temporary employment, and a few were independently wealthy and could live comfortably without working for at least a few months. But the majority of the new Christians were jobless and in need of help for the duration of their stay! Regardless of whether or not these people were prepared for a lengthy stay, the challenge was given for each of them to do everything they could to remain with the Jerusalem Brotherhood for at least a few months. It wasn't a mandate, but most of the young disciples *wanted* to stay and they knew it would be the best possible way for them to grow in their faith.

The out-of-town Christians accepted this challenge, even

knowing that their decision would cause a great deal of concern among their family members who were expecting them to return home within a proper time (and a few months would no doubt be considered absurd). And that led to another challenge: Not only would many of these displaced Christians need to be taken care of in Jerusalem, but they would need to make sure their families were being provided for back home.

With all that in mind, Zacchaeus issued a call for help. He said that the only way this massive need could be met was if all of us pooled our resources and took care of each other. And Zacchaeus never came across as if this wasn't possible. While he didn't know the income bracket of most of those in attendance, he did know the power of a changed heart, and how the first thing a godly heart desires is to take care of others.

Some of us were challenged to give large sums of money to the central treasury, which would be overseen by the apostles. Some were called to figure out how they could hire the out-of-towners at their places of business. Some were encouraged to open their homes (and their kitchens!) and invite two, three, four, perhaps even up to ten people, to become temporary roommates. Sure, everybody in the Brotherhood would have to make major sacrifices to pull this off, but Zacchaeus reminded us how much Jesus had sacrificed for us, and that was all we needed to hear.

The Widow's Words

After the challenge from Zacchaeus, Peter returned to the stage and thanked him for his inspiring testimony. He then introduced an elderly woman named Abigail to the crowd, and relayed the story of how Jesus had once praised her for offering up her two remaining coins to the temple treasury, everything she had to live on at the time. Like Zacchaeus, Abigail had also become a follower of Jesus during his days on Earth. She had been deeply moved to hear about his encouraging words after a few of the apostles found her and shared with her how much Jesus had been impressed with her giving. Abigail wasn't in good enough health to stand next to Peter for very long, just long enough for him to share with us about how much of an honor she said it had been to give all she had to a God whom she knew would give her so much more in return. When Abigail sat down, Peter honored her as a true hero of the offering plate, and encouraged us all to be inspired by her level of giving and her trust in God.

Before leaving the pulpit, Peter asked us to get down on our knees and pray. He thanked God for the powerful testimonies given that morning, then said a simple prayer that people would open their hearts in response to Zacchaeus' challenge. And boy, did that prayer ever get answered! In the next few days, pocketbooks were opened, property deeds were handed over to the leaders, priceless heirlooms were sold and plentiful amounts of worldly wealth were brought to the apostles and deposited in the Brotherhood treasury.

My Part of the Plan

After some powerful singing and our time of worship had concluded, a long line developed at the table where people were signing up to open up their homes to other Christians. And the best thing about that line was that Rachel was standing in it! Actually, we stood there hand in hand, awaiting our turn to offer up our home to at least two people, or even as many as four, if needed. And it was Rachel who was willing to double the offer! Initially, I had thought that two new roommates would be plenty, mostly because I wasn't sure Rachel would be ready for that challenge. But I must admit that at first I didn't think I could handle more than two newcomers, especially knowing what it would mean for our children and the difficulty of working out basic sleeping arrangements.

God had been moving in Rachel's heart that morning. And I hadn't even introduced her to the ten or twelve people I had in mind for her to meet! Her decision that morning to open up our home to complete strangers also opened up her heart even more to the truths of God. (I came to understand this spiritual phenomenon to an even greater extent in the years ahead—that when you give your heart to the needy and less fortunate, God will work to give you whatever you lack spiritually.) Turns out the two people who ended up staying with us for the next few months were a young married couple, Jonas and Elizabeth, and Elizabeth was a perfect match for Rachel—exactly the person she needed to present the truths of God to her. Rachel needed daily lessons from a caring and compassionate soul and the example of a dedicated lifestyle, and Elizabeth provided exactly that. With her help, soon Rachel realized her need to become a fellow member of the Brotherhood of Believers.

We stayed around for about two hours after the closing "Amen" of worship. I quickly did away with my list of "must-meets" for Rachel. I did get to introduce her to a few of those people, and I made sure she got a chance to meet my most intimate teacher of the truth, Thomas.

He was so loving and kind to her. He also bragged about me a bit and told Rachel how proud he was that I had taken a stand for the truth. And before we had a chance to leave, Rachel invited Thomas and his wife over for dinner that very night. Once again, I was blown away by her immediate desire to welcome my new spiritual family members into our physical family's life. Thomas gladly accepted, and their visit that evening was a final blessing in a day that overflowed with blessings on every front.

My Wife and the Word of God

Those next few weeks were equally exciting, from the Sunday worship celebrations, to the midweek meetings, to the miracles performed by the apostles, to the simple dinners we shared with Jonas and Elizabeth and other disciples. Life in the Brotherhood of Believers was more than I had ever anticipated. It was as though God was leading me little by little to the realization that being baptized had been the best decision I had ever made by far—and that no decision I would make in the future would even come close. Of course, the greatest event to take place after my baptism was the day Rachel said "Jesus is Lord" and I was able to baptize her into Christ.

But there were a lot of tears in those days leading up to her salvation. There were a few things she had to confess to me that really hurt me, like how she had pulled her heart away from me emotionally at times during our marriage, and had even hoped on a couple of occasions that I might look into securing a certificate of divorce so she could get on with her life. In addition to discussing those feelings, we also sat down with Thomas and his wife, Ariel, and Rachel shared the ways she had been hurt by my leadership through the years. She also listened to the few things I needed to be open about with her. The hardest thing of all was letting her know about the time I had been immoral with a prostitute. Initially, I thought that she didn't need to know about it since that was a part of my forgiven past. But I was quickly reminded that the hidden sins of the past still had an ongoing affect on our relationship, and that total honesty was a must if we wanted to have a marriage that would be a great example to others and bring honor and glory to God.

Rachel was incredible. After expressing her anger and sadness about my sinful interlude and receiving some specific direction from Ariel on how to best move forward in the situation, she put her hand on mine and expressed to me that the past was the past, and that our lives were now taking a new direction. Praise God for forgiveness! Praise God for new beginnings. Rachel embraced her new beginning about twenty-four hours later, and I had the privilege of baptizing her into Christ. I'm not sure if I was wetter from all the tears I shed that evening, or from the water we waded into so I could immerse her in obedience to the commands of God. What an amazing experience! Rachel and I were now not only united in marriage, but united in Christ. We weren't just husband and wife, we were brother and sister, an understanding that helped us deeply in working through all the challenges we faced in the years ahead.

New Beginnings

There were plenty of new beginnings during those first few months in the Brotherhood of Believers. I did things a lot differently at work, both in the way I treated my customers, and especially in the way I encouraged and helped my three part-time employees. I even shared my faith on a regular basis with my customers. Unfortunately, none of them made the decision to follow Christ in those first few months, although later on I did have a breakthrough with a man named Timothy. He, along with his wife and two teenage children, were baptized into Christ on the very same day I shared my faith with him, and they were close friends of ours for many years.

I saw a crippled man become totally healthy at the touch of Peter's hand and watched him dance like he was a young man in love for the very first time. I witnessed about five hundred more baptisms during the next few months. Each one of them reminded me of the best decision I had ever made and provided a golden opportunity for me to express my utmost gratitude to the God who had done it all.

I came to know Jesus in a more intimate way, understanding that he was still alive and could relate to everything I faced on a daily basis. I came to know many of the twelve apostles in a way that I now realize only a few had the opportunity to enjoy. And while Thomas always remained special to me because of his original impact on my Christian life, the other apostles were equally kind and helpful during my early years in the faith.

My kids seemed happier and more content after my decision to become a Christian. Funny how that happens when the head of the household leads the way! Money was harder to save and it sure seemed like we had much less of it back then, but somehow it didn't really matter. I was too busy enjoying my time in the Brotherhood to worry about money. And besides, I always knew that if I were ever to have a pressing financial need, I was in the best of all places to receive help.

Chapter Eight:
Money Matters

As I continue with this segment of the story, allow me to focus on a subject that I think most people aren't very excited to discuss. I hope you're not in the category of *most people!* I've been told by our leader that a large percentage of preachers in your day say that money is their least favorite subject to preach about, and that an even greater percentage of their listeners like it even less! Yes, we must talk about money—your responsibility as a Christian to give your first-fruits to the Lord, and the incredible blessings that will come your way once you grasp this all-important matter. This discussion is of utmost importance, especially for those who live in America and are constantly being bombarded with creative and cost-free ideas for capturing the American Dream.

Giving to God had been drilled into those of us who grew up in the Jewish faith. Even the most hypocritical Jew had a conviction about giving their money to God, even though they often gave in order to be seen and respected, rather than to honor God and meet the needs of others. And tithing was something every last one of us knew was an expectation—a no-brainer, to use your modern lingo! We were always being called to tithe. Our leaders had told us it really wasn't an option, unless of course we wanted to experience the withdrawal of God's abundant blessings. And except for the times when we arrogantly thought we could bypass that law of God without feeling any repercussions, we tithed. We had been taught from an early age that ten percent of whatever we had in our possession wasn't ours to begin with, but belonged to God. So for the most part, we made sure we tithed, regardless of where we were on the financial ladder of success.

Abraham tithed to Melchizedek. Jacob promised God that he would give a tithe of everything he possessed if God remained close to him and brought him through his trials. Where do you suppose he learned that concept? No doubt it was from his father, Isaac, who had learned it from his father, Abraham! Then Moses delivered the tithing expectation to the nation of Israel, even while they were in the desert and long before they had been blessed with an abundance of material goods in the Promised Land. And even what they did have in the desert had been bestowed upon them by God, much of it coming as a result of the many gifts they received from the frantic Egyptians just prior to their exit from Pharaoh's evil grasp. A few centuries later, Malachi implored God's people to immediately stop withholding their tithe and promised them an opened floodgate of blessings if they would repent of their ungodly habit.

Sure, our nation may have failed to live out some of the other instructions in the Law on a regular basis, but it wasn't very often that tithing was the culprit. We were taught that anything less than a tithe was actually taking what wasn't rightfully ours—stealing from God Almighty, if you get right down to it. And we knew there would be consequences for it. So most of the Jewish people always tried to give a little more than a tithe in their offerings, even if their hearts weren't totally into it—and that's a similar conviction to the one we held in the early days of the Brotherhood, since all of us were either Jewish by blood or by proselytism. Only now, as disciples of Jesus, we had plenty of reasons to be excited about our giving. So you might say that a tithe was just the beginning of our giving. Anything beyond that was what we commonly called a sacrifice—a gift that we gave, not out of obligation, but out of our own gratitude and initiative. And there were so many needs in those early days of the church, so we knew our money would be used for noble and urgent causes.

Needless to say, the leaders in our day rarely had to give lessons about the need to tithe. But over the years, I did hear a lot of lessons on sacrifice, money and having the proper heart while giving. Our leaders were convinced that the love of money was a root of all evil, and they wanted to make doubly sure that the devil wasn't able to woo us in that worldly and sinful direction. But I didn't mind those lessons. Actually, it was quite normal for other disciples in the Brotherhood to ask me about my financial state and how I felt I was doing with my regular offerings. We were family and felt we owed it to each other to help one another be our best in our giving. I welcomed the help. I knew I was just as susceptible to greed as the next guy was, and I was grateful that my brothers in Christ kept me on my tithing and trusting toes.

Before I ask you about your heart in the matter of giving, allow me this opportunity to share with you a few of the things I was taught during my time in the Brotherhood of Believers. And these are some of the same things I gladly passed on to people whom I had the privilege of teaching and training in my lifetime.

Why Do We Give?

The first lesson our leaders felt compelled to share with us was centered on making sure we understood why we gave. They wanted our hearts to be totally involved in whatever spiritual acts we engaged in, and giving wasn't any different. For me, the obvious reasons for why we obeyed God's commands were often enough to get me moving, but it never hurt to have additional motivations as well. The most obvious reason why we gave was simple—we gave to obey God! And that principle applied to everything in our spiritual lives: God says it, so that settles it! But that reasoning aside, there was way too much information in the Old Testament about giving to ignore its importance. And from what we heard the disciples say about Jesus' stance on money, we knew we had no other option but to be generous. No doubt there were plenty of other great reasons for giving, but even if I couldn't recall an additional one at a given time, who was I to say that God didn't already have hundreds of reasons for requiring me to give, even if he felt like he didn't needed to let me in on any of them?

Secondly, we gave to honor God. Giving was our way of telling God that we understood everything we possessed came directly from him in the first place. And every time I contributed some money toward the Brotherhood treasury, it was a reminder to me that God had given me everything I had ever owned or currently owned. Not only that, but it was a way for me to express trust in God's commands and in his ability to provide for all of our needs. And there were a few times when I gave first to the Lord, not knowing for certain where the money would come from to put food on my family's table for the rest of the week. But God always came through at those times, either with unexpected earnings at my place of business, an ability to sacrifice and live on less than I thought I could or even a simple helping hand from a generous brother or sister. And when I needed a little extra motivation to keep my heart in good giving condition, I always brought to mind the story of Cain and Abel, a true account in the Scriptures that shows the horrible outcome for a man who had forgotten the blessing and honor of giving his very best to the Lord.

I also enjoyed giving because it gave me plenty of opportunities to express my gratitude to God. I wanted him to know how deeply grateful I was for my salvation, my new family in the church, my job, my family, my home, my daily bread and so much more. It was just a small and simple way of saying thanks to him for taking good care of me. And besides that, it kept me from being self-focused and hoarding my wealth. Sure, I could have used all that money I gave to the Brotherhood for other things. No doubt it could have led to some nicer vacations with Rachel and the kids, some upgrades on equipment for my business, a bigger and better home or more opportunities for entertainment enjoyment. But I was investing in something bigger than those temporary things. I knew I was storing up treasure for myself in the heavenly realms—an eternal vacation, a life without the worries of hard labor, an elaborate mansion and heavenly enjoyment that would be far superior to any form of earthly entertainment. And though I must admit that, at times, I did feel I was missing out because of all the money I was giving to the Brotherhood, I now have no regrets for a single penny I gave to the Lord.

Another important reason I gave in a godly manner was to keep my heart close to God. I knew God wanted me to be free from greed and materialism, and giving was a great way of keeping my heart content and centered on what was really important. And I would often come to realize that I still had much more than I needed, even after giving to God. Simply put, giving was one fantastic way of keeping me from being consumed with myself and my own selfish desires.

Finally, I was convinced that I was giving to promote the work and worship of God, something I was more than eager to do. The money I gave through the years helped to provide for many wonderful things: Like more full-time leadership for the Brotherhood, travel requirements to bring about greater worldwide unity, gifts to the poor among us as well as to those who weren't members of the church, additional opportunities for the lost to hear the Word and for meeting various general needs of the members of the Brotherhood. My gifts helped to counter emergencies, both in the church and in the world, and also provided various things we needed for inspiring and meaningful times of corporate worship, especially during our Sunday resurrection celebrations.

How Do We Give?

We were also constantly challenged to make sure we had the right *attitude* in our individual giving—not simple acquiescence. These lessons were always reinforced with great examples from the Old Testament Scriptures, plenty of lessons and anecdotes from what the apostles had gleaned from Jesus and a regular dose of personal testimony from the likes of Zacchaeus, the poor widow who gave it all and many others who were modeling the right heart of generosity. The attitudes we were called to embrace were very basic, but challenging just the same.

First, we were called to be careful. The chilling story of Cain and Abel painted a clear picture of that in the Old Testament. The book of Haggai also ministered to my heart on a number of occasions, as I was reminded that I must always be careful to address the *needs* of the Brotherhood long before I addressed the *wants* in my own life. And the story of Ananias and Sapphira (one I will go into greater detail about in a little while) always made me stop and think before I gave my offering, especially if I was ever asked about my gift.

Once I had made sure I was being careful in my giving, I needed a humble attitude as well. I always tried to remind myself who had given me the job I had, and that as an Israelite living in the city of Jerusalem, where business was much more prosperous than most other places in our nation, I was quite fortunate to have all that I possessed. Most important of all, I continually reminded myself that I hadn't done anything to deserve my material blessings. I wanted to be like David when he offered an abundance of gifts to the Lord, both from his palace and from his personal treasure, for the construction of a temple that he actually never even saw. And I wanted to be like the four lepers during a famine in Elisha's day, who, after a few moments of selfish indulgence in a feast of rare proportions, realized their newfound riches were meant to be shared, not hoarded.

I also was called to trust when I gave to God. God wanted me to trust that he would meet my needs if I had the heart to give to him. God had always come through for his people in the past, so why should anything be different in the Brotherhood of Believers, or with the individuals who were a part of it? That's why it was always so good to spend time with Barnabas. He was always giving so much away to others. I can still remember the time when a few of us "concerned brothers" got together with him to express our fears that he was being a little too generous with his goods. We warned him that he needed to be more aware of the financial challenges that could come his way in the future if he wasn't more careful. Well, he didn't like that very much, and we quickly found ourselves on the learning end of that teaching encounter! Barnabas gave us a two-hour overview of our nation of Israel and God's providential care for us through the mountains and valleys of our existence, then topped it off by reminding us that Jesus had access to everything in the riches realm, but chose instead to live the humble and simple life. Needless to say, that was the last time we had a meeting with Barnabas to attempt slowing down his giving!

Along with showing our trust in our giving, we also were told about the importance of having a willing spirit when we gave. I always loved reading the few Old Testament stories about how God's leaders had to stop people from giving to the work of the tabernacle and the temple because they had already given more than enough. Wow, was that convicting! And it was something I experienced a few times in the Brotherhood. The most notable example occurred when myself and the other brothers and sisters in Jerusalem and Judea found ourselves on the receiving end of an incredible offering from the predominantly Gentile churches. They had gone above and beyond the call of duty to help us endure the severe famine our area was under for an extended period of time. The money they gave not only took care of all our needs in the Brotherhood, but we were also able to take some of the additional funds and meet the needs of many people not included in the church's membership.

Lastly, we were often taught that our attitude of giving needed to be a cheerful one. It was never to be done under compulsion—unless of course, the compulsion came from the word of God or the Holy Spirit. Now I want to make it very clear that this did not mean that we held back our gifts if we didn't feel like dancing in the streets at the moment the plate was being passed. Often times, the sheer act of giving made us cheerful! Our moods were never an excuse for not doing what was right and giving to God. But, thankfully, I felt excited about my giving a lot more often than not! And I could feel that way because I knew that all things were under God's control, and I trusted his promise to take care of my needs if I honored him with my material wealth.

In summary, the Brotherhood of Believers had a deep conviction about giving. God expected it, Jesus modeled it and the apostles preached about it—that was plenty enough evidence for us to obey the teaching.

It is my opinion that we actually had the most fun in the Brotherhood whenever we gave. It became something we grew to be experts in, you might say. But we never got to the point where we felt like we had arrived. There was always the threat of Satan's lies that could take hold of us while we were taking care of necessary matters in the physical world. And there was always another need in the church or in the world that demanded not only our attention but our available funds as well. Because of the words of Jesus, along with the encouragements and challenges of the apostles and the example of brothers like Barnabas and many others, we felt like this area of giving was one in which we could never relax.

Giving in Today's Church

But it's not as though none of us ever struggled with these expectations. We did for sure! But we always dealt with our struggles, whether filthy rich, middle-class or dirt poor. There were no exceptions! And giving to the Lord wasn't just preached about or addressed in a public forum. It was addressed in small-group meetings and one-on-one encounters. But the leaders didn't make us feel as if they didn't trust our hearts when it came to our giving. The bigger issue was that we didn't even trust our own hearts. And we were very aware of the power Satan possessed to cleverly twist the truth in this area.

Yet I've been told that very few people today open their hearts and checkbooks to be examined by other Christians. While I do hear that generosity and giving to God are preached about regularly, the question I have is this: Is it being practiced? I've been told that many wealthy people are giving much less than a tithe of their income. Perhaps that's because church leaders claim it's better to accept that amount rather than to challenge them on their giving, thereby running the risk of offending them and getting nothing instead. But it's not just the wealthy who are being stingy with God. Poorer people can be just as greedy with their money, and many church leaders aren't willing to spend the time addressing their hearts, either. Often, the poor are being let off the hook because their offering is so small. After all, why bother challenging those individuals to tithe when doing so would only increase their weekly giving by just a few dollars? And most of those in the middle class get little, if any, real challenges or correction on their giving. Why, if you offend too many of those individuals, the contribution may suffer—the budget may even be reduced to the point of needing to drop some long-standing programs or preachers!

So how's the giving going in your life, in your heart and in your community of believers? How did the information I just shared with you settle in your heart? Were you defensive about any of it?

Do you get excited when you drop your cash or check in the offering plate? How often do you talk about your personal finances or your family budget with other believers? Are you open to being challenged on your spending habits? Are you content with your giving, or striving to stretch yourself to an uncomfortable limit? How much do you trust in God to take care of your needs, even when things seem impossible? Do you tithe, or do you view that as just an old-fashioned, Old Testament concept? Do you strive to reach the level of sacrifice that the Bible talks about? And what exactly are you sacrificing? How would someone from a third-world country view it? After all, in many cases, the third-world vision of heaven pales in comparison to the earthly life people lead in middle-class America! Where is your money going—to build better buildings, or to better build up God's kingdom and the people in it? What can you do to free up more of your riches to be shared with those who have a whole lot less? Besides, what will bring you greater joy and more lasting rewards than knowing that you stretched yourself, giving as much as you could so that people's lives could be improved and their souls saved?

These are some of the questions that were asked of me. Sure, at times my heart didn't like to hear them. But that wasn't the issue. I needed to hear them. I needed to have them asked of me from time to time. I wouldn't have survived the all-out onslaught of Satan—his attempts to get me to love the world and the things of it—if not for the boldness of the members of the Brotherhood as they stepped into my financial space. And I'm completely confident in saying this: Neither will you! It saddens me to say that I saw more people leave the Lord during my time in the Brotherhood because of money and greed than any other issue. And I've been told that this is still the trend today. But don't let it be said about you.

Dig into your Bible to find the truth about giving and to expose the lies of Satan about money and possessions. Refuse to buy into any part of the prosperity gospel that is so prevalent in the religious world today. Better than that, expose it for what it really is—a bold-faced lie from the gates of hell. And be sure to allow others to spend time exploring your heart to discover any damage the world may be causing it. If you do these simple things, I'm certain that you'll significantly increase your odds of one day joining our Paradise Party, where money is no longer an issue.

Yes, we strove to do our best in the Brotherhood to use our resources to meet the needs of God's church, the needy and the lost. And I was so thankful to finally be a part of something so sincere, so serious and so significant when it came to matters of eternity.

Chapter Nine:
Liar, Liar, Hell's on Fire

Rachel and I grew tremendously in our faith during those first few months. It was nearly impossible not to grow with all the available opportunities to learn and spend quality spiritual time with other disciples. And the expectation to grow was always being put forth by our leaders. Yet it wasn't in a threatening way—almost the opposite, you could say. We felt so secure in our salvation, knowing that if Jesus had extended his amazing grace and mercy to us long *before* we were saved, just so we would have the chance to be saved at some point in the future, how much more would he be there for us during times of difficulty or on days when we just weren't clicking on all Christian cylinders.

But we also knew that if we weren't growing in our faith, something was terribly wrong with our faith. We had either forgotten the power of the cross and the forgiveness we had been granted at our baptism, or we weren't doing the basics of the faith very well—things like consistently learning the Scriptures and finding out more about the life of Jesus, praying on a daily basis, staying open with our struggles and sins and just hanging out as much as possible with the other disciples. Any absence of those four disciplines usually meant we were making ourselves vulnerable to believing the lies of Satan, thus allowing our hearts to be tempted to return to our previous lifestyles and religious hypocrisy.

Thankfully, I came to understand the power of Satan right away. As much as I could feel God pulling me toward him and his love, I could also sense that Satan was doing his hellish best to trip me up, take me down and turn me away from the truth. I'd like to take a few moments to share with you some of the lies that Satan thrust my way on a regular basis in those early days. I hope this will help to keep you on your toes, totally aware of how he may be working against you at this very moment. The lies I'm going to describe aren't in any particular order of significance, but they're all very vicious ones. And if you don't combat them with the truths of the Scriptures and the unbiased perspective of others in your church family, you will slowly but surely lose your conviction on spiritual matters. Even worse, you will lose your salvation and your reservation to join the rest of us here in Paradise.

The Consequences of Sin

One lie I always had to wrestle with back then was that my sin had little or no consequences. I would get barraged with this lie right alongside the temptation that accompanied it, making it much easier to convince myself that the sin I was considering really wouldn't hurt me or anybody around me. And I suffered through some rather rotten periods in my faith whenever I momentarily believed this lie—like the times I rationalized that it was okay to not be totally honest with Rachel or other disciples; or when I lashed out in anger at one of my neighbors who constantly ridiculed my new faith in Christ; or when I gave in to laziness by telling myself that prayer could wait until tomorrow. But we were always told that a man reaps what he sows and that sin does have consequences, even if those consequences aren't seen or felt for quite some time. Sure, God can and will forgive even our deliberate sins, but it's foolish to choose to take the route of iniquity when resisting sin gives you the opportunity to bring much greater honor to God—not to mention all the benefits of righteousness you'll gain!

He Loves Me, He Loves Me Not

Another big deception I had to keep battling was the lie that God didn't really love me all that much. I dealt with that one on a daily basis. I had a pretty guilty nature, thinking that I could never measure up to God's expectations and that he was constantly disappointed in me. Satan knew that if he could get me to doubt God's love, I would find it really hard to enjoy my walk with him, and that—best of all for him—I would eventually call for a complete separation. I would come to realize that a lot of that mind-set was instilled in me during my up-bringing. While I deeply loved and respected my father for all he did to take care of our family, I never really felt emotionally close to him. I rarely felt as though he was happy with my performance, whether in school, in my obedience to his household rules or at the carpentry shop where he was training me to one day take over the business.

I soon came to discover that most people in the early days of the Brotherhood struggled with believing that God really loved them. Something in our legalistic Jewish background had added fuel to that fire from hell. And Satan loved to capitalize on it! That's why we heard so many lessons on the love of God through the years. At times, I even felt like the leaders needed to be more concerned about preaching on a wider variety of topics, but I now see even more clearly why they felt the need to camp out on this subject so often. And even when the entire sermon wasn't centered on the topic of love, there were usually at least a few references to it along the way. And the more God's love was reinforced in my mind, the more I began to believe it and the more I felt at ease with my life, confident of God's grace and goodness in the midst of my desire to grow.

About Bad Company

Another lethal lie of the devil was one that we had to remind each other about on a consistent basis. And that was the lie that says you can be around whomever you want—people with good morals but who don't believe; people who claim to follow God but aren't maintaining high standards of righteousness or adhering to correct doctrines; people with no desire to please God whatsoever; and even the blatantly sinful—and you won't be negatively affected. Satan loved to plant the thought in my heart that these various types of "bad company" wouldn't corrupt my good morals or weaken my desire to serve God to the best of my ability.

Thankfully, I had access to the Scriptures, the advice of my leaders and some good, old-fashioned common sense to set me straight. That's why I loved fellowshipping with the members of the Brotherhood so much. They helped me to reach spiritual peaks of strength and integrity and to avoid the valleys of sin and mediocrity. For me, this usually meant that I needed to prioritize spending time with my brothers and sisters in Christ each week, If I did, and if I spent a good chunk of personal time with God trying to develop a stronger relationship with him, I knew I had a great shot of being the kind of man God wanted me to be—more like Jesus and less like my natural self.

I even had to be challenged to make some difficult decisions about the different people I had hired for my carpentry business. Even though I was the boss and in charge of their work schedule, I still had to be mindful of how their words and actions in my presence might have a negative effect on my faith. In my fourth month in the Brotherhood, I came to a deep conviction that I had to let one of them go because his anger and propensity to swear were beginning to rub off on me. I felt bad about the decision, and I did what I could to help the young man find work elsewhere, but it was either that or compromise my growth as a disciple. And that just wasn't an option! Thankfully, one of the other young men who worked for me became a Christian soon after my conversion, and the third one decided to work elsewhere after receiving some pretty strong persecution from his family and friends who accused him of working for a traitor of the Jewish faith. But even in that difficult situation, God's timing was perfect. I was able to hire one of the single men from out-of-town who had been baptized on the day of Pentecost, and he actually ended up moving to Jerusalem on a permanent basis, eventually becoming a part-owner with me in the business!

I think that when I was young in the faith I just didn't completely understand how spending too much time with unbelievers or immoral people could actually mess with my personal faith. Perhaps you still believe that lie. Are you finding yourself in situations where your faith is weakened because of the influence of people around you? Are you spending enough time with believers to counter the world's influence—enough time to give you perspective on how worldly people may be affecting you? Are you willing to examine this important area and even make some hard-line decisions about putting yourself in the best position possible to help you stay pure and grow as a disciple? What I discovered in the Brotherhood of Believers was this: The people who took great caution in this area always grew the most. And the people who didn't were the weakest among us, and many of them eventually ended up leaving the faith altogether.

The Road to Heaven

Another huge deception of the devil that I had to fight off was the lie that said the road to heaven wasn't a narrow one—or even worse, that all roads of religion ultimately led to God and a home in eternity with him. That was one lie I wanted to believe quite often, especially when I thought about my friends and family members who were religious but not truly saved. I had the most difficulty with this whenever I thought about my parents. Sadly, both of them had passed away from illnesses within a few months of each other when I was just seventeen, nine long years before I came in contact with the truth that could have saved them. They were, for the most part, good people; but looking back, I knew for certain that many of their beliefs were off in regard to what the Scriptures taught. Of course, they weren't alive to be introduced to Jesus as I had been. So for the rest of my life, I had to trust in God and believe that he knew their hearts better than anybody else (including me), and that he would be the perfect judge of their rightful places of eternity. My heart always wanted to believe that my parents were definitely going to be in Paradise one day. But I couldn't let my mind go there without having some proof to back it up in the Scriptures. Of course, now that I'm in Paradise, I know the whole truth. While I'm guessing you'd like me to tell you where my parents ended up, I've been given direction by our esteemed leader not to give that information away. He wants everyone on Earth to trust his love and righteousness in judging their deceased relatives and friends, and to stay focused on saving the living.

Then there was my younger brother, Jonathan. Growing up together, he always seemed to be a step ahead of me in his heart to honor God, and my parents made sure that I heard often about how proud they were of him for his commitment. On my father's deathbed, Jonathan had even made a vow to him that he would never disown the faith of Abraham, Isaac and Jacob and would fight to keep the one true religion alive and well, whatever the cost. Sometimes I even felt that Jonathan was more committed to his Jewish beliefs than I was to my Christian faith. Yet he refused to believe in Jesus. And for the first time in his life and mine, you might say the shoe was on the other foot. I was in position to lead him in the way everlasting. But initially, I felt like it wasn't my place to judge him, because God would do that. And while my attitude was right in many regards, I had to learn that it was my place to make judgments when the Scriptures had already pronounced them. If I didn't, I was either being a coward or a compromiser of the faith. And I wasn't about to be put into either of those categories.

My conviction about the truth did lead to a number of uncomfortable discussions with Jonathan, and a year or so after my baptism, he decided to no longer spend any time with me, Deborah or either of our families. I can't tell you how much that hurt me. I loved him so very much and we always had such a blast together before my decision to follow Christ. Whenever I started missing Jonathan, I was most tempted to cut him some slack and simply say he was saved, even though I knew it wasn't true. Had I ever told Jonathan that I believed he was still in good standing with God and simply agreed to disagree, it definitely would have eased a great deal of the tension in our relationship. But whatever peace that would have produced, it would have been both temporary and false.

Avoiding persecution, especially in the family, is quite tempting. One of the easiest ways to keep the peace is by withholding the whole truth about salvation from those you love the most. Don't do it! Compromise will only weaken your faith and lessen your loved ones' chances of making it to heaven. While you need to be gentle, polite and completely humble (always remember how you made it into the kingdom of God), you still have to be bold in your presentation and fearless when telling them exactly what the Bible says regarding their eternal destiny. Some of my Paradise pals have asked me to say this to you very strongly. They firmly believe that other Christians' courage was the biggest factor that helped them enter Paradise! They all agree that, had their loved ones beaten around the bush on the topic of whether or not they were really saved in the eyes of God, they wouldn't have become Christians. Granted, some of the people in my community initially gave their families and friends a really hard time when confronted with the cold, hard facts of where they stood with God. But they eventually made it. We all urge you to either start speaking the truth or continue to speak the truth to those you love, regardless of the reaction you believe you'll receive from them. After all, that's the only way they'll have a legitimate shot of making it to Paradise. Just be sure that you get plenty of help from others in the Brotherhood about how best to approach your friends and family, to make sure you're not being too soft or too insensitive in your presentation of the gospel.

Now I'm thinking this is probably a tender subject for you. There are so many religions and so many people who believe they're saved. The false doctrines about how to be saved abound: Sprinkling infants; going through confirmation; praying Jesus into your heart; asking Jesus to come into your heart; saying "The Sinner's Prayer"; being a "good enough" person; making sure your good deeds outnumber your sins and spiritual setbacks; having last rights administered to you by a priest prior to your passing; regular church attendance; or even just being born into a spiritual family or living in a Christian nation. But that's not what I was taught, what I experienced or what I taught others in regard to how to get saved. And I suggest you go back and do a very careful study of what the Scriptures really teach, insuring that you've obeyed them correctly and that you're teaching them correctly. Nothing else could be more important than making sure you've understood the truth about salvation and receiving the forgiveness of your sins. In my day, we were often reminded about Jesus' warning that many would be surprised on Judgment Day to discover that they weren't saved—nor had they ever been saved—despite their religious backgrounds and claims of good works. I'll have more to say on that subject a little later on as we discuss the topic of baptism.

More Vicious Lies

Along with the lies I've just described, here are a number of others that would occasionally catch me off guard during my days in the Brotherhood. I'll share them with you and mention just a few basic things about each one. My hope is that you'll look into your own heart and consider whether it's time for you to confront the devil's deceit and change your thinking about these matters.

Money produces happiness. All I will say about this is that my happiest times were when we were scraping to get by and when I was giving the most back to God. Happiness, I found, was in no way, shape or form dependent upon my economic status, but always centered on how grateful I was for what I did have and how content I was about the things I didn't.

God doesn't want to answer your prayers. I believed this lie on a few occasions. But I came to understand that it's not that God doesn't want to answer your prayers, but he has his reasons for saying "no." Maybe, if he did give you what you asked for, it would cause you more damage than good; or perhaps you wouldn't grow as much as you needed to grow; or maybe your prayer will eventually go into the "answered" column—just not in the time frame you've envisioned. All Satan wants to do with that lie is shorten your prayer times or eliminate them altogether out of your frustration with God.

People are the enemy, not Satan. That's a tough one to resist, especially during times of intense persecution when people are attacking you, or when someone at your workplace is making your life miserable and scheming to drop you a few notches on the promotion ladder. It was extremely hard to grasp this truth when people I loved in the Brotherhood started getting arrested, and some were killed, simply because of their belief in Jesus and their willingness to help people be saved. For you, your "enemies" might be your boss, your brother-in-law, your former best friend or the bully at school. Just remember that your struggles are not against flesh and blood, but against Satan and his demonic forces—the real enemies who use people to weaken your resolve.

The country you live in is in the government's hands, not God's. Believing that lie will get you caught up in petty politics and entice you to put far too much time into changing whatever it is you deem to be wrong in your government's practices. While I would definitely encourage you to vote and do what you can to help bring Christian principles to those in positions of leadership, your main focus must always remain on the kingdom of God and his sovereign rule over your life and the entire universe. God is now, has always been and will always be in complete control of this chaotic world. And he will move if and when he wants to move in order to change whatever government, official or law he deems necessary—with the goal of saving more souls. Let him lead. You simply focus on continuing to be a good citizen, paying your taxes in an honest and uncomplaining fashion and refusing to get caught up in the backbiting and slander that's become such a big part of politics and political campaigning. Pray for your president and other national and local leaders on a regular basis, just as we were challenged to pray for our governor, our king and even our ungodly emperors.

The outcome of a sporting event is incredibly important. While some of us in the Brotherhood enjoyed an occasional athletic event or physical challenge in the first century, I've been told that what we experienced is nothing in comparison to what you encounter in the twenty-first century as far as sports are concerned. The plethora of sporting events that you're exposed to can easily get you sidetracked with the unimportant. Does God really care who wins? I'm not certain of the answer to that. I would say, however, that God does care a whole lot more about the individuals on both the winning and losing teams, and because of that, I would make them your primary focus as well. Perhaps you need to analyze the amount of time you devote to the world of sports and make some spiritual adjustments. I will say this: Don't miss a meeting of the body for a sporting event if at all possible, and don't allow yourself to be changed from within based upon the performance of your favorite team. Just enjoy the game and give God the glory for the athletes and the abilities they possess.

You have to fight for your rights in this world. All I will say about this lie is that it's the complete opposite of what Jesus taught and how he lived while on the Earth. I was often reminded that I wasn't entitled to anything, that everything I had was simply a gift from God. If I was blessed with great freedoms, fine. If not, I needed to adjust my lifestyle and find inner peace within my circumstances. If I was ridiculed or persecuted for no apparent reason, I needed to rejoice in the opportunity to better understand what Jesus endured, and that I was developing a deeper spiritual resolve, one that I never would have acquired otherwise.

I shouldn't have problems if I'm following God correctly. While many of my problems did go away after I became a Christian simply because I was learning how to avoid them in the first place, I still faced the normal challenges of life, and even found a new set of problems that came with my newfound faith. I still had bumps with my wife. I still had to deal with grumpy and gruff customers at the carpentry shop. I still had to wrestle with staying ahead of the financial game. I still had to correct my children on their many moments of misbehavior. I still had to work on overcoming my lustful thoughts. I still had to discipline myself to stay in good physical shape. I still had to get help in resolving relationship conflicts, both in the world and in the Brotherhood of Believers. I still got sick on occasion. I still had to deal with the sadness I felt for how people were choosing to live their lives, as well as in my inability to convince them to live otherwise. I still had to deal with some of my own sadness and disappointments over unrealized dreams. I still got challenged personally by other disciples when they felt I wasn't living up to my calling as a Christian. Oh yes, I still had problems. But I also had a relationship with the problem-solver—Jesus—and I was reminded quite often to take heart, because he had overcome the world.

I must do things just right in my dealings with the lost or they won't become Christians. I can't tell you how many times I felt as though I had just given the Gettysburg Address of getting someone to heaven, only to see them respond with a resounding "no" and an unwillingness to surrender! And I can't tell you how often I felt like I had just fumbled every word that left my mouth, and would no doubt lose the salvation game because of it, only to watch an individual respond to my presentation with, "Could you tell me more?", and a short while later with, "Jesus is Lord!" Sure, as I've already mentioned, I tried to be prepared to share my faith, but, more importantly, God was in control. It was my job to share, teach and invite. It was people's job to respond righteously. That truth sure took tons of pressure off of me and my fellow believers. Once I learned this, I was able to laugh off some of the mistakes I made in sharing my faith, and also remain humble when I eventually acquired an ounce or two of eloquence. God draws people to himself. I was simply there to remind people of that and give them the simple steps involved in becoming a disciple.

There is no hell or punishment for those who don't become Christians. Satan loves to tell both the lost and the saved this particular lie. When the saved hear it, they shrink back into a comfort zone and become complacent in reaching out to the lost. When the lost hear it, they continue on with their sinful lives, unaware of the damage they're reaping, both now and for all eternity. And when the lost and the saved all hear it and succumb to it, all hope for the world's salvation is gone, and Satan wins. That's why I was determined to keep the truth about hell in my heart, just as I embraced the truth about heaven. Granted, one truth brought a lot more joy than the other, but thinking of hell motivated me to reach out as never before, and when someone finally was baptized in response to my sharing, joy overshadowed any sadness I might feel because of my convictions about hell.

Resisting the Devil

So how is Satan lying to you? Don't try to figure out the answer to that question alone. Invite a few people to get up close and personal with you, and figure it out together. You won't regret it. Keeping Satan at arm's length and knowing a good deal about his devilish tactics will keep you thriving in your faith and will protect you from falling into the ditches that he and his demons would love to strand you in along the road to heaven.

Thank God I had people in my life who were on the lookout for how Satan might be scheming against me. And I kept my eyes open as well for ways in which he tried to wreck the lives of my brothers and sisters in Christ. That combination kept me spiritually focused, and it greatly diminished the power of Satan, causing him to flee from me on a regular basis and focus instead on other possible victims.

Chapter Ten:
Brotherhood Growth

In addition to the personal growth Rachel and I experienced in those first few months as disciples, the Brotherhood was growing as well—both in our love for each other and in our numbers. At least three or four times a week, someone would come knocking on my door at home or at work to let me know about another baptism that was about to happen. We went to as many of those baptisms as possible, because we always felt that nothing was more important than someone's entrance into the kingdom. A few times, I wasn't able to get away to witness the baptisms, but just knowing about them brought incredible joy to my heart.

Many of the people who were baptized in those first few months had initially become interested (really interested!) after witnessing a miracle performed by one of the apostles. Now you have to understand that these weren't the kind of miracles that are supposedly being performed today by those in some segments of the religious world, especially the fakes and frauds you can witness with a little channel-surfing. These miracles were always whole and always very provable, unlike what you see and hear about today. If a man was crippled, he walked immediately, not after a few months of therapy. If a woman had been born deaf or blind, her senses returned completely, and witnesses were there to back up the claim. The apostles did it just the way Jesus did it. And for many of these people, both the recipients of the miracle and those lucky enough to witness it, they found a cure for their *spiritual* sickness as well. They reasoned that only God could perform those kinds of miracles, and they were motivated to stick around and listen to what the apostles had to say about Jesus and his ability to save their souls.

Opportunities for Outreach

We always got really excited whenever one of the major Jewish feasts was about to happen. We continued to enjoy them, even more so than before, as we were able to attach a deeper spiritual significance to each of them. But we also enjoyed them because we knew that thousands of people would come to Jerusalem to celebrate, a perfect opportunity for the name of Jesus to continue to be preached. We reasoned this to be one of the biggest reasons why God started the Brotherhood in Jerusalem. What better place existed than Jerusalem, with its influx of God-worshipers at least three times a year, and with all the members of the Brotherhood happy to share the truths of Scripture with them? While many of those among the first three thousand disciples had slowly but surely retuned to their normal places of residence, we could always count on a few new converts needing places to stay for a while after they became Christians during one of the feasts.

It was an incredibly exciting time in the Brotherhood of Believers. The number of men after just two years came to about five thousand, and the total membership of the church was more than double that figure. Every day, at least one new person was being added to our number, and God was pouring out his grace in ways that astounded all of us.

Solomon's Colonnade was always packed for our regular Brotherhood gatherings, especially on those Sundays that our leaders decided we would congregate there for worship. Talk about great singing out there! And although some of the Jewish leaders were, needless to say, not the least bit thrilled with our exploding population or constant use of the Colonnade, they didn't give us much grief those first few years. Either they were too afraid of our numbers and the possibility of an uprising, or they just figured we'd burn out eventually. But they were wrong in both cases! We knew there would never be a time to physically fight back in our own defense, regardless of how unfairly we were treated. And we also knew that we'd never burn out as a movement of God. Sure, a few individuals might decide to pack it in along the way, but we had heard the promise Jesus had given to his apostles about the gates of Hades not being able to overcome the church. And we knew the Brotherhood would keep on advancing until he decided to return as he had also promised.

We continued meeting together at the Colonnade until the great persecution came to town. But we spent most of our time in one another's homes: For Scripture discussions and times to learn more about the life and ministry of Jesus; for opportunities to help each other in our individual calling to follow Jesus; for evangelistic meetings in which our friends could hear the gospel preached by one of the Twelve; and for times of rest, relaxation and really fine cuisine. I think I must have spent time in about a hundred different homes during those first few years. And I'm pretty sure that at least five hundred different people came to visit mine. But we loved it. What better place than a home to convey the truths of Jesus and the love of God? We could serve people, feed people, offer them a place to stay, make them feel like family and so much more—all the things Jesus did for the twelve apostles and those he came in contact with while he walked the Earth.

Those early days were amazing, and some of my greatest moments as a disciple happened during that time period. Now don't get me wrong. I enjoyed all my time in the Brotherhood of Believers. But some of my most precious memories come from those early days. And I'm so thankful that I was in a situation where I could grow and gain momentum in my faith. It was a perfect setting to help me and the other disciples keep Satan off of our backs, out of our hair and away from our hearts. As someone in the Brotherhood quipped one evening while he was directing a time of Scripture study for the young disciples, "You can't keep a bird from flying over your head, but you can surely keep it from building a nest in your hair." And we helped each other to live nest-free as best we could. Praise God that the truth was marching on in my heart, giving me the foundation I so desperately needed to survive some of the difficult and painful days ahead.

Chapter Eleven:
The Truth About Baptism

Before I spend any time telling you about some of the battles I faced with persecution during my time in the Brotherhood, I think it's important to talk frankly about a subject that I've heard is quite controversial in your religious world today. Most of us in Paradise have a hard time understanding the difficulties modern people have with this teaching. Baptism and its purpose were always crystal clear to us. Our major controversies usually centered on matters of the Law and our need to submit to it, and whether Jesus really was who he claimed to be. (These were two of the biggest areas in which Satan tried to use false teachers in my day, and unfortunately, he had his share of victories.) But right now, I would like to talk about my understanding of the subject of salvation and how baptism is so intricately involved in the entire process.

I urge you to do your absolute best to remain open to what I'm about to say, as it is a matter of heaven and hell! The last thing we want is for you to believe that you've experienced the new birth Jesus taught and commanded, only to discover at your death that you had completely missed the proverbial boat. Again, please remember that I'm not questioning your sincerity of heart or your level of commitment to what you believe, nor am I disputing your desire to follow Jesus. I'm simply addressing what you believe in a doctrinal sense—and we were always told that doctrine holds equal footing with the need to carefully examine your lifestyle as a Christian. If you come to understand that you've done something incorrectly or embraced a salvation doctrine that turns out to be false, don't fret or feel as though you've wasted all these years thinking you were a true follower. Perhaps those years were well spent, preparing your heart to one day be humble enough to admit you were wrong. Perhaps those years will give you even greater conviction in the future about the lies of Satan, and maybe in that time you've developed a circle of friends whom you can now help to see the light as well. And besides, any adherence to the teachings of Jesus is no wasted effort. It has no doubt kept you from a lot of sin and helped you to see through some of the world's false promises. And lastly, perhaps your experience will make you even more grateful for the salvation you'll soon receive, and more amazed at the patience of God in giving you this much time to come to a correct understanding.

On the other hand, what I'm about to tell you may simply be a great reminder of the truths you already hold onto with courage and conviction. If that's the case, my hope is that my words will help you to steer away from compromise and watering down the truth. I know that doing so will be challenging, as no doubt you find yourself in the minority position on the subject of baptism. I know you're constantly being blitzed with false teachings of salvation, like praying Jesus into your heart and intellectually accepting Jesus as Lord. It would be easy for you to accept those teachings as truth, or close enough to the truth, so that you don't have to become involved with trying to correct them. No doubt that would make your existence in the religious world somewhat easier; certainly, fewer people would feel as though you're misguided in your understanding of the Bible. But life as a disciple isn't about finding the easy or popular way. It's all about sticking to the truth, whether that leads you down a difficult, dangerous or deadly path.

No Compromise

I've been informed that many followers of Christ have been doing just that—saying that while they believe in the truths of salvation and that baptism is a necessary element in that process, they can't say with certainty that those who believe otherwise are lost and in danger of the fires of hell. But that's exactly why you have a Bible— to teach people the clear and simple truths of salvation and that God expects every single individual to practice obedience to those truths. If you can't be certain about how someone gains entrance into God's kingdom, then of what can you be certain? And wouldn't God have made this matter of salvation one that could be easily understood by everyone—young and old, uneducated and intellectual? So allow me to take you on a journey toward a better understanding of the subject of salvation by sharing what I was taught about how I (and everyone else in the world) could experience the wonders of salvation in Christ.

First, the message of salvation was simple. Whether it involved believing in Jesus, coming to repentance or being baptized—all of these components were quite easy to grasp.

I Believe

In believing in Jesus, we knew it was much more than an intellectual assent. It was a belief that involved embracing his Lordship and his teachings. If we believed in Jesus, we believed everything he said and we knew we had to accept it wholeheartedly. If he said that lust was something we had to master in our hearts as well as in our bodies, then we made that our focus. And if we felt as though that type of radical mind-set wasn't necessary in our efforts to remain pure, then how could we ever call ourselves believers in Jesus in the first place? If he said we had to make it our goal to tell others about him, how could we do anything less? If we concluded that submitting to his great commission was open to various interpretations and that each individual could do as he pleased in that area, then again, how could we call ourselves his disciples?

Yes, it was that simple. Yet today, there are millions who call themselves believers in Jesus, yet have no intention of following his teachings. Millions claim to be saved in Jesus but aren't focused on letting others know about that salvation. And millions more believe in Jesus but won't deal with each and every sin in their lives. Simply put, this is not true belief, and this type of belief has nothing to do with salvation in Christ. In my day, we were taught and always reminded that if we believed in Jesus we had to obey him. Jesus' own brother, James, made this point crystal clear when he wrote that even the demons believed, but that belief didn't mean they were saved. And none of us wanted to be equated with one of Satan's henchmen!

Do you believe in Jesus? What does that phrase mean to you? Do you understand that belief is much more about the way you live than what you believe in a purely intellectual sense? Do you see the fallacy of the popular view that theoretical, intellectual belief is enough to save you? Are you willing to admit that you need a biblical belief and that you should quickly discard the one you've perhaps come to accept from the American definition?

A Change Will Do You Good

Now that your foundation is solid in regard to what is meant by belief in Jesus, we absolutely have to talk about repentance. Again, this topic is one that's quite fuzzy in today's religious climate, but one that was quite fixed in mine. Repentance meant change—a complete change! It was a radical turn from one way of living to another. It was a decision to stop doing whatever you needed to stop doing to align yourself with Jesus, and a similar choice to start doing whatever you needed to start doing for the very same reason. It wasn't about just feeling bad, although that was a very important beginning point of the process. It was about action.

Remember when John the Baptist refused to baptize a number of people in his day simply because they failed to comprehend this point? They wanted to be forgiven through baptism, but they hadn't made a decision to turn over their entire lives to obeying God. So John gave them specific direction on what they needed to do to indicate they were ready for the waters of baptism. And we were also told stories of how Jesus didn't accept anyone and everyone who asked to follow him—he challenged them to repent first. Many turned away because they could not—or would not—accept his standards of repentance and righteousness. And I vividly remember Peter's message to me on my day of salvation. That message of repentance was loud and clear. I had already felt so much sorrow for my part in the death of Jesus. And I felt even more sorrow when I came to realize who he actually was. My heart was cut and I felt incredibly guilty for how wrong I had been about Jesus. Peter knew that was how I and many others were feeling that morning, but he still took the time to deliver a strong message of repentance. He expected our feelings to turn into actions. He expected us to make a radical change of heart and lifestyle if we wanted to gain salvation in Christ. And while I made that change in a very short period of time (within the day), there were many other people through the years who we refused to baptize because we could see in their lifestyle that they hadn't submitted to the teaching of total repentance. Some of those people were held off for a day or just a few days. Others took weeks or months; some even longer than a year. But we refused to compromise on this subject. If Jesus called people to repent, who were we to soften the blow? If Jesus expected an individual to turn away from greed, who were we to allow them to continue to glory in their financial prowess? If Jesus called people to love their enemies, who were we to baptize people who had bitterness in their heart toward a fellow human being? If Jesus expected someone to deny themselves daily, who were we to hold them to it for only a few days of the week?

No, we knew all about repentance. And we practiced it daily, not just during the time preceding our baptism. It was a lifetime decree, not a momentary one. This was the message of repentance I heard during my time in the Brotherhood of Believers. But is it the one you're hearing today? If so, then why is it that millions of people are allowed to "come to Christ" without a word of repentance being preached to their ears? How is it that ministers offer people the precious blood of Christ while refusing to challenge them to deal with the blood on their own hands? And, most importantly, what did you hear about repentance when you were invited to join God's kingdom? What expectations were put upon you regarding your old life of sin and your new life in Christ? What scriptures were you shown to deepen your understanding of this all-important topic? How often have you heard the subject of repentance preached in your church? How many times have you been challenged personally on the need to repent of sin in your life? Have you been willing to deal with the sin you see in the lives of other people in your church? Are you willing to confront them and call them to repentance? When you're trying to help someone enter God's kingdom, how much time do you devote to the subject of repentance? How much are you willing to wrestle with the sin you know is in their heart, and are you willing to call them to change the same way Jesus did with every last one of his potential converts?

Just because someone believes and is baptized, that doesn't automatically mean they're headed for Paradise. Repentance is the key here—it's dealing with your heart and surrendering everything to the Lordship of Jesus. If baptism was all that mattered, I would have frequented all the pools in Jerusalem and pushed as many people as possible into them on a regular basis. But salvation is much more than getting wet. It's about being willing to change anything and everything in your life that doesn't match up to what Jesus taught or how he lived. He was, and still is, the standard for righteousness, and our leaders never allowed us to compromise that point. I simply want to encourage you to do the same.

The Big Splash

Let's conclude this part of my story with some important discussion on the act of baptism. Keep in mind, however, that this next topic is third on my list of salvation components. Now I'm not saying that baptism is third in importance! All matters of salvation are equally important, but baptism is third in the sense that it is the third step in the salvation process. After all, each of us had to learn how to walk before we could run. And we had to learn how to talk before we could carry on a meaningful conversation. In the same manner, any teaching you might hear on the subject of baptism that isn't first preceded by thorough discussions on belief and repentance is probably a waste of time. If you have already learned about baptism, before you take the big splash, I would urge you to go back and learn the truth about belief and repentance—two subjects that Jesus and his apostles talked about a whole lot more than baptism.

But once we taught a person about the correct understanding of believing in Jesus, and once we knew they had grasped the truth of repentance and were actively engaged in it, there was just one final lesson that needed to be taught—baptism. It was the moment we received our salvation in Christ. It was the point in time when we came into contact with the life-saving blood of Jesus. It was the moment when we were added to the number of saved souls and our names were written in the Lamb's Book of Life. It was the exact instant when all of our sins were wiped away and we received the indescribable gift of the indwelling Holy Spirit. That was what I heard from Peter on that amazing day of Pentecost. And the more I learned about the subject of baptism, and the more I taught it to others, the more amazingly clear it all became. It's the same clear message I feel burdened to pass along to you today.

Allow me to share a few of my convictions on this all-important subject. And let me ask you to be honest with yourself as to whether or not this is what you were taught or what you currently claim to be true regarding the subject of baptism. If not, thank God you've been listening so far, and thank God I've been allowed to spend some time with you on this once-in-a-lifetime mission. This is exactly the primary goal of my mission—to give people the chance to make sure they've done things right, and give them another great opportunity to be saved. And if this information about baptism is something you presently believe and are currently teaching others to believe as well, praise God that you've been introduced to the truths of salvation, and please keep standing firm in your convictions. Allow me to give you five keys to understanding the truth of the controversial subject of baptism.

The Motivation for Baptism

First, let's discuss *the motivation to be baptized.* Why should someone want to get baptized? Why should someone end up being baptized? Based on my own understanding and the constant teaching of the apostles, the answer came down to two basic things:

First, baptism gives honor and glory to God. In my time, nobody got baptized who wasn't first excited about doing it because God commanded it. The joy of obeying God was an intrinsic part of someone being saved through baptism. It wasn't for show, and it wasn't just for personal safety (escaping hell). It was primarily for God, a promise to him that our lives would be drastically different from that point forward. Second, baptism was for *us.* Now, that may sound odd to you at first, perhaps even a bit selfish. But one of the main reasons

I got baptized was because I knew I was lost, and I wanted nothing more in my life than to be saved. I was greatly motivated by the hope of Paradise and the ultimate goal of living forever in heaven with God and Jesus—as were thousands of others who were baptized during my time in the Brotherhood of Believers.

This dual understanding—that baptism was first and foremost to honor God, and second, to save ourselves from the corrupt generation in which we lived—was the perfect combination that unlocked the forgiveness vaults of heaven.

The Meaning of Baptism

Next, we were very aware of the *meaning of baptism*. Contrary to what many preach and believe today, it was not at all about "an outward sign of inward grace," or a ritual we performed simply because God told us we should. We knew what baptism entailed, and we knew what we would receive once we properly submitted to that teaching.

In baptism, we were identifying with the death, burial and resurrection of Christ himself, as we also died to ourselves in repentance, were buried in a watery grave and rose up to a brand new life upon our exit from the water. I remember being told by Thomas to do everything I could to picture what was happening in that brief moment of baptism—that I was actually participating in the gospel of Jesus and identifying myself with him. And what a beautiful moment that was for me, a time I will never forget.

We all knew that this brand new life we had been promised had everything to do with getting rid of the old (our sin) and being given the new (God's Spirit). And we were all very eager to start over in our lives. I know I was especially excited about a new beginning. I had so much guilt and doubt about my life before baptism, and I couldn't wait to know that my sins had been forgiven and that God's Spirit was living powerfully in me. I knew I was carrying my sins into the water, and that upon my exit, every last one of those sins would be gone, remembered no more by the one I had hurt so many times.

I knew my sins were still on my record as I approached the water that afternoon. I didn't receive forgiveness when I felt cut to the heart over my sin. I didn't receive forgiveness when I made a pledge to God to be drastically different. I didn't receive forgiveness when I decided I would live and abide by the teachings of Jesus. If that had been the case, I'm sure Peter would have told me so. But it wasn't. The one who had been given the keys to the kingdom was using those same keys to unlock the way for me and three thousand others to find salvation in Christ. And he specifically said these words to all of us there that day: *"Repent and be baptized, every one of you, in the name of Jesus Christ for the forgiveness of your sins. And you will receive the gift of the Holy Spirit."* It was that clear! It was that simple!

But sadly, I've been told that few people hear this message in churches today. Many religious, churchgoing people do not view baptism as the point in time when they receive forgiveness. Most are led to believe that they've already been forgiven beforehand, and that their upcoming baptism is simply an outward expression of thanks to God for the forgiveness they already enjoy. But that teaching just isn't true. It isn't what Peter taught. It isn't what any of the other apostles taught. And that's because it wasn't what Jesus taught. He had drilled the exact meaning of baptism into the apostles' minds—receiving the forgiveness of sins and entering into a saved relationship with God. But not only did Peter and the other original apostles teach this understanding of baptism, everybody they influenced was teaching it as well—from Phillip to Paul, from Timothy to Titus, from Priscilla and Aquila to the one who penned the letter to the Hebrews. Forgiveness came at the point of baptism, not days, weeks, months or years before, and not days, weeks, months or years after.

But not only did we receive forgiveness at baptism, we were also promised the indwelling gift of the Holy Spirit. And, wow, was I ever grateful to hear that! I knew that baptism wasn't just about forgiveness, although I couldn't wait to get a clear conscience and a clean slate with God. But it was also about receiving the power of God to keep me from returning to my old ways of sin and selfishness. And I knew I couldn't do that on my own power, or just on the basis of how fired up I was to be forgiven. I needed the power of God, power I hadn't possessed up to that point in time, power to keep me away from my sinful past.

Nobody who gets rid of their old and grungy furniture is satisfied with sitting on the floor after that. No, they go out and purchase new chairs and couches. Nobody who trades their near-death, clunker car in to the dealer leaves the lot without some new wheels to get them where they need to go. And no one throws away an old pair of jeans without purchasing a new one. Otherwise, you'll end up furniture-less, car-less and naked—none of which would make much sense. So receiving forgiveness without an additional promise of help to live out my life of discipleship wouldn't have been very exciting for me. But I never had to worry about that, because Peter had told me (as had Thomas) that, upon being raised from the waters of baptism, I would immediately receive God's glorious gift of the Holy Spirit—the power available to help me keep changing and continue to be my best for God—something I was so excited about doing.

No, the Holy Spirit didn't come to live in me before my baptism. While I'm sure that the Spirit had moved over and around me on numerous occasions to help protect me and bring me to the point where I could decide to serve God, the truth was that I'd never had the Spirit living in me moment by moment until the day of my baptism. And no, the Holy Spirit didn't enter me a few days, a few weeks or a few months after my baptism. I got it right then and there. How else could I have faithfully lived out those first few weeks, when my life seemed to turn upside down on a daily basis, and with so much to learn and experience? How else could I have kept my composure when friends and family questioned my sanity about my decision to follow Christ? How else could I have made the changes Rachel said she noticed daily? It certainly wasn't about my effort, though I did work in conjunction with the Spirit. But the Spirit was always leading me. I was simply a follower.

Sure, certain miraculous gifts of the Holy Spirit were given to a number of believers in the first-century Brotherhood, like those in Samaria, Ephesus, Corinth and other places where the gospel message was being introduced for the very first time. But the miraculous gifts were used primarily as signs to unbelievers in hopes of inspiring them to listen to the message of salvation being given by those who possessed them. And except for one rare time when Peter had to be knocked off his high-horse of religious prejudice so Gentiles (Cornelius and those with him that day) could be included in the invitation to salvation, those who were granted these miraculous manifestations of the Spirit already had the *indwelling* gift of the Holy Spirit. If they didn't, and the indwelling of the Spirit had to be given at another point in time, then Peter had deceived us. But Peter was no liar. He reassured us that we would receive the gift of the Holy Spirit upon our baptism. And we undoubtedly did!

So does your story agree with what I've described thus far? Is this the message that was preached to you? Was this your understanding of your baptism? When you prepared to be baptized, did you comprehend that you would be participating in the death, burial and resurrection of Christ, receiving forgiveness of all your sins and acquiring God's Holy

Spirit? If not, I want to let you know that you did not hear the gospel correctly, and therefore, you did not have the salvation experience that I did in the early days of the Brotherhood. Again, don't let that fact anger or shock you. Let it motivate you to go back and read the Scriptures again. Let it inspire you to make sure you've done it correctly. Nothing could be worse—or more tragic—than allowing your pride to stand in the way of submitting to the simple meaning of baptism.

The Mode of Baptism

Next, we must talk about the *mode of baptism.* This was an easy subject for me to grasp, because we Jews were very familiar with ceremonial washings. And although baptism was in no way just another ceremonial washing, we understood the concept of taking something dirty and using water to make it clean. And I know this is one of the reasons why God chose baptism as the point of salvation—it makes so much sense and is so incredibly simple to understand. When you have something that gets dirty, you go and wash it. When you have sin that needs to be cleaned up, you enter the waters of baptism and get them washed away as well.

But many people in the religious world today do not teach this simple truth. I've been told that sprinkling and pouring are practiced by some of the largest religious groups in the world. But I never saw any of that in my day. Everyone who wanted to be saved was fully immersed in water, and everyone we baptized was old enough to understand why they were doing it. Don't get hung up on how long your religion and its teachings have been around—get hung up on what the Scriptures teach about the mode of baptism. Peter never commanded us to repent and be sprinkled. The word *sprinkle* was a completely different word in our language, and all of us who got baptized back then totally understood the difference between sprinkling and immersing. But Peter told me to "be immersed." That's what the word you translate as "baptism" meant in the Greek language, the language in which the New Testament was originally written.

And doesn't that make sense—to bury and fully immerse someone? Jesus didn't get partially buried. And nobody buries half of a person or just the forehead—they put the entire body away or under ground! And baptism is the very same burial process. And that's how Jesus himself was baptized. Even John the Baptist baptized people in places where there was plenty of water so they could be fully immersed. Whether it was Jesus, John, Peter or any of the other leaders in the

Brotherhood of Believers, none of them taught anything but immersion. That was the mode I submitted to, and that's the only mode that is acceptable to God and included in his salvation process. Again, if you didn't experience it that way, don't fret! Search out the Scriptures and make a decision to honor God by obeying the truth, not the traditions of men.

The Moment of Baptism

The *moment of baptism* is also a critical issue. And when I talk about the moment of baptism, I'm talking about the time when it finally happens. When can someone experience that moment of salvation? When is someone ready to take the plunge? Well, all I can tell you is what I experienced and what I saw in others during the first century. Simply put, it was always a matter of trust and teamwork. The trust part involved trusting that God would make it obvious when a person was truly ready to be baptized. Had they understood enough? Had they repented? Were they willing to confess "Jesus is Lord" both then and for the rest of their lives? Were they really doing it for the right reasons? We knew that God wanted people to be saved a whole lot more than any of us did, yet we also knew that he wasn't interested in people getting baptized who didn't have the right heart in doing so. So we believed that God would work to help this difficult question find an easy solution. And that solution involved teamwork.

It was always a team effort: The work of God, the efforts of the teachers of the truth and the hearts of the people who were hoping to be baptized. If the teachers of the gospel were hesitant to baptize someone, we felt this was a clear sign that the person being taught needed to take things deeper in some way. Not that the teachers were always right in their hesitation, but we also knew it was never right to administer baptism to another individual if we didn't have a clear conscience about doing so. If we felt any reservation, we simply needed to have further discussion about the individual's readiness, or else bring in some other disciples to assess the situation. And obviously, if the person wanting to be baptized was hesitant to any degree, we always waited to baptize them until it became their all-consuming desire.

Again, that didn't mean their hesitancy was from God. It might have been prompted by the devil. Even so, we never felt good about baptizing someone who wasn't totally excited or confident about what was going to happen to them. I remember a number of times having to sit down with someone in this position and help them work through their doubts or fears. But it was well worth the effort—much better than baptizing them out of sheer excitement and emotion in hopes they would get there someday.

Most of the time, those hesitant individuals ended up being baptized. But there were also a few times when those small doubts turned out to be much bigger than the people led us to believe. And when a teacher of the gospel had doubts about a student's readiness, and if a student of the gospel was also questioning their decision, those were very clear indications that everyone involved should pull back and figure out the next step in helping that student turn the corner. And while we sometimes felt tempted to get caught up in a number's game and find excitement in all the baptisms taking place, we knew in the long run that baptizing individuals prematurely was about the worst thing we could do—for them, for God and for the entire Brotherhood of Believers.

Sometimes, the person who wanted to be baptized felt they were ready, but their teachers didn't. That could cause a few challenges, and it sometimes did. But one of the ways we came to agreement when that happened was by observing the humility of the student when discussing their desire to be saved. Any sign of pride or angry impatience might indicate that the person simply needed a better understanding of Jesus' humility.

But usually, none of those scenarios happened. Most of the time, the teachers and the students were on the same page, and it sure led to a whole lot of baptisms. In my case, I had wanted to be baptized a few hours before I actually was, but Peter had been given the keys to the kingdom, and who was I to question his timing strategy? He expected each of us there that day to make sure we understood what we were being taught and what we were getting into if we ended up being baptized. And I'm so thankful I had that time with Thomas to shore up my doubts and settle in my heart that I truly wanted to be a follower of Jesus.

The Message of Baptism

Finally, the *message of baptism* was clear as well. And that message was evident, not only to the one being baptized, but to everybody who happened to be there to witness it. The message to those being baptized was that God loved them deeply and was welcoming them into his family and the glory of being forgiven by their Creator. The message was that of God's acceptance and his desire to save them for all eternity. The message to the many witnesses of baptisms was virtually the same—that God was into the saving business and that he loved to do it as often as possible and for all different kinds of people. I saw rich and poor, young and old, educated and uneducated people from all nations and backgrounds be welcomed into the Brotherhood of Believers, and every last one of those baptisms was a miracle in my opinion. God's desire to extend his love and mercy to those of us who had done nothing to deserve it always boggled my mind. But I wasn't about to argue with him! I loved being one of the members of his family, and I loved whenever I heard about another family addition. We could never be big enough! When could we, as a church, be satisfied with our growth and numbers? Never! While numbers were never to come into play when we were teaching a potential convert, we wanted the church to grow as fast as it possibly could, because it meant more souls were being saved. And we knew that God would take care of the rest and guide us through any problems we might encounter along the way.

Wow, that was a lengthy overview, wasn't it? But it needed to be! To close this segment of my story, allow me to summarize the teaching of baptism: It was *simple*, it was *sensible* and it *saved*. I invite you to further study out this crucial matter in the Scriptures, and then do whatever it takes to align yourself with the truth—the truth I was taught in the first century by those who heard it from Jesus.

Chapter Twelve: The Challenges

My first few years in the Brotherhood of Believers flew by rather fast. And before I knew it, I had been a faithful disciple of Jesus for three thrilling years. My marriage was stronger than ever. My kids were growing in their knowledge of God and his expectations for their young lives, and Rachel and I were growing in our understanding of the kind of parents God expected us to be. My work as a carpenter was moving along well, recovering from the slump I faced when a handful of steady customers decided they could no longer do business with me because of my belief in Jesus as the Messiah. My relationships in the Brotherhood were growing, and I was gaining tremendous confidence in my ability to help others, both inside and outside of the church. I was gaining strength and stability in dealing with the many temptations I faced daily, especially in regard to lust and sexual impurity. I felt great about the number of brothers who I felt close to and could be open with at any time, knowing they would give me excellent spiritual guidance. I was happier than I had ever been and so excited about what the next few years would bring for me and my family.

The Spiritual Battle Rages

Now if that description leads you to believe that everything was easy for me during those first three years, you couldn't be farther from the truth. I also experienced a number of very challenging episodes during that time, all of which God used to paint the overall positive picture I've just described onto the canvas of my life. I'm of the firm belief that life is never easy, especially when you come to a deeper understanding of the spiritual battles that disciples of Jesus face on a daily basis. And life wasn't always easy for me in those early days. Nor was it a walk in the park throughout the remainder of my time in the Brotherhood of Believers. But meeting the challenges head-on and gaining a spiritual perspective about each of them were huge keys to my spiritual survival. Those attitudes kept me faithful about hurdling each potential roadblock, and patient as I waited for God to work everything out for the good. But I sure had plenty of help along the way.

I also had to fight hard to overcome my tendency to become easily agitated by the imperfections I saw in myself and in others, as well as those I witnessed from time to time in the leadership of the church. But unlike what many do today when they become dissatisfied with something in their congregation of believers, I didn't have the option of finding another church down the street where I'd be more comfortable attending. Nor should I have been given that option! Going that route would have been completely contrary to the prayer Jesus offered for complete and absolute unity in the Brotherhood just prior to his death, and it would have only served to heighten my selfish desire for things in the Brotherhood to be just the way I liked them.

Sure, there were always a few groups of people in every part of the world who decided to separate themselves from the Brotherhood of Believers and start their own little movement. Most of them did so because they found it difficult to submit to various Brotherhood authorities, or else they thought they had a better idea than Jesus or the apostles did about interpretations of the Law and matters pertaining to unity. And upon their departure from the Brotherhood, most of those splinter groups were out recruiting new members and welcoming anybody interested in joining them in the promotion of their varying legalistic interpretations and practices. But we in the Brotherhood were often reminded that when it came to matters of the Mosaic Law, differences of opinion, relationship challenges or addressing situations in the church we weren't all that fired up about, it was all about taking the higher ground of humility and working together to come to a resolution on truth and potentially divisive matters. And whenever I was tempted to journey on the lower terrain of "my-way's-better-than-your-way", God used the Scriptures, as well as some disciples who had much more of a spiritual grasp on resolving conflict than I had, to calm me down and challenge me to develop a godly mind-set. They reminded me that God was very serious about his people being life-long partners and working through any awkward and unresolved situations. And he was none too happy with anyone being prideful and promoting their own agendas.

I often wonder where I would have been without the help of Thomas those first three years. He, Barnabas and three or four other brothers kept me from freaking out and forgetting the path and promises of God on a regular basis. God used them to remind me often of Satan's presence in the Brotherhood and his many easily accessible paths to destruction, one of those being the hellish philosophy that says "the more religious groups available to the general public, the better off everyone will be." They helped me fight for unity at all cost during those times when I was inclined to stick my heels in the ground and separate instead. And they reminded me that heaven would be the great equalizer for my willingness to fight off those urges to divide, and for my commitment to continue traveling instead on the more challenging road of Brotherhood oneness.

Rachel was also very instrumental in helping me. While it was often easier for me to accept challenges from the brothers, she was almost always right on-target when she corrected me as well. My manly pride made it a bit more challenging to submit to her, since God had called her to submit to my leadership. But thankfully, I learned the importance of doing just that—after all, Paul did point out in his letter to the Ephesians that all disciples should *"submit to one another out of reverence to Christ."* I can't tell you how much Rachel helped me through the years to trust in God and take a big break from my wayward ways of thinking.

I wanted you to know all of that before I shared about the various challenges I experienced in the Brotherhood. Because without the people God put in my life to help me, I'm pretty sure my faith would have cracked, and I would have eventually broken off my relationship with God and his people, no doubt arrogantly justifying both along the way. And I'm absolutely sure that unless you have similar people who help you find faith through your individual challenges and those temptations to do it your way, you won't make it, either.

The Pain of Persecution

One of the biggest challenges I faced during those first few years in the Brotherhood was trusting God through the various episodes of persecution that hit me personally and the church as a whole. Granted, there were some much-needed times of peace for us as disciples, but it sure seemed like most of the time we were smack-dab in the middle of some big attack, either on the church or on us as individuals. At first, I had difficulty understanding why God would allow such evil, and why he didn't just choose to eliminate the enemy altogether so we could be about the business of building the kingdom. And why couldn't I launch some spiteful arrows back at those who were regularly aiming them at me? Why wasn't it okay to give them a substantial piece of my mind? Why was I being called to love those who hated me and gave me the hardest time? Or why couldn't I just ignore them and shut them out of my world instead of coming up with a plan for how I could be a blessing to their life? Wasn't I being a wimp when I turned the other cheek? And wasn't I teaching my kids the same level of weakness when I instructed them to embrace the very same retaliation strategy?

While those questions naturally entered my mind whenever I faced persecution of any kind, thank God I got my brain washed often with the Word. I also got help from the wisdom of the brothers who knew me best and from people who had spent lengthy amounts of time learning from Jesus himself about the proper way to deal with the enemy. And when persecutor after persecutor became worn down by the love they were given from the brothers and sisters, and subsequently made the decision to join our happy family, I was reminded of the simple reason why vengeance was all God's business and none of mine. It was especially humbling when Saul made his radical transformation and joined the ranks of the Brotherhood of Believers. Nobody predicted that one! And most of us didn't even believe it after it had happened. We surmised that it had to be a clever attempt by the dark side to infiltrate our ranks in hopes of destroying us. I guess you could say we got that one way wrong! Nobody did more for our cause than Saul did. And nobody was more helpful to us than he was in our attempts to remain patient with our persecutors.

The Apostles Lead the Way

But persecution wasn't an easy thing to endure. My first major experience with it came when I heard the news that the church leaders—the very same men who had poured out their lives to help me and so many other members of the Brotherhood—had been arrested for preaching about Jesus. Now it was getting serious. It was one thing to be brushed off by those who opposed us, or even to be sworn at on occasion. And it definitely stung when some of my steady customers had decided to take their business elsewhere. (But those individuals were soon replaced by dozens of others from the church who wouldn't think about taking their business to any other carpentry shop than mine!) But to be thrown in jail for what you believe! And to be treated that way by those who arrogantly claimed to have the market on God and his kingdom—well, those things made it even more difficult to grasp.

I remember it like it was yesterday. My good friend, Daniel, came by my home and told me the news. I was so upset. I wanted to go out right then and give those hypocritical Jewish leaders a piece of my mind. That is, until I heard the second part of the story—the part Daniel didn't initially divulge because of my immediate rebuttal of anger. But when I calmed down, Daniel told me that the apostles had been released and had been incredibly bold in telling the authorities they had no plans to stop in their efforts to promote the name of Jesus..

That was a relief to me. But more than anything, it was a rebuke to me. As if God couldn't have kept them out of jail! As if God couldn't have caused the Jewish leaders to practice restraint instead of throwing them in jail! That simple but profound truth sure helped me out a lot that night, and it helped me tremendously in the days ahead when the persecution intensified and some truly remarkable people even lost their lives at the hands of the Brotherhood enemies.

After telling me the entire story, Daniel informed me that the apostles had encouraged an impromptu get-together that night for anybody who could make it. Those able to attend were to meet at the same house where some of the biggest evangelistic meetings had taken place over the past few years—the home of Barnabas, one of the wealthiest men in the group, but more importantly, one of the most sacrificial and encouraging. You could always count on being encouraged a great deal if you set foot in his home. Whether by giving you a warm hug, a warm meal or a warm fuzzy feeling, Barnabas always made you feel like a million bucks. On this night, about two hundred of us managed to squeeze our bodies into the main living area of his home, and it was a night I will never forget.

Peter led the meeting and told us the details of his and the other apostles' imprisonment, and he especially highlighted their response to the Jewish leaders' orders to shut down our outreach operations. After reminding us of the fact that persecution was a way of life for God's people in the Old Testament, that it was something Jesus had often predicted and that nothing happened outside of God's control, he asked us all to join him in prayer. We prayed for our enemies, that God would be patient with them and bring out the good-hearted ones and rescue them from the dominion of darkness. Peter quoted scripture in his prayer, a reminder to each of us that the earthly threats of the Jewish leaders were insignificant to a God who resided in heaven. And he prayed for us to be bolder than ever, that we wouldn't allow the persecution to cause us to shrink back in our efforts to save as many as possible, but that we would be emboldened to speak and preach as never before.

Bolder than Ever

I was so moved and convicted during that time of prayer. I felt so ashamed of my thoughts about retaliation, as if that would have brought about growth and goodwill for our group of disciples! I felt so embarrased that love wasn't my first instinct, but that anger reigned instead. And I felt more inspired than ever before not to allow Satan and his threats to deter me from my number one cause—testifying to the gospel of Jesus Christ, just as I had been doing since becoming a member of the Brotherhood.

When the prayer was concluded, something extraordinary happened. The room we were all sitting in actually started shaking. It was as if God was in attendance and all of his heavenly angels were there as well applauding our efforts. It seemed like the room shook for minutes, but we all concluded that it was probably more like fifteen seconds—plenty long enough to know that it wasn't some small earthquake or something we were all making up in our minds. No one else's house in Jerusalem shook that night. And there were no reports from any experts about an unexpected earthquake hitting the area. But Barnabas' house did shake that night, and we were all shaken in our faith because of it. But we were shaken in a good way—just enough to know that we needed to continue to stir up the world with the message of Jesus.

On my way home that night, I must have shared my faith with about twenty-five people. I couldn't help but preach about what I had seen and heard. I was more convinced about what I was involved in than ever before, and I was determined to find at least one person who would listen to what I had to say that night. Turns out I didn't find one, but five. Each of those five individuals accepted my invitation to Solomon's Colonnade for our worship time the following Sunday, and two of them, Omar and Eli, were baptized within the next two weeks! While more than twenty people I met that night didn't want anything to do with Jesus or my invitation to learn more about him, I remained focused on the five who were willing to give him a chance. And while only two of those five eventually made it into the Brotherhood of Believers, Omar and Eli could now be used by God to find twenty-five more. And besides, what if I hadn't shared with anybody that night? Those were the type of positive thoughts I did my best to carry with me whenever I was out and about among the general public.

Unfortunately, there were a number of nights and days when I gave in to fear or busyness and passed people by right and left on the busy streets of Jerusalem. While I wish I could go back and live those days differently, I'm so thankful that God moved my heart that night to share with those twenty-five people. To this very day, Omar and Eli often look for me in Paradise to thank me for stopping them in their tracks and telling them the good news of Jesus.

That was my first intense encounter with church-wide persecution. Later on, an even bigger episode occurred in which the apostles were arrested, re-arrested, beaten, threatened and flogged severely, leaving a few of them with lifelong scars. Thankfully, they weren't killed, and God continued to use them to strengthen the Brotherhood and lead thousands more to Christ. They actually thanked God for their opportunity to suffer for the name of Jesus, and we were all convicted once again about how little we understood what being "strong in the Lord" really meant. I'll gladly give you more details on that inspiring incident later on in my story.

These apostles were tough. And they always told us not to be amazed at their strength, that they were simply doing what they saw Jesus doing, and that he never expected any praise or added popularity because of it. And that's the attitude we ended up adopting whenever we were personally persecuted. It was simply just another part of the spiritual program. All godly men and women of the past had experienced persecution, so who were we to think we could escape it? And it was also God's way of making us tougher and testing us as to whether or not we were really in it for the long haul.

Personal Persecution

Like everybody else in the Brotherhood, I had to endure my fair share of personal persecution. Aside from the previously mentioned loss of sales from a few regular customers, Rachel and I had a few real challenging situations with some of our closest neighbors. Of course, we wanted more than anything to be a light to our neighbors. After all, they would likely see us more often than anyone else would, and we would have ample opportunities to talk with them in passing. So not too long after Rachel was baptized, we put together a little plan of our own for reaching out to them. We decided that the wisest method would be to invite them into our home, because that's where they could really witness our lives on a personal level, and we hoped that some of their defenses would be eliminated as a result. And while that did happen with a few of our most distant neighbors, that was far from the case with the two families who lived right next to us and the one who lived across the street.

I'm not sure which one of the three was the most challenging, but Rachel and I spent many hours in prayer, asking God to provide us with patience so we wouldn't take things personally. One of the neighbors even went so far as to put up a sign outside our home, as well as one outside my business, that said *Jew Hater.* That one hurt in a number of ways. We loved our Jewish heritage. As a matter of fact, most of us in the Brotherhood maintained many of our Jewish practices during our first years as followers of Christ, and we attended the various yearly feasts with fervor and fresh perspective, and we were in better touch with our Jewish history than we had ever been. I was more inspired than ever before by Abraham, Moses, Elijah, Daniel and all the other prophets and powerful men of God. And, of course, my Lord was Jewish as well. So me being a Jew-hater was about as far from the truth as anything could have been. We tried confronting them in love with what they had done, but they always said that they were only speaking the truth and that people deserved to hear it. They actually felt the sign was something God was pleased with and they hoped others would imitate their zeal in humiliating us! The good news, however, was that the sign in our yard became a topic of conversation for a number of people, and strangers and visitors to Jerusalem even approached me to question me about it—one of whom became a Christian as a result.

No, not even that satanic sign was powerful enough to keep the kingdom from advancing. But it sure did cause me quite a bit of angst. I even have to admit that I was embarrassed a few times about it, and I questioned whether or not I had the strength to keep on fighting with the weapons of Christ rather than those of the world. But I endured it all. After taking down the sign a number of times in those first few weeks, only to see our neighbors put another one right back up, Rachel and I decided we would just leave it be and allow it to remain there as a sign to God that we trusted his judgment in the matter. And it wasn't more than a week or so later that the sign came down for good.

I wish I could tell you that those neighbors became disciples, but they didn't. They actually became so infuriated by our response and our unwillingness to back down that they moved out of the neighborhood altogether. I guess they just didn't like to see all the joy taking place at our home, especially during our house church times when fifty to sixty disciples would converge upon our dwelling to enjoy times of prayer and worshiping God.

Another one of our neighbors simply stopped talking to us. We had been fairly close to them since moving into the neighborhood after our wedding, and we had been in each other's homes for dinner on a number of occasions. Our kids were about the same ages and the father of the family had a business fairly close to my carpentry shop. So we had a lot in common, and it proved to be helpful in building what I considered to be a pretty solid friendship. But that all changed after we became disciples.

We made what we thought was our best attempt to help them understand our decision to follow Jesus, but they wanted nothing to do with it. We even invited them over for dinner a number of times, but the wife would come to the door alone to tell us they had no interest in spending any more time with us. They even gave us the cold shoulder whenever we were out in the yard or saw each other on the way home from work. It hurt us a lot. But again, other disciples helped us to realize that even Jesus got that kind of treatment and that we shouldn't take it too personally, always remembering the words he had shared with his apostles about similar persecution he had received: *"They hated me without reason."*

But we had invested a lot of time and love into those neighbors, and we were just plain saddened that they treated us that way. And what made it even harder was that they taught their kids to treat our kids in the same rude manner. A friendship that once involved laughter in each other's presence, parties in each other's homes and walking together to school and synagogue turned to absolutely nothing. And we could tell how hard that was for their kids, not just ours. We knew they wanted to remain friends with our children, but their parents just wouldn't let them. And it wasn't easy explaining everything to our children, who were then ten, nine and seven years old. All we could do was trust that we were setting a good example for them, share some simple truths to help them realize that God was very near and remind them of what the apostles had told us concerning the harsh treatment Jesus had received when he was a child. We made a commitment to pray for those neighbors before each and every meal and also before going to bed. So the kids got to see us living out what we had been taught by the apostles, the very attitude they had seen played out so beautifully in the life of Jesus. After all, that's what the cross was all about when you get right down to it—Jesus giving the maximum for people he knew would have little or no interest in giving him even the minimum.

Again, I wish I could tell you that this story had a happy ending, but it doesn't—at least not completely. While neither of the parents ever became disciples, we were thankful that one of their kids, Matthew, eventually saw the truth and became a Christian a few months after turning sixteen and leaving his parents' home to live on his own. My son, Joseph, had managed to stay in some contact with him through the years. And after hearing about Matthew's upcoming marriage, Joseph attended his wedding, gave him a generous gift and shared with him how much he had been praying for him and his family every day for the past seven years. He was very moved by Joesph's gestures, and eventually told him how deeply embarrassed and angered he had felt by his parents' treatment of us. Joseph met with Matthew a few weeks later and began studying the Scriptures with him and his new wife, Adah. They were both baptized a few days later and were some of Joseph's closest friends throughout the remainder of his time in the Brotherhood. Rachel and I were even privileged to take on the role of being Matthew's unofficial adoptive parents after his own parents disowned him upon his confession of Christ and baptism.

Insiders

Our difficulties with the neighbors who lived right across the street weren't quite as dramatic, but the strange developments in our relationship took a while for us to understand. They were so friendly to us after we got baptized. They had always been nice, but not this nice. They had us over for dinner and even seemed really interested whenever we talked about Jesus and our decision to follow him. Their kids continued to play with ours, and it seemed as though our relationship was headed in a healthy direction. Rachel and I had high hopes that they would become disciples someday. Not to mention that it was such an encouraging diversion from the way we were being treated by our two other sets of neighbors. But we were wrong about that!

It turned out that they had been asked by one of the synagogue leaders to pretend to be interested in Jesus and in a friendship with us, simply as a way of finding out more about what we believed and exactly what we did during our meetings. I guess I should have recognized what was going on when they came to four or five prayer meetings in a row, then stopped coming altogether. But I wasn't tuned in to their evil strategy, and when I talked to some of the church leaders about how bad I felt for missing the signs, they encouraged me not to feel guilty. While I'm certain I could have gained better insight into their motivation to befriend me, I was simply trying to focus on the joy of (finally!) getting closer to one of my neighbors and having the opportunity to share my faith and life with them. I completely expected myself to become angry after I discovered what they were really up to, but by that time, God had changed my heart a whole lot. The compassion I felt for my neighbors' lost state completely overshadowed my desire to give them a lengthy rebuke for their deceit and duplicity.

That kind of thing happened a lot in those early days, as the Jewish leader were quite curious about what was really taking place in our individual and collective lives. But a few years later, after failing to compile the kind of juicy gossip or controversial information they had hoped to discover, they stopped doing that and turned to more overt strategies. But we really didn't care that they were spying on us. We realized that almost every time we met together, either in a small-group setting or a large gathering, at least one individual in attendance was working for the Sanhedrin. But we had nothing to hide in our meetings. We wanted people to know everything they could possibly know about who we were, what we were doing and our desire for others to know about Jesus. And a few of those Jewish spies even ended up being baptized as a result! I wish I could tell you that my neighbors were some of those fortunate individuals, but they weren't.

So between those three sets of neighbors, we experienced a myriad of challenges and emotions. But each of those situations was used to strengthen us and make us more determined that we would never lessen our zeal for God or lose our faith in Jesus.

Quitters and Qualifiers

Another huge challenge for me during my first years as a disciple was watching people turn away from following Jesus after being baptized. This was a very hard pill to swallow. Contrary to the popular modern doctrine of "once saved, always saved," we in the Brotherhood of Believers knew that people could disown God and lose their salvation. While the "once saved, always saved" teaching definitely tickles a lot of people's ears, it is so far from the truth.

To begin with, it isn't at all logical. That philosophy didn't work in any other area of life in my day, and I'm certain it doesn't work in your day either. Think about it: What farmer could count on his crops coming in annually if he only plowed and planted every four or five years? What employee could rely upon a regular wage if they didn't show up for work and follow their boss's instructions? What athlete could expect to receive the victor's crown after refusing to compete according to the rules? And what soldier could expect to remain in good standing with his commanding officer if his focus was anywhere but on the battlefield?

Not only was that teaching illogical, it was also unbiblical. Too many stories in the Old Testament proved beyond a shadow of a doubt that God expected people to finish the race, not just enter it. God kept an entire nation (minus two) out of the Promised Land because of their disobedience. And he kicked an entire nation out of the Promised Land years later for similar acts of rebellion. Prophet after prophet warned God's people of developing the attitude that says, "I'm safe and sound regardless of how I live." God saved his harshest admonitions for people who chose to think in that manner. It was also clear to us that many had turned away from Jesus during his three years of earthly ministry, and none of them, especially Judas, were told that their desertion was inconsequential.

And finally, this misguided belief was unspiritual. Feeling that your salvation is absolutely secure, no matter what you do, has never done a thing to turn anyone away from temptation or sin! What man or woman has ever raised their level of righteousness by believing that even a head-first dive into unrighteousness will have absolutely no eternal consequences? The once-saved-always-saved teaching is—and has always been—a false teaching. And many of the New Testament writers did a marvelous job of making that point abundantly clear.

So when anybody made the decision to turn their back on Jesus and return to their old religion or their old way of life, we all went through a grieving period, especially if the person was someone we had spent a lot of time with in the Brotherhood. And while we were always amazed by the number of baptisms we witnessed in the church, we were equally amazed—dumbfounded, even—that people could actually turn away from the greatest man to ever live, the greatest community to ever exist and the greatest opportunity ever given for eternal rewards.

Of course, most of the people who turned away felt as though they were still following God when they departed, only in a slightly different way (and I imagine people say the same thing today). Most of those who turned back to the Jewish faith said they felt fine in doing so, as the Jewish faith had been around a lot longer than the Christian faith had. Even those who went back to the world often said they felt like it wasn't going to be that bad. They thought their lives would now be much more stable and sound, since they had learned some valuable morality lessons during their time in the Brotherhood. Others admitted to being in the wrong about their decision, but said they just didn't think they could continue to live as disciples, especially in the midst of some pretty stiff opposition. A few of the individuals who left, however, claimed that they were simply taking a spiritual sabbatical. They had the arrogance to say that they would come back to the Brotherhood as soon as they'd had the chance to sow their wild oats.

But our leaders were always quick to give us the real truth when we heard those lies about leaving the kingdom. Every last one of those people had left the faith. They had quit their pursuit of God and his will for their lives. They had decided to exit the narrow road and travel instead on the road of least resistance. They had done the worst possible thing to Jesus they ever could have done—they had broken their promise of persevering through thick and thin.. And there were no good excuses for making such decisions.

There was never a good reason for leaving the one and only kingdom of God, and there still isn't in the twenty-first century. And we knew that their chances of ever returning were slim. Sure, a number of people did have a prodigal son experience, and we were so thankful that God always left the door wide open for people to return to him. But very few of those individuals who left the faith during my days in the Brotherhood ever returned. And while we were encouraged to keep in contact with those who left, to keep them on our hearts and prove that our love for them was unconditional, we couldn't keep knocking on closed doors. We needed to spend the majority of our time teaching people who expressed a sincere interest in God, and helping our faithful brothers and sisters to remain strong.

Not that this was cold and insensitive treatment, because Peter and the other leaders always reminded us that it was God who would restore people to himself. The prodigal son came back because God humbled him, not because anyone treated him in a certain way. We were simply encouraged to always remain ready and willing to open wide our arms of restoration to anyone who was brave enough to return to the fold. And we were equally ready to plan a spare-no-expense "welcome back" party.

The apostles' advice in this regard was so good for me to hear, because I always felt guilty if I wasn't able to track down a deserter and bring them back to the fold, especially if it was someone I had taught or baptized. But I also knew that I had to remain focused on my task at hand—that of continuing to testify about the gospel of grace to lost souls. And from what the apostles told us, this was Jesus' mind-set toward those who turned away from him. While Jesus always did everything he could to convince people to stay inside the circle of true disciples, and although he was faster than anyone in history to put up the "Welcome Home" sign, he never begged people to follow him or tried to make things just right for them so they'd feel more comfortable in their discipleship.

Too Close to Home

The hardest scenario I faced, however, was with my daughter Miriam. She was baptized at fourteen years of age, married a wonderful disciple named Zerah a few years later and continued to serve God in great ways for many years. But a few years after she and Zerah moved to Antioch to help the church deal with its explosion of Gentile growth, something happened to their faith, and hearing that news broke my heart.

They both stopped attending the meetings of the body and said they no longer desired to serve God in their original capacity. What was I to do with that? Was I to employ the same strategy with my own flesh and blood as I had with others who had left the spiritual family? And what would our times be like together now that we had much less in common? Actually, would we have anything in common anymore? Rachel and I needed tons of advice on how to treat Miriam and Zerah, and thankfully we had plenty of people who could help us think straight on this matter. And it wasn't often that thinking straight was my first reaction. I was usually tempted to react in an emotional and extreme way—I either wanted to give Miriam and Zerah the biggest rebukes of their life, or to love up on them like never before and pretend everything was fine. I was regularly told that the rebuke option wasn't a very wise one, but the loving part had its down side as well, at least the kind of "loving" strategy that I was determined to employ.

In the Brotherhood, we were often told that the answers to these and other extremely difficult questions came down to a matter of balance. Loving Miriam and Zerah was definitely something I needed to continue to do. But I couldn't just treat them the same way that I always had—as if nothing had ever happened. Something had happened. Actually, the worst possible thing had happened, and Miriam and Zerah needed to hear from Rachel and me that we were very disappointed and concerned, without making them feel like they weren't welcome or wanted in our family any more. But the biggest challenge for me was dealing with the tremendous sadness I felt about the whole situation. I can't tell you how many tears I cried when I first heard the news. I can't tell you how many hours of sleep I missed just sitting up worrying about Miriam's and Zerah's future and whether or not they would ever soften their hearts enough to be restored. And the biggest challenge was not being right there with them so we could help them develop a change of heart.

Thankfully, I had plenty of people who were willing to listen to every last one of my thoughts and concerns, and who also put me on the best possible path for helping Miriam and Zerah return to the Lord. So many people prayed for them during their departure from the truth. They were both well known and respected in the Jerusalem church and the other churches of Judea, as they were some of the first second-generation children to get baptized. In addition to offering prayers on their behalf, a few people from Jerusalem who knew them best even ventured to Antioch, as we did on one occasion, to reach out to them and encourage their return to the Brotherhood. But during all that time, no one ever said that Miriam and Zerah probably needed this time away from the Lord so that one day they could really appreciate what they'd had in the first place. No one ever said that, because it was as far from the truth as the Earth is from the sun.

If time spent away from God and in the world was something God felt fine about, no doubt there would have been plenty of scriptures promoting that belief. If it were a positive means of deepening an individual's resolve to never leave the Lord again, surely Jesus would have made that point clear with the apostles. The truth of the matter is that God never wants an individual to turn away from him and his expectations. Any time spent in the world and away from truth is hazardous time indeed. Life outside of God's direction leads to sin, and sin brings consequences. And if your child has made a decision to leave the Lord, or if they have resisted his call of discipleship and are living outside of his will, you should never look at that in a positive light. While God wouldn't want you to panic and park in only negative spaces, he certainly wouldn't want you to be naïve about your child's spiritual condition, and he certainly wouldn't want you to assume that they'll make it back to him eventually. Such assumptions can weaken the intensity of your efforts to help them return to God. But if your child has turned away from the truth, I fervently hope that they will make it back and that your story will end as happily as mine did.

Praise God that the balancing act we embraced was effective, and both Miriam and Zerah had a change of heart and bounced back strong for the rest of their lives. And I came to find out that their faith-less decision to leave the Lord and the Brotherhood of Believers came down to this: They had both felt so overwhelmed after Miriam gave birth to twins that they slowly but surely lost their faith. During those first few weeks after the babies were born, they ended up missing a number of Brotherhood meetings, they weren't growing in their knowledge of the truth as they had in the past, and they were quickly becoming overwhelmed with the cares of the world and the worries of life. And they totally stopped sharing their faith in order to attend to what they felt were more important matters, even though they had always been known for their enthusiastic evangelism.

Paths to Persistent Faith

Miriam's and Zerah's struggles helped to deepen my conviction about a few things I believe are most necessary to gaining and maintaining a strong faith—growing in your knowledge of the Scriptures, faithful attendance to all the meetings of the body and reaching out to the lost. That may sound over-simplified when you first think about it, but whenever I was engaged in those three disciplines, I always felt on top of my spiritual game. And whenever I was helping someone who had become weakened in their faith over time, their struggles typically boiled down to them neglecting their involvement in one, two or all three of those activities.

After all, keeping your nose in the Scriptures gives you plenty of reminders about how the power of God can help to keep you strong in your faith, and it provides you with many examples of people just like yourself who faithfully endured times of testing and tribulation. I always came away with a no-excuse mentality whenever I read the Scriptures. They reminded me that God wasn't going to excuse my lack of faith, and that people in much more challenging circumstances than mine had already shown that the battle could be won.

If I was determined to attend every possible meeting of the body that I could, and if I decided to go there with an attitude to give, I knew that my chances of staying strong multiplied. At Brotherhood gatherings, I could always count on being encouraged, being challenged and being offered more tools of the discipleship trade to fend off the devil's advances. Being at the meetings of the body built my faith, even when I didn't realize it—those days when I ignorantly felt as though I had just put in a few hours of time honoring God and had received nothing in return. God was working even when I thought he wasn't, simply because I had remained committed to his plan of not forsaking the Brotherhood assemblies.

Evangelism was another key that helped me to maintain a strong faith and keep a fresh perspective on the difficulties I was being called to endure. Sure, my challenges were many; and they were quite troubling at times. But I always had God and the brothers and sisters to help me fight through adversity. And whenever I taught the Scriptures to the lost, it didn't take long for my heart to overflow with gratitude. I would quickly realize the many advantages and blessings I had as a direct result of being a part of the Brotherhood of Believers. Most of the people I reached out to had no answers to some of the easiest challenges in life. Most of them had no idea about how to overcome the difficulties in their marriage or parenting. Most of them had been hit hard with the consequences of their sin, and seeing their suffering always made me grateful for the ways God had spared me by saving me when I was still fairly young.

I'm absolutely certain that if you aren't doing well spiritually at the moment, neglect of one, two or all three of these spiritual disciplines lie at the root of your problem. On the contrary, if you're doing well as a follower of Christ and feel as though you're at or near the top of your spiritual game, then you're probably engaged in all three of these spiritual practices on an ongoing basis.

Welcome Home

I was so encouraged when I heard the news that Barnabas (who at the time was one of the main leaders in the Antioch church) had experienced a breakthrough with Miriam and Zerah. He had spent a numbers of hours with them, helping them to understand some of what I just shared with you—that getting wholeheartedly back into the spiritual game would lead to a renewed heart of faith. Simply put, he called them to act themselves into a better way of feeling, not to feel themselves into a better way of acting. That was great advice, since they didn't feel at all as though they could regain their former spirituality, even though they had only been away from the Brotherhood for about a year. And little by little, with the help of Barnabas and others in Antioch who met with them a few times a week, Miriam and Zerah got their spiritual hearts beating again and were ready to be restored.

The final event that helped their hearts to be fully restored came when they heard an amazing apology from Barnabas and a few of the other leaders in Antioch. With tears, Barnabas and several others apologized for their insensitivity when Miriam first gave birth to the twins. They realized that they hadn't understood the challenges of raising twins, and that they could have and should have done much more in a practical sense to ward off the devil's discouragement. They regretted that they hadn't served them by making sure a few sisters were there to provide a break from the daily grind of child-rearing, and by encouraging more disciples to just drop by more often to allow Miriam and Zerah the chance they needed to recover from the daily effects of emotional and physical fatigue. Those humble words of Barnabas and his fellow leaders were the straw that broke the deceiver's back and paved the way for Miriam and Zerah to return to God. And to no one's surprise, in the years to come, they became extremely instrumental in helping others find their way back to God as well.

Weaknesses and Sins

I faced a number of other challenges in the Brotherhood through the years. Some came about simply because I didn't always put my own selfish nature to death on a consistent basis. Others came as a result of Satan's schemes and his desire to make my life as miserable and confusing as possible. A few came as a result of the errors of my brothers and sisters in Christ and the times when their sins reached into my personal space to cause me grief.

As far as the challenges in my life that I had no business blaming on Satan (though I'm sure he and his demons were busy planting seeds of selfishness in my heart), or anybody else for that matter, probably the three biggest were these: First, being over-zealous about things that I didn't fully understand; second, not seeking enough advice about important matters (which, I would come to realize, played right into the hands of my over-zealous and reactionary tendencies); and third, not spending enough time in prayer so I could rely upon God's strength to see me through difficult situations. This, too, stemmed from my biggest overall problem, one that sums up the root issue of these three sinful tendencies—pride!

I remember a few occasions when I made mistakes in sharing my faith with fellow Jews. At times, I gave out some incorrect information about Jesus, or talked about a prophecy that I felt certain referred to him—only to discover later that I had been wrong. I wanted so much to see my Jewish brethren be converted to Christ, and often I felt as though I only had one shot to make that happen. Sometimes when I felt the conversation moving in a bad direction, I foolishly shared some information that I thought might be able to hold their attention a bit longer—information that I wasn't completely sure was correct. No, I didn't tell out-and-out lies, but as a young disciple of Jesus, my mistake was in simply wanting to have all the answers instead of being humble and admitting that I didn't know, then returning to someone more mature to get clarification. After a few of those mistakes, I learned to tell people, without being embarrassed or feeling like a fool, that while I didn't know the answer to all their questions, I knew people who did. It was so freeing to go into conversations with that mind-set, knowing that I didn't have to have everything all mapped out in order to help people find spiritual treasure. Actually, it was even more powerful to watch how God worked through my humility in those cases, and to see a few people come to Christ once they had welcomed my invitation to get together with someone who could explain it better than I could.

I also suffered a few times from pride toward others in the Brotherhood. I always felt a big burden to help my brothers and sisters in Christ come to conviction about any particular sin in their lives, but it took me a while to learn how to be effective in my presentation. I often jumped to conclusions and was way too eager to offer quick solutions for their sinful behavior. I soon realized that I was a pretty poor listener and that I wasn't allowing people to share their struggles with me in a thorough enough manner. I was even told that some people were afraid to talk with me at times, because they just didn't feel I really loved them or wanted to help them change. Sure, people knew I had conviction about right and wrong—and I needed to possess that quality, as does every disciple of Christ. But having great insight about someone's sin without also possessing the greater ability to make them feel loved and believed in was (and still is) a complete waste of time.

I ate a lot of humble pie in those early years whenever I had to apologize for my gruff and gravelly style of confrontation. But I was so grateful to those who were brave enough to tell me how I had hurt them and others by my behavior. The hardest one for me came about a week after a friend of mine named Nicolas got baptized. He told me that he felt like I had been more interested in seeing him get baptized than in loving him and being his friend. Wow, did that ever cut to the heart!

Another time, I'm ashamed to admit that I even stopped a brother in his tracks when he was on his way to serve someone in need. He was taking a few bags of groceries to a major persecutor of the church whose wife was near death. I told him that this family had done much damage to the church, and that there were certainly other more deserving people who could benefit from his generosity. Caleb was a fairly young disciple at the time, and he looked up to me as someone he needed to trust and respect. So he listened to my advice and took the groceries instead to one of the couples in the church that I told him needed the help just as much. Needless to say, when a few of the brothers got wind of what I had told Caleb, they had a long talk with me about my judgmental and unloving spirit. They spent about an hour reviewing with me the approach of Jesus with his enemies, and it was just what the doctor ordered. I admit my heart was a bit defensive at first with how strong they were making their points, but my sin needed to be confronted sharply so I would grasp the significance of my erring ways. And I'm glad to say I quickly saw how far I had strayed from the path of God. The very next day I came by Caleb's house with an apology and an even bigger bundle of groceries to take to that family.

My tendency to neglect my prayer life was a struggle I battled with until the day I died. Thankfully, I heard many lessons on prayer at the Brotherhood gatherings, and I often paired up with people who struggled with the same weakness, just to allow some built-in accountability to rule the day. But it wasn't as though I didn't enjoy talking to God. Some of my greatest moments as a disciple were in times of prayer—whether prayers of rejoicing, or times when I cried out and bared my soul to God. But I constantly battled with the belief that prayer had more power than fervent and feverish human effort—and I struggled with this in every area of my life, from teaching someone about Jesus, to watching my marriage grow, to finishing an important project at work, to anything else that I knew required at least some effort on my part. My problem was that I felt that success was much more dependent on my effort than it was on God's. And this is quite embarrassing to share with you, but I even got a bit critical of the apostles on occasion because they prayed for long periods of time, and I felt as though they were praying a bit too much and should be working and spending time with people a little bit more. Thankfully, those thoughts were few and far between, and I'm glad I had the example of godly leaders to remind me to tap into the source of real power, which of course lay outside my physical capacity. And Rachel always set such a tremendous example for me in this area. She prayed about everything. And she prayed until she either got the answer she wanted, or until she realized that God had said "no" because he knew what was best for her and for those around her.

A Praying People

But prayer dominated our movement. We had prayer meet-ings, prayer vigils, prayer chains, all-night prayer sessions, prayer lists, answered prayer celebrations, prayer worship services, prayer lessons, prayer accountability, prayer partners and more! We were known for a lot of things in those days, but we especially wanted to be known as people who prayed. If that was our reputation, and if that reputation was indeed deserved, then we knew God would be pleased and would deliver us from whatever challenges we were facing. We knew that by praying often, we would not only be close to God, but that others would recognize that our focus was clearly on the God we claimed to love and follow.

At this time, I think it would be appropriate to ask you a few questions about your prayer life. How much do you pray? How often do you pour out your soul to God, both in times of joy and in times of sorrow? How often do you pray with others in the Brotherhood of Believers? How much are people in your church accountable to each other in this all-important area? When was the last time you felt as though you really made a commitment to regular, daily prayer? Do you have a regular time devoted to prayer each day? Do you find other times during the day to slip away for a few minutes and get reconnected with God? Does God get to hear how you feel about what you're going through right now? Does God get to hear how grateful you are for all the blessings he has heaped upon you? Do you feel as though you're growing in your prayer life? Are you in a position to teach others about how to pray more powerfully and passionately?

These are the kind of questions you should ask yourself about your payer life. And these are some of the things you need to make sure are being incorporated into the life and structure of your church family. If not, and prayer takes a back seat to other areas of your faith, the power you may be experiencing right now will only begin to wane, and Satan has you in a position where he knows you will eventually fail. More time on your knees will make the difference in your life and in your church. More time crying out to God instead of crying about all the problems you face will bring you amazing perspective about those very same problems. More time spent busting out in thankful praise for what you do receive from God will put you in a much better position to be happy and content about the things you don't receive. More time spent bringing your requests before God than before man will ensure that those requests are heard and responded to in the best possible manner. More people praying on your behalf means it's much more likely your petition will carry the necessary clout. And more prayer groups gathering across your city to pray for a spiritual harvest will ensure that you'll meet more open hearts in your daily efforts to bring salvation to your fellow man.

Help Is Available

Very soon after joining the Brotherhood of Believers, I learned the important spiritual discipline of seeking advice. It only took a few times of seeing my wife in tears over my insensitive directions for her life and schedule to realize I needed lots of advice about my marriage! After a few valuable times of learning from married couples we admired, I came to understand that even though I was Rachel's God-appointed leader, the sisters (especially the married ones) had a much better understanding of what she needed as a wife and mother than I did. From then on, I often ran my ideas by at least one other sister before sharing them with my wife. Early on, most of those ideas were met with strong resistance by those godly women. And I was given some valuable (not to mention much better) suggestions for how to present my thoughts and plans to my wife. Even after I identified the triple-tangled root of my problem (insensitivity, pride and an arrogance that assumed, "I'm not a woman but I still know what she's feeling"), I still got a lot of consistent input from the women Rachel was closest to in the Brotherhood. And she couldn't have been more grateful to me for choosing this course of action in our relationship. I can't tell you how many arguments we avoided because I chose to seek advice. And thankfully, Rachel also sought a lot of direction from the married brothers who were in my life.

Probably the biggest personal challenge I faced throughout my time in the Brotherhood was dealing with the guilt I felt about the time I had committed adultery with a prostitute on a business trip. Even though Rachel had showered me with her incredible grace and forgiveness, and even though I knew God had forgiven me completely for that awful sin, I still had a problem forgiving myself. I felt as though I had to live my life making it up to Rachel and to God. Not only that, but my lack of discretion that terrible day left me with haunting memories, and I often begged God to take away the mental pictures that kept coming back.

Thankfully, a few of the disciples helped me to realize that some of those awful memories I faced were God's way of keeping me from traveling down similar paths in the future. I knew how awful the guilt of adultery was, and I knew how terrible Rachel had felt after learning I had cheated on her, and I wanted nothing to do with anything close to a repeat performance. On a few occasions, business brought me back to Sychar where the adultery had occurred, and I even passed by the very house of ill-repute that I had wandered into in my pre-Christian days. I must say that it was quite tempting (in spite of my hatred for the sin) to want to go right back in there and repeat my mistake. The desires of the flesh were strong, and lust was something I always had to work hard to overcome in my life. Thank God I got some good advice about how to put myself in a better position to resist temptation during the few times I returned to that city.

The first time I returned there, I decided that I was just too weak and susceptible to sin, and I didn't trust myself at all. So to cover all my bases, I asked one of my closest friends in the Brotherhood to join me on my trip. He was there with me every step of the way, and his presence took away almost every possible longing I had to return to the folly of sin. I even paid for his entire trip. It was well worth it to me to make sure I did everything I could to resist any temptation, and also to show my wife that my repentance was real. I actually took another brother on my second trip, and things went fine once again. A third time I went alone, thinking that I would be strong enough to endure any possible evil that Satan might place in my path. And I was! I did, however, decide that my third trip there would be my last. Though I was confident that I would never be unfaithful to my wife in that manner again, it wasn't worth it to me to keep bringing the thought and the temptation back into the picture. Sure, I lost a bit of business by not going back there ever again, but what I lost in revenue I gained in respect from my wife and in confidence in my heart—the confidence that came from knowing that Satan had failed to win in his battle to get me to return to my sinful ways. Not that I didn't struggle with lust and impure thoughts on other levels and in other places, because I certainly did. But I continued to practice high levels of openness with my brothers in Christ, and played it incredibly safe whenever I found myself in situations where I thought the demons of adultery might be waiting to take me down once again.

The Sins of Others

I also faced a number of challenges because of other people's sins, but I don't want to spend too much time discussing those, nor should you spend much time dwelling on that subject, either. After all, I certainly didn't want anybody in the Brotherhood reflecting on the ways I had hurt them, and I especially didn't want any of them living in a state of bitterness and resentment toward me.

But I was hurt on occasion by people's lack of insensitivity toward me and my family. I was hurt by a few of the brothers who didn't keep their promises to pray for me, and by the times when people occasionally forgot to keep important appointments with me. And sometimes I did feel like people didn't understand the demands of my job, and therefore weren't in a position to give me very good input about my schedule and my devotion to the meetings of the body. But whenever I got to feeling as though people had let me down or were causing me strife, I was reminded of the parable of the unmerciful servant that Jesus had told his disciples (and they often recounted to us). That parable helped me to realize that forgiveness was the key to great relationships, not perfection. I had hurt a number of people with my own weaknesses and sins, so who was I to hold their mistakes against them? I knew (we all knew) that forgiveness for others was the biggest test of our Christianity, and the biggest expectation of a God who had completely forgiven us and who remained in the forgiving business on a minute-by-minute basis. There was never anything more refreshing to me than to know that one of the brothers or sisters had forgiven me of an offense. And I always felt so unburdened in my own heart whenever I was able to offer similar forgiveness to others.

Then there were the many times when the sins of unbelievers came to our doorstep. Whether it was from persecution, basic unkindness or the temptation we felt to become bitter at God and them for their lives of relative ease compared to ours, we were all battling against pride and ungodly thoughts of retaliation. It was especially tempting to give into the pride of looking down upon those people for their ignorance of spiritual matters. But all of these attitudes fell woefully short of the grace Jesus exhibited on the cross when he prayed for his enemies: *"Father, forgive them, for they do not know what they are doing."*

I often talked with people who were struggling with forgiveness, and shared about my personal encounter with Jesus at his death. I felt such gratitude for the patience he had displayed toward me, and I did my best to encourage my brothers and sisters to embrace his path to patience in regard to the unbelievers they encountered: Turn the other cheek. Pray for your enemies. Remember your past. People aren't the enemy, Satan is.

You, too, will do well to keep these same attitudes in mind when people try to make your life a little more difficult than it should be. Your patience, your prayers, your understanding of your sinful past and your practical but humble understanding of their ignorance will allow many of your current enemies to turn their lives over to God and join your happy band of believers.

As Far as it Depends on You

Yet I'm told that many preachers and their parishioners are quick to pick their enemies apart, especially those who've chosen a political position that they feel goes against the values of Christianity. Petty name-calling, plenty of retaliation, protests and poor examples of Christ (who daily and deeply loved his enemies) are the actions that often rule the day, instead of praying for those same individuals and putting on a robe of righteousness that, in the long-run, will expose their spiritual nakedness. My friend, this should not be! Help one another in your efforts to treat your enemies with the utmost respect. Challenge one another to feed your enemy, not fry them! Do not allow a single word of hatred or bitterness to escape your lips. Honor the words of God and never speak an evil word against the leaders in your life, both those in the church and those in the world. Flee from your political pursuits and throw away your sermons that slander the leaders of the land. Put your greatest enemies at the very top of your prayer list. And most important of all, let God do his job of judging, the job he has done often and perfectly since the creation of the world. Devote your time to loving and teaching, the very things God has called you to do on his behalf.

In the following segment of my story, I'd like to share about some of my greatest difficulties in my first decade as a Christian. Some of my biggest challenges during that time came as a result of the sinful actions of three individuals—two of whom were Christians. Allow me to share about those individuals and what their actions did both to challenge me and change my heart for the better.

Chapter Thirteen:
Difficult but Glorious Days

I could tell by the look on Rachel's face that something had gone terribly wrong. I was returning home that evening after about ten hours of work, and it looked as though Rachel had been crying for at least that long. My immediate thought was that something bad had happened to one of the kids, or that she had just received news that her father had passed away. My greatest hope was that I could be used by God to bring her the encouragement she needed to endure whatever was tearing apart her heart.

As soon as I opened the front door, Rachel got up from the table in the dining area and came running toward me. She threw her arms around me and couldn't stop sobbing for the next few minutes. I was trying to get her to talk, but even when she did make some effort to tell me what was happening, her words didn't make much sense. Finally, she calmed down and shared the dreadful news: Ananias and Sapphira were dead. She didn't have all the details, just something about how they were caught in a horrible lie and that God had meted out his discipline in an immediate and final way. She said the leaders had called a meeting of each of the house church groups for the following evening so they could adequately convey what had really happened and why the punishment was so severe, as well as squelch certain rumors that had already begun circulating.

I must admit I had many thoughts during those following twenty-four hours—primarily that the punishment was way too severe and that if one-time deceit was the issue, then nearly everybody in the Brotherhood deserved a similar fate. But I was able to take captive those initial thoughts by recollecting how God had always treated me and my friends in the church with fairness and grace whenever we sinned. So I concluded that something about this situation must have been terribly ungodly and unusually grievous.

Rachel and I had enjoyed a fairly close relationship with Ananias and Sapphira. I wouldn't say we were best friends, but we had spent a few evenings together at each other's homes, shared a number of positive spiritual conversations through the years and always made a point to fellowship with each other at our large Brotherhood gatherings. They seemed to be a solid couple in the Lord, and nothing I saw would have ever led me to believe that they were causing trouble or were a threat to the church's well being. I later discovered that those who knew them best had regularly counseled them about issues of greed and integrity, and some had even warned the couple that they didn't seem serious enough about repenting.

The Explanation

Rachel and I were fortunate to be a part of Peter's group meeting the following evening. The mood in the room was somber and intense that night, and I heard similar reports from the other brothers and sisters who met throughout Judea that evening to discuss the matter. Peter opened the evening's events with a prayer that helped put all of us a bit more at ease. But the emotions in the crowd that night were all over the map—some said it was about time they were disciplined, and that the couple had been a real drag on those who had worked closely with them; others said that if this was how they were going to be treated in the days ahead, they didn't see how they could ever relax and enjoy their walk with God. Others were somewhere in the middle, most of them just wanting a clear understanding of the situation so they could process it in a proper way, and so they could share the facts with unbelievers who would no doubt be curious as to why two members of the Brotherhood were suddenly put to death.

After the prayer, Peter walked us through the entire scenario, beginning with the most recent history of discipleship in the home of Ananias and Sapphira. That alone did me a world of good, and it sure helped me to see that God hadn't been harsh at all in his decision to put them to death. I would actually come to see it in just the opposite way—that through their deaths, God was displaying his mercy to the rest of us, especially to those members of the Brotherhood who, at the time, weren't acting very serious about their decision to let Jesus be the Lord of their lives. And there were definitely a handful of those individuals present at every meeting that night.

Peter went on to explain the actual events of the day and the terrible thing Ananias and Sapphira had done to bring about their deaths. The church had just recently been given a challenge to consider how we could take it higher in our giving to God. There were still so many needs to be met in the church, and we always wanted to get in a better position to be more aggressive in building up the church with new conversions. We had a series of lessons preached to us over a period of three weeks that gave our hearts the chance to respond to the challenge in the best possible way. And Rachel and I were grateful that we had been able to sell a few items that meant something to us and give that money to the church to use as the leaders felt was best.

Most everybody I knew in the Brotherhood had been able to give something, and a few were still working on it, hoping to give their offering within the next few weeks. Some disciples hadn't been able to give hardly anything, and that was perfectly okay in the minds of our leaders. Those who lacked the funds to donate usually spent extra time praying for the contribution to be a huge success, or even working the crowds in Jerusalem to help their fellow disciples find prospective buyers for the items they were hoping to sell. Nobody was ever told what to give or how much to give—we were simply told the kind of heart to have about our giving, and always urged to be honest with others about the extent of that offering, should we be asked. Our leaders always wanted our hearts to be purest when it came to giving, and this recent collection effort was no different.

Ananias and Sapphira were fairly wealthy, but they had always appeared to be generous. No doubt their donations had been used by God to bless the lives of many other people in the years since they had joined the Brotherhood. But there was a strong message that God felt he needed to deliver about their lack of integrity, and Peter spent most of his time making sure we understood that. He wanted our trust in God's wisdom and goodness to continue to pervade our hearts and minds just as it had prior to their deaths.

Ananias and Sapphira had actually sold a piece of property they owned, and Ananias had come to deliver the proceeds of that sale to the apostles, as all of us had been encouraged to do. Before that delivery, he and Sapphira had decided to keep back a portion of those sales (something they had every right to do), but to still make it appear to the apostles and others that they were giving the entire amount. As God often did in those early days, he had endowed Peter and the other apostles with some pretty special miraculous gifts to be used to get the early church off to a good and wholesome start. He was determined to lay a solid foundation for the Brotherhood for the years to come. And this was one of those times when God decided to let Peter in on the information that he had known ever since the idea had formed in the couple's hearts several days earlier.

Whether it was the pride of wanting to be known for doing

something special (trying to keep up with disciples like Barnabas), the greed of desiring worldly wealth or just the arrogance of trying to pull one over on the leaders of the church and put God to the ultimate test, their sin in the situation was severe. All Peter said for sure was that Ananias and Sapphira had decided to lie to the Holy Spirit and act as though they were outside the sphere of his influence. All of us knew that was a big mistake. If there was one thing we were always reminded of in the early days, it was that God was with us every step of the way and that every act we committed, whether good or bad, was in his full view. And we knew that God would deal with all our thoughts and actions at some point in the future, even if we ourselves eventually forgot about them!

Expressions of Pain

Peter remained very calm that evening. He knew that many of us would need to express our frustrations about how things had been handled in the situation and that it wouldn't help if he shut us down too quickly. He also realized that others would need to display grief over losing people they loved. Granted, Peter and the other leaders expected everybody to get on board with God's wisdom in the matter, but they also realized that allowing people to spew their frustrations and feelings without being judged for them on the spot was an important element in the human equation. And there were a few individuals at our meeting that night who did just that.

It was especially difficult for their closest friends, some of whom felt as though the couple had recently made some headway in dealing with their struggles. They thought a little more time would have been helpful to get them to the point of true repentance. But Peter reminded them that God knows best about timing in matters of life and death and that he would never make a decision that wasn't best for the greatest number of people involved. Hardest hit were the people who had been introduced to the faith by Ananias and Sapphira. They had looked up to them in many ways and were overcome with discouragement that their spiritual leaders and teachers of the faith had been so deceitful.

After Peter shared all the facts, he then allowed us to ask questions. And it was amazing to see how patient he was in answering every question and how wise he was to put an eternal perspective on each of his responses. There were a lot of questions that night, but each of them boiled down to three major categories: First, how did this all work together with the love of God? Second, shouldn't they have been given an opportunity to repent after being confronted about their sin instead of just being killed instantly? Third, could we expect similar things to happen in the future?

The meeting went on until one in the morning. Some people had to leave a little early, but most of the brothers and sisters were able to stick around, and all of us felt so much better when we finally finished. Not that we were happy about their deaths, because we still felt incredibly sad. But we felt a great sense of relief and an even greater level of understanding of the grace and fear of the Lord, and those things served as huge stepping stones for us in our personal faith.

Making Sense of It All

Here's what I remember about the answers Peter gave to those three questions. First, God's love did not falter with the deaths of Ananias and Sapphira. Peter reminded us that what we view to be harsh and unfair from our earthly perspective is often just the opposite from heaven's point of view—and that God's ways were well beyond ours. Who were we to question the actions of an all-loving God? Somehow, some way, this tragic event was perfectly in line with the love of God and with his efforts to give every single person the best possible chance at making it to heaven to enjoy the benefits of eternity with him. Second, the couple had been given an opportunity to set things right. Through divine intervention, Peter had somehow known that Ananias and Sapphira had each lied about the amount they had received from the sale of their property. And Peter had given each of them a clear chance to tell him the truth. Upon hearing their lies, God must have felt that an immediate and absolute response to their actions was the best thing for them, the best thing for the church and the best thing for unbelievers interested in becoming members in the future.

Peter was also quick to remind us that discipline in this manner did not necessarily mean eternal separation from God for the people involved. That was God's ultimate business, he said, and he reminded us that Ananias and Sapphira might well be going to Paradise despite their sin. He told us that the lesson wasn't about us sitting in judgment of the people who had been punished, but about learning a greater and deeper measure of the fear of the Lord so we would never give in to the temptation to be deceitful.

Peter reminded us of Uzzah in the Old Testament, a man who was immediately struck dead when he touched the Ark of the

Covenant—yet we're never told whether or not Uzzah was ushered into Paradise upon his death. From my perspective in Paradise, I obviously have the complete story as to their eternal destinies, but again, I have been given strict orders to keep that information a total secret. After all, if you spent your time analyzing what you believed to be God's fairness of lack thereof in matters of eternal destiny, you might find yourself in worse shape than did Ananias and Sapphira.

Peter also reminded us that we would never know what God would do with our individual lives, and that we needed to trust in his judgments and decisions every step of the way. The most important lesson we should take from this event, he said, was that God is serious about telling the truth and that there's no place for arrogance or pride in the Brotherhood. Our attention to these matters would be the greatest safeguard against similar events occurring in the future

The few weeks after their deaths were tough. While I felt at peace about what I had heard from Peter that night, and while I was even used by God to help a few others to ultimately get the right perspective, I must admit there were a few times when I returned to thinking, "Unfair, unfair!" Thank God I had access to the Holy Scriptures, and I could quickly get back on track when I spent just a few minutes remembering God's gracious dealings throughout the history of our people. If anything, I discovered that God was consistently way too nice, if that were even possible. He always had given our entire nation and individuals within our nation many more chances than they deserved, And I reasoned that if God had always been that gracious, then surely he had acted graciously in the lives of Ananias and Sapphira. I also came to believe that God had probably given them a lot more chances to repent than even Peter himself had realized—and that God would judge them perfectly in regard to their eternal place of residence.

But even in coming to greater levels of understanding and appreciation of the love of God, the fear of the Lord was in high gear those next few months. And there were a great number of conversions during that period. At the same time, a large number of people decided to stay away from our fellowship completely, too afraid that the God we served would similarly judge them if they made an appearance. But the good thing about that decline in visitors was that these troubling events were being used by God to keep any spies away from the Brotherhood for at least a little while. And we also had very few problems with hypocrisy among the membership during the following weeks. Peter and the other brothers who led meetings that night even encouraged us to pair up in the next few days with someone and have a confession session, just to make sure our hearts were free of any secret sin. And most people gladly complied with that direction. Meetings took place all over the city and all over Judea where a number of disciples lived in the surrounding towns and villages. Most of those meetings took place that very night, and the rest of them happened within a day or two.

I came to a much better understanding about a few very important things as a result of the deaths of Ananias and Sapphira, and I would like to share those with you at this time. I believe it is of the utmost importance that I discuss these truths with you, as I've been told that many churches are far from where they need to be in these all-important matters.

The Fear of the Lord

The first of these matters involves having a correct understanding of the fear of the Lord. We had it back then, and we took it up a notch or two whenever a situation like the one with Ananias and Sapphira occurred. From the Scriptures, we knew that the fear of the Lord was the beginning of both knowledge and wisdom, and we had healthy amounts of it in our spiritual lives. Yet in spite of this great fear of the Lord, we weren't walking around as depressed deadbeats, fearing that God held us over the fires of hell by a single thread and that one sinful slip-up on our part would likely mean being dropped into the flames.

Actually, just the opposite occurred. We enjoyed our lives even more because of our fear of the Lord. The simplest explanation for our joy is that we used the fear of the Lord to keep us away from sin, and the less we sinned, the more we enjoyed our lives. And we always knew that even if we did sin, the Lord had grace for people with hearts of repentance, and we always believed the door to mercy would be open when we dealt with our sin in a decisive manner.

But there were enough stories in the Old Testament that taught us to have a deep level of respect for the power and wrath of the Almighty God.

We knew the story of Sodom and Gomorrah and learned quickly that sexual sin was nothing we should be toying with in our lives.

We were aware of the Israelites' golden calf and the partying that took place around their idol of choice—the same party spirit that God quickly snuffed out upon Moses' return from the mountain.

We knew of God's ultimate response to continual grumbling

and complaining by his people, and we wanted nothing to do with poisonous snakes coming into our personal space and taking bites out of our joy.

We knew all about faithlessness and doubting the power of God, and we wanted nothing to do with spiritual wandering for any length of time, let alone forty years.

We knew about partial obedience and how God responded to even his top-level leaders when they chose to walk that unholy path, and we wanted nothing to do with a future that was anything like King Saul's after he ignored the clear commands of the Lord.

We knew about lapses in moral judgment and what terrible consequences adultery could bring by reading the story of David and Bathsheba, and we wanted nothing to do with the sin and strife that followed him for many years as a result.

We knew the dangers of ongoing complacency and religious hypocrisy whenever we read the stories of captivity and temple destruction, and we wanted our invisible kingdom to be as strong as possible for as long as possible, so we steered clear from simply being religious and putting too much confidence in our godly heritage.

God used these and numerous other stories of old to keep us in line and to encourage us to remain faithful always. We lived in the fear of the Lord, and the deaths of Ananias and Sapphira only served to deepen our respect for God. Sure, a few people ended up leaving the Brotherhood over this situation, but that's typically the case when God tests an entire group of people—hearts are exposed during times of testing, and we lost some once-devoted people in the few weeks following.

Living in the Fear of the Lord

So let's talk about the fear of the Lord in your life. Do you have it? Do you carry it with you in your daily activities? Do you teach the importance of it to your children and to others you're trying to bring into the kingdom? Do you understand what it really means to fear the Lord? Do you believe that a proper fear of the Lord will bring you more joy? Or do you see it more as a threat to take away pleasure from your earthly existence even though, in the end, it will help you get to heaven?

However you answer these tough questions, you have ample opportunity to understand the fear of the Lord. And believe it or not, you're already practicing a proper fear of something at this very moment, and that fear is keeping you from harm and bringing you greater blessings than you would have experienced without it. Consider these following examples:

The sun is the first analogy that comes to mind. To ward off the dreaded sunburn, you use things like sunscreen, umbrellas, baseball caps and sunglasses, and you're (I hope!) wise enough to avoid the sun altogether at certain times of the day. Who doesn't practice one or more of these safety measures before stepping outside to confront the awesome power of the sun?

Understanding the fear of the Lord is really no different. To properly follow him and to prevent yourself from the damaging effects of the unyielding power of sin, you must employ a number of spiritual safety measures. If you choose to do so, you will be protecting yourself and doing what you can to avoid the pain and problem of sin. Continuing with my celestial analogy, nobody stares at the sun for very long without damaging their eyes. And nobody steps out unprotected into the heat of the day without paying the consequences. Sadly, Ananias and Sapphira did both and were burned for it. Don't let the same be said of you. Learn from their folly the way many of us did.

People who are poor swimmers certainly practice a healthy fear of the water whenever they're around it, and especially when they're in it. To keep themselves from the possibility of drowning, they wear life jackets, stay away from the edge of the boat or the dock and avoid the deepest parts of the pool. And they'll take most of these precautions without even thinking about it. Even good swimmers have a keen respect and fear of the water, and if they're wise, they don't push their luck by treading water that's well over their head for long periods of time or by swimming too far from the shore.

Driving an automobile requires a certain fear of the road—and a fear of other drivers!—if you want to avoid the pain of tickets, crashes and even deadly accidents. After all, aren't the safest drivers often the most defensive drivers? Don't simple things like wearing a seat belt or traveling slowly in bad weather conditions typically result in fewer injuries and fatalities? Doesn't careful respect for the speed limit usually result in a happier and safer existence for drivers by and large?

And how about when you're positioned in high places or on steep embankments? Don't you respect the possibility of falling from those locations enough that you'll make absolutely sure you don't tumble to your death?

These are just a few of the times when you practice a correct sense of fear, and they all can be used to help you come to a better understanding of the importance of fearing the Lord. Bottom line, there are certain things you must do to prevent yourself from falling under the judgment of God. A few basic decisions will not only keep you from the dangers of sin and its consequences, but will also allow you to enjoy your life much more as a result. Knowing what God has said about sin, knowing the possibilities of a terrible fall if you get too close to the edge, knowing your tendencies to succumb in certain situations, knowing some solid truths about the nature of God and knowing a lot about the schemes of Satan—all of these can help you get the most out of your Christianity and keep you from the damning effects of sin. But if you go out into the sun without sunscreen or a cap, or if you swim in the middle of a deep lake without a life jacket or a boat nearby, or if you drive like a madman without wearing a seat belt, or if you don't pay close attention to where you're walking while on hilly terrain, then there's no guarantee you'll be safe, and an even bigger chance that you'll suffer a number of consequences from your actions—consequences that could be deadly. The same is true in a spiritual sense in your efforts to resist temptation and say "no" to the sin Satan would love you to commit.

So now answer my questions again: Do you have a proper fear of the Lord? Do you live your life in the fear of the Lord?

Or do you have more respect for the sun than for the one who placed it there in the beginning?

Do you have a greater respect for the water or for the one who once flooded the world with it?

Do you take greater care as you drive down the street, or as you walk down the narrow road?

Do you fear the possibility of falling from a high place in greater ways than you fear falling away from the living God?

Do you concern yourself more with what the doctor says about your physical health than with what strong disciples say about your spiritual maladies?

Do you exercise greater caution with a possible bear or mountain lion in the nearby woods than you do with the possible attacks of Satan (the real roaring lion and a bear of an enemy) that can happen in your own backyard?

Do you prepare more for your tests at school than you do for your final eternal exam that will mean the difference between graduating to heaven or hell?

How enthusiastically do you study the nuances of your sports opponents, hoping to win mere games, compared with the way you study the nuances of your sinful nature, hoping to resist the ways Satan might try to capitalize on your weaknesses?

Do you study out the fear of the Lord very often and what it really means to practice it? Do you read those Old Testament stories as though they're fables or as though they're true and valuable lessons that you must learn from today?

Do you hear many sermons in your church about the fear of the Lord and how it leads to greater levels of righteousness?

Do you believe that God acts differently (more passively) nowadays in doling out punishment and that you therefore have plenty of time to get things right? Or do you believe you're under the leadership of the same God who made the Israelites wander for forty years because they were unwilling to take his warnings seriously?

Do you think you can simply do as you please and there won't be any consequences for your actions, whether they're immediate or long-term? Do you think God doesn't care about the sin you're committing right now, which perhaps nobody else sees or even suspects? Do you suppose that on Judgment Day God will pour on the love juices and allow you and many others to slip into heaven because he just couldn't send you, or anybody else for that matter, to hell?

An Absence of Fear

In the Brotherhood of Believers, we practiced, believed in and taught all about the fear of the Lord, and I'm enjoying Paradise at this very moment as a direct result of my correct understanding of that very important topic. Yet I hear that many churches today rarely talk about it—if ever—and even if they do, they only say that we need to show proper respect to God, in much the same way that we would be polite to our boss or next-door neighbor. Many individuals and churches never dive into the subject of sin. It is rarely, if ever, talked about in strong and serious ways from the pulpit. Actually, many churches choose not to even talk about the fear of the Lord for fear that their members and visitors will be offended by the subject. Whatever the case might be for you or your church family, you must embrace the fear of the Lord, even if nobody else in your church family or spiritual circle of influence is doing so at the time. You have a personal responsibility to live in the fear of the Lord as we did, and you must expect others to do the same. Better yet, find yourself a family of believers that understands the importance of fearing the Lord, and make sure the people expect one another to repent daily of any lukewarm behavior or sin when it's pointed out in their lives.

The other thing we must talk about that's closely related to the subject of fearing the Lord is church discipline. Though the story of Ananias and Sapphira doesn't fit that subject exactly, it certainly does help us better grasp the way sin must be dealt with in the lives of Christians. In my time, we knew—from the Old Testament Scriptures, from the words of Jesus and from what we saw and heard from the apostles and our other leaders—that we were expected to follow Jesus' standard, and that we should conduct ourselves *"in a manner worthy of the gospel of Christ,"* as Paul later told the church in his letter to the Philippians. If we decided to act outside of the parameters that had been set for us by the head of the church—Jesus—we knew there would be consequences and a confrontation. We couldn't just continue on our sinful path. We could certainly count on having a meeting with at least one of our fellow disciples, and should that meeting lead to our repentance, that would be the end of it. But should we persist in our sinful direction, no doubt one or two others would set up a follow-up appointment with us, and the warnings would become much more intense in nature. But this was reasonable.

Why should anyone in the Brotherhood of Believers have expected anything different? If Jesus was our Lord and we were refusing to submit to any of his expectations, could we really expect the leaders to turn their backs and allow us to set our own standards of righteousness? Could we really expect our brothers and sisters to simply ignore our actions or turn the other way for fear of how we might respond to their challenges?

Thankfully, we didn't have too many situations in which people's sins were brought before the entire membership of the church, or when we had to withdraw our fellowship from an offending and unrepentant member. But one of the biggest reasons it didn't happen very often was because we knew it was a very distinct possibility for each and every one of us. So we weren't about to risk finding out if the apostles' bite was as big as their bark. And when Ananias and Sapphira died as a result of their sin, we all took our conviction about unrepentant sin to a much deeper level and there were very few people who tried to hide their sin over the next few years.

Granted, a number of people still walked away from the church after that. But that's something we expected to happen. It happened in Jesus' day, so we knew that it was a real likelihood in our time as well. But that was how things were supposed to operate in the Brotherhood. Most people who weren't keeping in line with the teachings of Jesus knew that living a hypocritical lifestyle in the church wasn't an option, so they simply left when their wayward heart kept them from wearing the badge of true discipleship. It didn't matter whether someone was poor, middle-class or wealthy; a leader, a layman or a long-time hero of the faith; a brand-new disciple, a ten-year veteran of the Brotherhood or someone who had been faithful for more than forty years— everybody was expected to live a righteous life and continue to display ongoing repentance when necessary. As I told you earlier, Ananias and Sapphira did well financially, and their deaths meant that their contribution would no longer be a part of the Brotherhood budget. But obviously their regular contribution was of little or no importance to God—the righteousness of the church was his greatest desire. Above all, he wanted to have a group of people who would live for his honor, refusing to blaspheme his name to nonbelievers. God had seen enough of that in the Old Testament days, and he desired a much different body of believers in his church.

Is that what you see today in your church? Is regular confrontation for sinful behavior a part of your church's business? Is your church willing to challenge a member's unrepentant anger just as much as they would that person's ongoing adultery? Are they as strong in their stand against greed as they are in their statements against homosexuality?

Do people who give large sums of money get large amounts of pampered treatment from the leaders?

Are there people you know right now in your church who are living a life contrary to the one Jesus has called them to live, and are they getting away with it?

Are you involved in sinful behavior that nobody is calling you to repent of right now?

Is there a double standard in your congregation, so that older and more established members are allowed to have less of a commitment to Christ than the younger and newer members? Or perhaps it's the other way around.

Are people allowed to reach a stagnant stage of growth in their spiritual lives, as if they're "good enough for now"? Or is there a constant expectation for every member to strive to be their best for God and keep growing at every stage of their spiritual lives?

Are people allowed to come when they want, give when they can and share their faith when they feel like it?

Are people allowed to carry bitterness and resentment in their hearts toward their fellow members in the church?

Are there ongoing conflicts between members of your church, yet those same people still come to the same assembly to worship the God of love and forgiveness?

How about you? Do you have any of these things going on in your heart at the moment?

Settling Matters Quickly

In the Brotherhood of Believers, we were not permitted to allow bitterness and resentment in our hearts toward any human being, whether they were saved or lost. When we had relationship conflicts, they were addressed, and we worked to settle them until they were completely resolved. We never tabled a relationship conflict by saying that it would all be worked out once we got to heaven. We wanted peace now, and we were called to do everything on our part to see that that peace was achieved.

After I had been a disciple for about three years, I encountered a stressful situation with a brother in the church named Gershon. Gershon had become a Christian about two years after I had, and he had a woodworking business in Jerusalem, somewhat similar to mine. At first, I was excited about his conversion and I was even hoping that we would be able to help each other in our efforts as Christian businessmen. But about nine months after Gershon's conversion, I found my heart really struggling with him and his business approach, as it appeared that his company was moving in a much better direction than mine.

While I was receiving some persecution on a fairly regular basis because I stuck up for the Lord and refused to cower to the Jewish leaders who threatened to see to it that my business would fail, it looked as though Gershon was steering clear of all of that trouble. I couldn't help but wonder if he was lowering his standards a bit and giving in to compromise to maintain his normal revenue and respect from the unbelieving Jews. And it sure didn't seem like Gershon was interested in spending much time with me, almost as though he saw me as a threat instead of a help to him. All of these feelings caused me to distance myself from him. But it hadn't always been that way—in those first few months after Gershon became a Christian, I had always searched him out on Sundays during fellowship to see how he was doing and to set up some time to spend together during the week. But after those suspicious thoughts about Gershon entered my heart and mind, I actually did my best to avoid him altogether.

For the first few weeks, I didn't say anything about it to anybody. I just figured it would go away. Maybe it was just me and my selfish heart that was causing all the problems. Even worse, I decided to just keep quiet, assuming that soon enough someone else would notice Gershon's erring ways and call him to repentance. That, I thought, would be a much better approach than a fellow businessman challenging him on what I perceived to be sin. But neither of those things happened. My heart didn't change, and I didn't see anything happening on Gershon's front either. I even was deceitful a few times with the brothers who asked me how I was doing and how my relationships in the church were going. That was a question we heard quite often, as our leaders informed us that Satan would work just as hard to sow seeds of discord inside of the church as he would on the outside, and perhaps even harder. After all, if he could cause strife both in and among the Brotherhood, the affected individuals would be too distracted and discouraged to share their faith. So even though the brothers asked me straightforward questions, I hid what I was really feeling.

During that final week while I was waiting for a revelation and a resolution from the Lord, I met with some brothers to discuss how we were doing spiritually—another perfect opportunity for discipleship pruning. And the question was asked of me again: "Is everything okay in your relationships with other members of the Brotherhood?"

I responded quickly by saying "yes," but this time my friends weren't so sure about my response. They pressed the issue and asked me again. Again I answered "yes," thinking my second positive reply would be enough to shut down that line of questioning and we could move on to other things I was ready and eager to talk about with them. But that never happened. One of the brothers there felt strongly that something was a little bit off with me and that I wasn't being open about it with the group. He didn't know quite what it was, but he simply said he had noticed that I hadn't been as joyful on Sundays as I had in the past. He said he felt that something was bothering me and stealing my joy, especially during worship, the very time I usually looked forward to the most. He spoke for about two or three minutes, reminding me that honesty was always the best policy and that anything and everything could be worked through if I was just committed to that end.

And I was.

Tears began to fall from my eyes, and I quickly apologized to the brothers for my deceit. I then shared my struggles with Gershon, doing my best to be as real as possible about what exactly was causing my heart to feel the way it was toward him. I knew that everything I was feeling wasn't totally right, but I had always been encouraged to share my innermost feelings, regardless of whether they were totally accurate or not. God, we were reminded, would work through those feelings, but he always did his very best work when people were totally vulnerable with one another, even when it was embarrassing or potentially hurtful to others for a short time. The brothers thanked me for finally sharing the truth, but they were very strong as well in pointing out that Satan had won a battle with me. Thankfully, the war wasn't over by any means. They challenged me on my deceit, and even more on my lack of faith that God's way (the way of honesty and allowing others to help you through your challenges) always works, and that I had trusted more in my own ability or in the mere passing of time to clean up the mess. And they were right on all fronts.

But beyond being right and simply letting it go at that, they wanted to help me get the situation completely resolved. One of the brothers there said he was going to talk to Gershon, and suggested that we set up a follow-up meeting to allow both of us the opportunity to put our feelings toward each other on the table. They were fairly certain Gershon had a few problems with me as well, as relationship conflicts, they said, were rarely one-sided. Or perhaps he had been deeply hurt by the way I had treated him recently, or discouraged by my withdrawal of what was once encouraging and warm fellowship. Or maybe our time together might even expose that I was right about his lack of righteousness in his business dealings. I didn't go into our meeting assuming that my concerns would be accurate or the major emphasis of our time together, but I did know that the meeting would at least give Gershon an opportunity to change whatever he might need to change.

Resolutions

We got together the very next day. That was something that happened all the time in the Brotherhood. Relationship conflicts were handled as soon as possible. Jesus' words about settling matters quickly and resolving conflict before you approach the worship altar were spoken often in the church. We knew that if Christians couldn't get along with the help of God and one another, how would non-Christians, with all of their relationship hang-ups, find any comfort in our fellowship?

The meeting went well, although it was quite awkward at the beginning. Gershon was doing the exact same thing that I had done the day before, not being as honest as he needed to be about his feelings. I did have a few moments of frustration with him, as I could tell he wasn't being up front with us. But who was I to look down upon him for that? I had gone on for a few weeks with my dishonesty, and it took the brothers three times to finally drag the truth out of me. At least Gershon got it right on the second chance in his first meeting with the brothers! And when he was finally open about his struggles, I was so convicted.

As it turned out, Gershon was giving in to fear about his business dealings, but his reasons, though wrong, were quite compelling. His in-laws, who were not disciples, were both in very poor health, and they needed to be fully supported by him and his wife. They had even come to live with them recently. Gershon didn't make great money in his business, and the pressure to support his entire family was more than enough temptation to gain worldly friends in an unspiritual way.

So, yes, I was right about my observations, but Gershon's compromise had all occurred in the hope of keeping his business thriving and food on his family's table. As a businessman, husband and father myself, I sure could have been a lot more compassionate. I apologized to Gershon for not finding out about his situation and figuring out how to help him, and for letting him down as an older brother in Christ. He felt so bad for his behavior. And he made a commitment to get the help he needed to change. Gershon even asked me if I would be his discipleship partner for a while, someone he could seek help from when it came to being righteous in the business world. I was humbled and honored to do so, and we made a commitment to developing a strong friendship with one another.

One of the greatest things to come out of our meeting, besides our resolution and subsequent friendship, was that the other brothers became aware of Gershon's financial challenges. He hadn't wanted to bring anything up in the beginning, because he always knew there were so many ongoing needs to be met in the Brotherhood. He just figured he would buckle down and figure it out himself. I guess you could say Gershon was doing the same thing with his financial challenges as I had done with my observations and feelings about him—waiting for time or luck to turn the situation around, instead of working through God's people and his Spirit to bring the matter to a spiritual resolution.

But when the brothers heard just how much Gershon needed some help to assist his in-laws and make ends meet, they brought the matter to the apostles, and he was given enough money to cover his in-law's expenses for the next three months. And the leaders were quick to tell Gershon that if he needed additional help, he should let them know about it right away, and that they would make sure he was cared for appropriately. But the three months would give him time to take his mind off of the worries of the world and focus on being a better businessman for God—something I was so excited about helping him to do.

And did God ever come through for him! During those next three months, Gershon's business did better than it had in a long time. I still had to remind him once in a while that he needed to stay righteous in certain dealings, but he was more than eager to continue to discuss his business integrity with me. A relationship that had been headed for disaster turned into a remarkable friendship that blessed my life for many, many years! And it came as a direct result of the conviction we shared in the Brotherhood of Believers—that we must call people on the sin we see in their lives, or even what we perceived to be inconsistent behavior in their lives. And whenever we couldn't resolve conflict ourselves, we were expected to follow the plan of God and allow others in the church to steer us in a better direction, trusting that the Spirit of God would work powerfully in our individual and collective lives.

Time for a few more questions. How many new and improved friendships might you develop in the months and years ahead if you allow honesty to rule your heart and let others help you work through your relationship conflicts? How might your children benefit from this pattern of living? How many people in your church could you help if you simply played your hunches and got into their hearts? Sure, your hunches might not always be right, but from my experience, they often are right on target—and this also holds true for others' concerns about you! God absolutely loves turning what looks to be a problem and a pain into a remarkable blessing, and this is what I often saw in the Brotherhood when we trusted him enough to lead the way.

Getting Back to Normal

After our initial shock over the deaths of Ananias and Sapphira began to wear off, the church was able to get back to the business of saving souls. We continued to experience great results with our outreach efforts. We were actually meeting and studying the Scriptures with a lot fewer people than we had in previous years, but those we did manage to get into spiritual discussions with usually had hearts that wanted to do whatever was necessary to get right with God.

The biggest reason for both of these trends had a lot to do with the outsiders' response to the tragic deaths of Ananias and Sapphira. A number of people simply stayed away from us after those events, thinking they might be the next victims of God's wrath, or that the Brotherhood, with its hard-line mentality, just wasn't the place for them. It actually provided for a very peaceful few months in the church, as even our most fervent persecutors took a break from their usual attacks on our movement. On the other hand, those who had even a hint of openness to the gospel beforehand were greatly motivated to learn the truth. They took the time to research our movement much more intensely, thinking that there had been way too many strange occurrences the past few months to simply write us off altogether. That, along with some of the amazing miracles the apostles were enabled to perform through the power of God, stirred people's hearts like never before.

The church was growing, the respect of our movement was spreading and we were primed for more peace and prosperity in the days ahead. That lasted about a year. I guess I should have been more aware that the tranquility couldn't last forever, but I was so enjoying the times of peace that I forgot to guard my heart against what took place after that.

The Jewish leaders were soon back on the attack, filled with jealousy about how fast the Brotherhood was growing and furious that a number of their own people had left their synagogues and aligned with us. So a plan to arrest our leaders was put in motion by the members of the Sadducees group, and it wasn't long before Peter and the other apostles found themselves back in the public jail. I guess the Sadducees should have been aware that God had the master key for every cell door, because it wasn't long before all of the apostles were back in the streets testifying to the gospel of God's grace, just as they had been doing the previous day.

But we knew that this time the Jewish leaders were posing a much more serious threat to our movement. And if not for some wise direction from one of their own, a man named Gamaliel, many of the apostles would have probably been put to death right then and there. But just to make their point as clear as possible, and to inflict as much pain on our leaders as their consciences would allow, they flogged the apostles and ordered them to discontinue their preaching in the name of Jesus.

We were all expecting the apostles to take a heavy hit with this latest threat. Surely they would retreat at least a little bit and figure out the best alternative strategy for advancing the gospel. Surely they would need a few weeks to recover from their injuries and regain the strength to preach the Word as powerfully as they had in the past. Surely they would tell us all to be a bit more careful with our evangelism, sensing the real threat that we were all facing. We were wrong on all counts.

The apostles had a meeting with all of us that next day, and they had never been more fired up. Sure, they were physically in quite a bit of pain, but their resolve to serve the God who had changed their lives was deeper than ever. And they put the entire Brotherhood on a daily evangelism campaign that was greater than anything I had ever experienced in my five years as a member. We went from house to house, doing our very best to find even just one open soul. But we found a whole lot more than that. The number of disciples increased rapidly over the next few months, and the church just kept getting bigger and bigger. We lost a few members along the way, those who decided to quit amid the intense persecution and threats to their safety. But most of the Brotherhood remained intact and intense about their purpose in life—to save as many as possible!

Attacking the Problems

The growth of the church was amazing, but like everything else, it brought with it a few daunting challenges—the biggest one being that we had to make sure every single member's spiritual and physical needs were met. We faced a very challenging time in which many of the wonderful Grecian widows were somehow being overlooked in receiving their daily food provisions. But as I saw so many times in the Brotherhood, we didn't allow the problem to swallow us up or get us navel-gazing. The leaders proposed a plan, one that allowed the widows to be cared for and the apostles to avoid being distracted from doing the work Jesus had called them to focus upon—prayer and ministry of the Word. We selected seven fantastic brothers who were allowed to use their talents in finances and organization, and they gladly spread their spiritual wings to address and correct the problem.

Once again, many more souls were added to the Brotherhood as a result of fixing the problem at hand. We even started to see a number of the Jewish priests become disciples, something we had only seen on rare occasion before this time. They testified that the love they saw expressed in the Brotherhood just couldn't be denied or attributed to man-made means. They had also been moved by the level of conviction that kept us from backing down from what we believed to be true. Love and conviction: These two qualities helped them get past their previous biases and disagreements with the church, enough evidence to open their hearts long enough to properly investigate what was actually going on in the Brotherhood.

In the meantime, it was amazing to see those seven men rise up and lead. They had already done so much in the church, and it was obvious that they were the right men for the job, as each of them hailed from a Greek background and possessed great passion to take care of those they considered their own. Two of the men, Philip and Stephen, even went on to greater levels of leadership after they had helped to correct the problem with the Grecian widows. Philip worked for many years as an evangelist, and he was quite instrumental in helping to spread the gospel to a few challenging areas. Sadly, Stephen didn't live that long after his rise into leadership, but his impact was equally stirring.

Today's Solutions

Allow me to take just a moment to ask you a few questions about how you address problems in your own life and how your church deals with its challenges. I've been told that many churches in your day are great about fixing the problems they face— but, sadly, they devote all of their time and resources to those same problems. Consequently, they have little or no time left to grow numerically. Other churches are even dividing their congregations over how to go about fixing problems. Some do appoint leaders to tackle certain ministries and pressing situations. But unfortunately, they choose men and women who have no business whatsoever leading anything—those who can't even fix the problems in their personal lives! Others get so caught up in how and who to elect to positions of leadership that they end up with more of a problem than they had in the first place!

I'm also told that many individuals have difficulties in dealing with the personal problems they're facing, even contemplating leaving the faith as a result—challenges like losing a job, staying positive during a health crisis, overcoming a relationship strain, dealing with rebellious children or countless other potentially deflating situations. I came to understand through the years that problems were simply God's opportunity to show his power and help me turn my weaknesses into strengths. And there were plenty of people to provide assistance in making sure I did just that.

So how do you deal with a crisis? Are you solution-oriented or problem-focused? Are you a complainer or a complier? Do your problems cause you to pray more or less? Do your problems take you deeper into the Scriptures to find solutions or deeper into the world to find sympathy? How does your church attend to its known weaknesses? Are you available to your church as part of the solution, or are you already too busy with other things? Do you struggle with jealousy when others are chosen to serve in some special capacity?

Every human being and every church has problems. We had many in the first century, and I had many in my personal life—none bigger than the challenge of dealing with my father-in-law, Nathan, the man I tried harder to love than almost anyone, but the one who responded to me with the most negativity. I had numerous bouts of mini-depression whenever I was around him and even when I thought about him, and the relationship also caused a lot of strife between Rachel and me, although she seemed equally angered and discouraged by his response to our decision to follow Jesus. But despite a few minor setbacks, with God's help and with reminders from my leaders about how to handle the situation in a righteous manner, I was able to soar above the problem.

I found much comfort in knowing that God would use my patience and persistence with Nathan to work on his heart like nothing else ever could. And it was the arrival of Saul in Jerusalem and the death of our beloved brother, Stephen, at Saul's hands that started to bring God's amazing power into clearer focus for me. These incidents instilled in my heart the conviction that truly God would cause all things to work together for good, as long as I continued to love him and stay dedicated to living out his purposes in my life.

Chapter Fourteen:
The Enemy Comes to Town

It wasn't long before the Jewish leaders requested reinforcements for their ongoing war against the Brotherhood. Jews from Cyrene and Alexandria came to town, as well as others from Cilicia and Asia, all with the expressed purpose of figuring out the best possible way to snuff out our expanding movement. Stephen, in the meantime, was being used by God to influence hundreds of people to come to Christ, and the combined Jewish opposition paused in their attacks on the apostles and targeted the new kid on the preaching block instead.

Saul had been recruited for the evil mission as well. A well-known Jew who had been rising up the ranks in the Sanhedrin, Saul hoped to reach greater levels of leadership by showing strong loyalty to the cause of eliminating Christianity. I had even met Saul a few times in my younger years, as he had come to Jerusalem on many occasions to teach in the synagogues, and was himself taught at one point by Gamaliel, the highly acclaimed rabbi.

Saul and his companions had come to town with one mission in mind—to stop what they called our crazy and out-of-control movement before it took over Jerusalem and put an end to peaceful relations with the Roman Empire. But they had another reason for concern, one they didn't admit publicly: The defection of many Jews to Christianity had meant a substantial hit to the synagogues' pocketbooks.

Knowing they had no charge against the Brotherhood that could persuade the Romans to banish us completely, the Jewish leaders resorted to a plan that smelled of Satan: They lied and looked to rid Stephen from the Earth without the approval of the ruling body in Jerusalem. False accusations were brought against him, and those lies served to bring the level of animosity among the Jews to a fevered pitch, causing them to lash out in anger toward Stephen for his supposed crimes against the temple and the laws of Moses.

While their tactics were lower than low and straight from the gates of hell, and while this brief story ends with the death of one of the greatest men in the history of the Brotherhood of Believers, Stephen was used by God to preach one final and breathtaking sermon, one that still resonates in Paradise for its boldness and beauty. Stephen's lesson was both informative and insightful. He was polite while preaching, yet powerful, laying out the truth as boldly as he knew how. He was calm, yet challenging. And even when he was being struck with the very rocks that would lead to his death, he was forgiving, yet firm. I wasn't there, but a few men in the Brotherhood were able to witness the events of that day and shared of his courage. And later, we often heard the inspiring story from Saul, the very man who was largely responsible for Stephen's execution.

It was Saul—the one-time arch-enemy of the church—who told us how Stephen's sermon affected him even as he was organizing final plans to stone him. It was Saul who told us that Stephen's method of love and non-retaliation was one of the sharpest tools used by God to soften his heart and prepare him for his later encounter with the living Christ. It was Saul who shed many tears a few years later while relating his sorrow for putting to death such an amazing man. But before Saul did or said all of those things, Satan used him to make life as miserable as possible for those of us in the Brotherhood. And he was successful on many fronts.

A Thorn in Our Flesh

Saul's efforts in traveling from city to city to put disciples in jail caused some in the Brotherhood to cower and deny their faith. His threats against the church caused some disciples to shrink back from their normal evangelistic fervor. For a period of time during his early reign of terror, most of us were constantly looking over our shoulders during our daily routines, just waiting and wondering if it was our turn to get attacked for our faith. Saul's vicious orders to put Christians to death caused much grief for those who lost their loved ones. And his involvement in Stephen's assasination led to the church's biggest challenge yet, and the most intense few years of my life up to that point—the scattering of all the disciples from Jerusalem. But once again, God used that dastardly move by Satan and one of his principal pawns to accomplish his own purposes. As a result of the disciples' scattering, I experienced some of the most incredible moments in my own life and witnessed some of the most phenomenal growth the Brotherhood of Believers ever experienced.

I guess we shouldn't have been surprised by the actions of the enemy in those days, but in some ways we were. How could these men treat us in such a horrible way when all we were trying to do was offer them the truth and give them the greatest gift they would ever receive? How could people threaten to kill the very same people who were treating them with such kindness and consideration? How could we, the people who sought to bring our city great blessings, be targeted for elimination?

These were just a few of the questions we asked of the apostles when things got really sticky and when we sensed the situation was only going to deteriorate. The apostles were always quick to remind us that they, too, had some of the exact same questions for Jesus whenever they received unfair persecution during their years with him. They had been amazed as well at the harsh treatment heaped upon the kindest, most caring and best example of love they had ever witnessed. And they often relayed to us the things Jesus said about persecution and his enemies:

"They hated me without reason." That was the answer most often given to them by the Lord. Persecution would occur in our lives, even while we made every effort to promote peace.

"Father, forgive them; for they do not know what they are doing." That was another insight they learned from Jesus about how people could carry out the wickedness they did against him during his time on the planet. Zeal without knowledge was at its peak during the crucifixion, and intelligence levels amongst the opposition hadn't increased much in the few years following.

"You belong to your father, the devil." Many of our enemies practiced persecution simply because their hearts were hard and they loved nothing more than to make life as difficult as possible for those who opposed them.

And these were the very same reasons why many of us in the Brotherhood of Believers were constantly being misteated by those who dared to call themselves lovers of God and caretakers of his eternal truths. So we did what the apostles said they saw Jesus do in each and every situation where the flesh was ready and willing to fight fire with fire—we allowed both of our cheeks to become red with the marks of non-retaliation and we walked a second mile with our enemies, hoping to seize the opportunity to reach deeper into their hearts with the love of God on the additional leg of the journey.

Fighting to Stay Righteous

But those acts of submission didn't come naturally. There were a number of times when I wanted to give the Jews a healthy dose of retaliation. There were times when I prayed that God would wipe the bad guys off the face of the map so we good guys could be about the business of teaching people how to love. But then I would realize that they couldn't learn how to love if they were dead, and my heart would feel convicted for verbalizing those feelings. But I was always encouraged by other disciples to voice my angry thoughts, despite how ugly or ungodly they were in nature—first in prayer to the God who welcomed them and who could turn them from complaining to compassion, and second to the brothers and sisters who felt some of the same things I was feeling but who could also lead me to higher spiritual ground. But it wasn't easy, and I suppose it isn't easy for you, either, when you're doing your best to be the salt of the earth but people keep peppering you with insults and unfair treatment. But I always forced myself to remember how it must have been so difficult for Jesus to respond to his enemies the way he did—and yet he continued to display perfect humility until his final breath, even while undergoing the excruciating ordeal of crucifixion.

"If they persecuted me, they will persecute you also." The apostle John always reminded us of these words of Jesus whenever persecution was fiercest. Who was I to think I could respond differently than Jesus had, and yet still please God? So I and the other brothers and sisters buckled down for what we knew was going to be the most challenging time of our Christian lives. We exercised our spiritual muscles more than ever in order to maintain a tight grip on our status as true followers of Jesus Christ. And even though we felt ready to deal the devil another blow by throwing more love-water onto his fire of hatred, it was much more challenging than most of us had thought it would be. But it was simply another opportunity for us to grow stronger in our faith and to feel more excited than ever about one day escaping the cares and worries of this world.

So how do you deal with similar challenges in your life? Where do you go to take out your frustrations, and where do you go to find peace and love to replace them? Are you even doing enough spiritually to catch the devil's attention? Does he even feel the need to recruit a few troublemakers to make life a bit more difficult in your world? Not that being persecuted as a Christian automatically amounts to a stamp of approval from God—but if you rarely experience persecution on any level, you should be a bit concerned that you've shrunk back in some area of imitating Jesus.

I've even heard that many churches and individuals in your day have gone years—even decades—without a hint of trouble from those on the outside. That just doesn't seem possible to me, if those same people really are striving to change their own lives and influence the world. Darkness does not respond well to light, and what harmony is there between righteousness and wickedness? Not that anybody or any church should go on a panicked search for persecution. Far be it from any of you to be crazy enough to bring trouble on yourself intentionally. But simply doing some of the basics of following Jesus—things like reaching out to the lost, challenging people on their sin and refusing to overlook mediocrity and lukewarm behavior in your own life or in the lives of your fellow disciples—will produce at least a small amount of friction in your faith.

So I ask you to take a careful look into this important area of discipleship and consider whether or not your peaceful existence is indicative of your compromise as a disciple of Christ. It's not that I want you to suffer or endure hardships. And it's not that I'm envious of how easy many of you have it compared to what the first-century Brotherhood experienced. It's just that I can't deny the words Paul wrote a few decades after the death of Jesus, a clear reminder that persecution would be a normal occurrence for true disciples: *"In fact, everyone who wants to live a godly life in Christ Jesus will be persecuted."*

The phrases "in fact" and "will be" must resonate in your heart and mind. Paul didn't say "in theory," he said "in fact." He didn't say "could possibly be" or "there's a really good chance there'll be," he said "will be." And he was merely uttering the exact same words Jesus had spoken to his disciples on numerous occasions, the very same words we frequently heard from those men as well.

So now that I've made it clear that persecution will be a part of your life as a disciple of Christ, please take a few moments to answer these questions:

First, if you do receive persecution, is it brought on more by your righteousness or by your misguided zeal? And if the persecution is a result of your strong walk with God and your desire to promote his ways in the midst of many perils, do you shrink back when it continues, or do you outlast the opposition?

And how do you find the spiritual energy and resolve to continue turning the other cheek with an enemy when you want to put a fist to theirs?

Do you have people in your life who can check your pulse, calm you down and call you to imitate the example of Christ when you're being singled out or slandered?

Do you have any patient people in your life who will let you blow off some steam with them, but who also will call you to befriend your enemies instead of fight them?

Do you have people urging you to voice your complaints to God before voicing them to anybody else? Will those same people call you to end your times of prayer with the commitment to do what's right, just as David did so many times during the constant battles he fought to stay righteous while the enemy was seeking to destroy him?

Do you have a place of refuge you can go to after a long and hard day in a world that doesn't appreciate your stand for truth?

Do you have anyone who will challenge you not just to avoid retaliating against your enemy, but to go the whole nine yards and love them as well?

Do you have people in your life who can sense when you're shying away from speaking the truth because you're tired off all the consequences it brings—the same people who will call you out of your fearful and comfortable lifestyle and help you to continue your life as a true disciple of Christ?

I'm so very thankful that I had people like this in my life. And I'm even more excited that I had a God to pray to who wasn't shocked by my retaliatory and sometimes unrighteous feelings. Not only that, but I had a Savior who had modeled the perfect response for how I was to treat people who were making it their goal to bring pain and suffering into my life. And I always had what I called my ace in the hole—my personal memory of watching Jesus perform his masterpiece of love in a theater where hatred and animosity were seated everywhere.

Without these spiritual aids, there's no way I would have responded righteously to persecution, and I'm sure I would have missed many opportunities to make a positive impact on malicious and misguided souls. And those very things helped me and many others in the Brotherhood of Believers to spiritually survive and thrive in the midst of the most intense period of persecution during the next few years.

Chapter Fifteen:
Wherever We Went

There was very little time to gather our belongings for the trip out of town. Mere hours after Stephen's funeral, the apostles informed us that Saul was masterminding an intense plan to destroy us one by one. Many of our homes and properties would likely be confiscated in the next few days, they said, and it was up to each household to determine what valuables they would remove, if any, before the authorities came to claim it all. Sad as it was to realize we would soon be losing most of our treasured earthly goods and that we might never return to our beloved Jerusalem, we did our best to cling to the joy of knowing that we had better and lasting possessions elsewhere and an eternal city that God was preparing just for us.

While we fought hard to keep that joy in the center of our hearts, we were also pretty anxious about our immediate future. But it wasn't like we fled the city in complete fear. Sure, we wanted to avoid imprisonment or escape the sword. We wanted to enjoy the lives God had blessed us with for as long as possible. And we would have loved to have done that right there in Jerusalem. But we also knew that we needed to do our best to stay alive so the gospel could go out to a lot more people. The Brotherhood boasted a very large membership by this time, but not nearly large enough in our minds. We had to go elsewhere, and we were told that this temporary setback needed to be viewed as God's way of getting the message out to many more people. Little did we know that not only was the message going to reach a lot more people, but an entirely new group of people would soon be grafted into the family tree.

Deciding Where to Go

While we in the Brotherhood were thrilled about this exciting new opportunity, it didn't come without tremendous practical challenges. Finding consistent work, staying afloat financially, relocating our children and finding appropriate ways to continue their education, explaining our hurried move to family and friends outside of the church, leaving people who had been making great headway in their decisions

to come to salvation—these were just a few of the discouraging realities
we dealt with in the following weeks as we tried our best to get settled
in new places throughout Israel and still make an impact by witnessing
to people in the towns and villages where God led us.

None of us in the Brotherhood were exactly sure how long
we'd be gone from Jerusalem, but we assumed that we should seek
permanent residency in another town, just in case we were never able to
return. Having that mind-set would be better for our hearts anyway, because we knew that in order to please God and help others find him, we
had to stay focused on the present. We couldn't constantly look behind
us to what we had left. Nor could we long for a homecoming that might
never happen (except the true homecoming we'd one day experience in
heaven). We knew the story of Lot's wife, and we also knew the radically different mentality that Abraham possessed when God called him
from total security in Ur of the Chaldeans to tent-living in the middle
of the desert. We all wanted to follow in Abraham's footsteps, and nobody cared to go the pillar-of-salt route. But at least we knew we weren't
being booted out of Jerusalem because of our sin as our ancestors had
been some six hundred years earlier. We were being rudely ushered out
because of our unbending conviction to share the good news of Jesus
and his resurrection with everyone we came in contact with, whether
they were fellow residents or visitors to our great city.

While we didn't have very much time to determine where it
would be best for us to go, Rachel and I felt we had two viable options
for relocation—Bethsaida or Caesarea. Bethsaida seemed like a good
choice at first, so we set our hearts on relocating there and beginning a
new adventure as disciples. Thankfully, Bethsaida was one of the many
locations where a number of our fellow disciples would also be finding
themselves within a few days, some of whom were related to a few
of the apostles who hailed from there. And the apostles had strongly
encouraged us to do our best to move with a group of disciples so we
would have constant encouragement in our difficult transition and so
we would immediately have a functioning church family in our new
place of residence. But there wasn't much time for careful organization
or counting the number of other brothers and sisters who would be
joining our caravan. We would need to totally trust in God's guidance
and his ability to take us where we needed to go.

There were about fifty of us who were in the group heading
to Bethsaida. Some of the people going there were already our close
friends. Others were those we only knew as faithful men and women

of God. But we were confident these relationships would be used by God to keep each of us from feeling sorry for ourselves and to provide a great source of encouragement through the difficult times ahead, the times we all knew could produce regular bouts of sadness and self-pity. And we all understood that, in our new locations, we couldn't cleverly hide among a large and fired-up group of people, and we couldn't rely on others to carry the bulk of the workload in the church, as some had done in the large Jerusalem fellowship. We were now going to be the up-front people. We were now going to be the leaders, the worship organizers, the advisors, the examples, the movers and shakers of the Bethsaida Brotherhood.

A Change of Plans

While we felt Bethsaida would provide us with a great situation spiritually, the biggest challenge was going to be finding work and permanent housing there. Some of those moving to Bethsaida had relatives they would be staying with, but most of us weren't that fortunate. I would need to either figure out a way to set up shop in Bethsaida and find steady clientele as soon as possible, or I would need to hire myself out to one of the other carpenters in the city. Both of those options seemed overwhelming to even contemplate, and I guess you could say that a huge wave of doubt and discouragement came over me just prior to the first leg of our journey there, and I just couldn't shake it.

Just minutes before leaving for Bethsaida, I pulled aside another brother in our caravan and shared my insecurities with him. While he did challenge my lack of trust in the same God who had miraculously saved me and blessed my life for the past ten years, he was also very sensitive with me, knowing this was probably the most difficult time any of us had ever faced, and knowing that we would all need large doses of grace and goodwill throughout this trial if we were going to survive spiritually. And while he desperately wanted for me and my family to move to Bethsaida with the rest of the group, he also sensed that my faith wasn't at that level (even though it should have been), and he talked with me about the other options that wouldn't put me in such a tight spot financially.

That was the open door I needed. I knew my decision about where to relocate wasn't a black-and-white issue. There were no bright and clearly written signs in the sky or cross-shaped cloud formations to tell me or my brothers and sisters which way to go. I didn't have any specific dream or vision that spelled out clearly where I should or shouldn't move. This decision came down to where I believed it would be best for me and my family to live, and I knew that God had always worked through the other members of the Brotherhood to guide me in a godly direction.

This situation was no different. There was a strong level of maturity among the brothers and sisters by that time. Eight or nine years earlier, I might have been told what to do instead of someone helping me to come to my own decision. And in many cases back then, that would have been better for me, because I was a young disciple who lacked wisdom in many areas. But by now, most of us in the Brotherhood had a much greater level of trust in God, and we especially knew that even in our weaknesses and possible mistakes of judgment, God would work together for the good in our lives. So the greatest issue to me wasn't whether I moved to Bethsaida or another city. The most important thing was going there (wherever there was) and committing to be my best for God!

After talking through the issue with that brother for a few minutes, I mentioned to him the one option that would allow us to move and not need to worry right away about the financial side of things. But at the same time, I wasn't totally sure that this plan would work, either, and I didn't know if it would be best for our hearts. But if it didn't work for some reason, I would still be in a similar spiritual situation to the one in Bethsaida—trying to find work and, thankfully, still living among a number of faithful disciples who were moving to that city as well.

Moving to the Coast

Caesarea was our choice. We would move to the Mediterranean coast instead of the shores of Lake Gennesaret and see what God had in store for us on our new adventure. Why Caesarea, you might be asking? While it was a few miles closer to Jerusalem than Bethsaida was, it was also more densely populated and would likely provide me with greater opportunities to begin my own carpentry business, or at least to get hooked up with a larger and more established business. But the biggest reason I felt Caesarea would be the better option was because my father-in-law, Nathan, lived there. Being with him could provide an amazing opportunity for outreach, as well as give us a good chance of being able to live rent-free until I could save enough money to either rent or build a place of our own. While this option might seem like it was the easy way out, I also knew there would be a number of difficulties in moving to Caesarea, and dealing with Nathan's animosity toward me would pose a huge challenge to my heart.

Nathan was a bitter man. Oh, he hadn't always been that way, and deep down, there was a very giving and faithful man of God just waiting to be discovered. But the last I had known of his attitude toward me and my newfound faith had been one of deep anger and resentment. You see, Nathan was a deeply religious man, committed to the cause of Judaism, meticulous in his attempts to adhere to the laws of Moses and a man who never missed the local synagogue services. Rachel was his only child, and that's where the bitterness story can begin to be told. Nathan's wife died while giving birth to Rachel. Her death was a severe blow to his heart, and while he devoted himself to being the best father he could possibly be for Rachel, he never dealt with the hurt and pain of being left without a wife to love and grow old with and a helpmate to raise his daughter.

Since the moment of his wife's death, Nathan devoted his time to two main things—giving his beloved daughter the best possible life, and working to make as much money as he could. Somehow he felt that the more money he made to provide a secure future for her, the better father he was. Nathan always had a substantial amount of money thanks to his father's thriving business in the shipping industry, but once he had more time to devote to his work after his wife's passing, he became consumed with it and became a wealthy man in the process. It was his desire to give Rachel the absolute best things in life. If he couldn't spoil the woman he had chosen to love for life, at least he could spoil the daughter he had been given. And he did a fine job of that. Rachel had everything, more than she ever wanted or needed. But Nathan was extremely over-protective of Rachel, and that's where I come into the picture.

Love at First Sight

Nathan brought Rachel to Jerusalem when she was twelve. Being wealthy, and with the ability to leave his business in capable hands, Nathan often traveled the world, and he had decided to bring Rachel to Jerusalem so she could experience the "city of God" firsthand. His plan was to spend five or six years in Jerusalem, giving Rachel the chance to grow into adulthood there, and giving him the opportunity to help her find an upstanding Jewish lad whom she could marry. Though he would need to make occasional trips back to Caesarea to check up on his business, Nathan would do his best to make Jerusalem his new home. I'm personally grateful for that decision, because not long after their arrival to Jerusalem, I caught sight of Rachel at a synagogue service. I was fourteen at the time, and very interested in the opposite sex, you might say. I wasn't even aware of her father's income bracket at the time; I just wanted a chance to get to know her. And while arranged marriages weren't exactly the norm in my day, I did know that I would need to do a good bit of schmoozing and convincing if I wanted a shot at a relationship with Rachel. But I was committed to that cause.

During the next three years, Rachel and I became great friends. When I turned seventeen, my father sat me down and had a serious talk with me about the carpentry business and also about how I should take care of business if I wanted to take my relationship with Rachel to the next level. I had a lot of respect for Nathan, and he always seemed open to Rachel and me spending the necessary time together (with much supervision, of course) to develop the type of relationship that would warrant a decision to get married. And while I was incredibly nervous about learning whether or not he would give me the go-ahead to marry Rachel, my love for her had reached the point of no return. But before I could even muster the courage to bring up the subject with him, Nathan scheduled a time to meet with me, and Rachel was the focus of our discussion. After what I think was about three hours of hearing Nathan describe just how special and important Rachel was to him, and how he had always lived for her and wanted only what was best for her, and how he was expecting me to carry the torch in that regard as well, he told me he thought Rachel and I were ready to take the next step in our relationship.

Rachel and I were married about a year later, and the first few years of our marriage went well. Nathan continued to live in Jerusalem, though by now he was going back and forth to Caesarea on a much more regular basis. He had been so generous in giving us the funds to build a great home of our own in Jerusalem, even though I'm sure he would have loved for us to live with him instead. And when my mother and father passed away during our engagement, Nathan stepped into my life in a huge way, and I was so thankful for his love and support during those trying days. But upon hearing news of some problems in the shipping industry, Nathan felt it best to return to Caesarea for an extended of period of time—perhaps, he said, for good. Though he did ask us to accompany him on the journey and even to consider relocating permanently with him, I think he knew that moving there wasn't best for us. So we said our goodbyes, and it was a very difficult time for

Rachel. But I will say that God used Nathan's departure to bond our marriage in ways that wouldn't have been possible had he stayed. Rachel was a daddy's girl all the way, but she needed to move on from that so our relationship could reach the level God had intended it to reach.

An Unfortunate Change of Heart

During the next seven years, Nathan visited Jerusalem ten times, and we were able to make two visits to Caesarea to see him. Our relationship was still moving in a positive direction, and Nathan often thanked me for taking such good care of the daughter he so deeply treasured. Then I became a disciple of Jesus, and all of that changed.

It was about four months after Rachel's baptism that we took a trip to visit Nathan, telling him the news of our conversion and sharing with him our newfound convictions. We weren't sure how he would respond, but we knew there would be some level of resistance. We just didn't realize it would be so intense.

Nathan had definitely heard about the new movement spawning in Jerusalem, and all that he'd heard was from a negative perspective. He had learned of the large numbers of people who had been leaving the Jewish faith to join what he called the sect, and he had felt sure that Rachel and I would be wise enough to keep a good distance from the dangerous group. So when we told him about our conversions and how much we were locked into our new belief, he had no room for us in his heart. He shut us down so fast we couldn't believe it.

Rachel was crushed. From a father who would give her everything and more than she ever wanted, to a father who wouldn't give her the time of day so she could explain her new beliefs—it was as though her whole life lost all the joy she had been experiencing as a disciple. Sure, she had known there were no guarantees about how her father would react to the news of her conversion, but she had been counting on their close relationship to carry the day. And she had never doubted that he would at least give her the chance to tell him the entire story.

That never happened. Our talk was incredibly brief compared to what we had been hoping for—only about twenty minutes or so. Nathan was just this side of a fit of rage throughout our time together, and he informed us that, as far as he was concerned, we would no longer be considered family. The regular yearly gift he had gladly sent us (money that we had used to provide some additional comfort to our lifestyle) was no longer going to come our way. He said that he would not be coming to visit us in Jerusalem any more, and if we ever visited

Caesarea again, we shouldn't try to arrange plans to see him.

While Nathan did eventually loosen up a little bit in regard to those threats, and though he did come by our house a couple of times just to see Rachel, our relationship was still quite strained. He had concluded that I was the main cause of Rachel's departure from the Jewish faith and that, had it not been for me, she never would have given in and joined such an absurd religion. He blamed me for her decision to follow Jesus and even stated quite bluntly on a few occasions that he never should have allowed Rachel to marry me—that he had seen this coming and had never felt sure about my motives.

Of course, I had never heard any of those things from him before, and his words were so deeply painful. Rachel and I needed so much encouragement and nurturing during the next few months, but even so, we never really got over it. While our faith was solid, and while we knew that our love for Jesus needed to be displayed above and beyond our love for our family, it hurt like crazy, and we cried buckets of tears about how much we missed having Nathan in our lives. But we were especially sad that he was so closed in his heart about hearing the very things he needed to hear in order to find salvation in Christ.

We prayed for him every single day, and the kids did as well. It was probably just as hard on them as it was on Rachel and me. After all, they had never met either of my parents or Rachel's mother, and now he had decided to stay away as well. So that left them essentially without grandparents. Thank God there were so many elderly brothers and sisters in the church who sensed their pain and did everything they could to fulfill that role in their lives for the next number of years.

Fear and Faith

Now you can see why the thought of returning to Caesarea was so challenging, and how difficult it would have been to ask Nathan if he would let us stay with him for a short while until I could find work. Call me crazy, but I really felt like this was the time to go after his heart again. I reasoned that, if he would just allow us to live with him for a brief while, he would see the incredible changes in our hearts and how our lives were better than they had ever been. And I figured that he would be at least willing to have the three grandchildren around him, even if he didn't want to see me and Rachel very often. But by that time, Joseph and Miriam had already been baptized, and I knew Nathan wasn't going to be very excited about that when he heard it. But even if he did decline our request for lodging, we would at least be in his city. Perhaps the church in Caesarea would flourish. If so, then Nathan would get a real chance to see the Brotherhood for what it really was, instead of just hearing about it from other bitter and misinformed Jews.

After discussing the matter with Rachel and coming to a final resolution about our sudden change of plans, we got hooked up with a few of the brothers and sisters who were moving to Casearea. We were so emotional at the time, as we had said our goodbyes to my sister Deborah and her family just a few hours earlier, as they were headed back to Joppa where many members of Ethan's family lived.

During that first day of our trip, I couldn't help but think that I had made a really stupid decision. Part of me wished we were still going to Bethsaida instead of thrusting ourselves into what would surely be an exceedingly painful time in Caesarea dealing with Nathan. But painful or not, I finally settled in on the belief that this was God's will for my life and my family. I prayed and prayed for God to open up Nathan's heart so that he would let us stay with him. I have to admit that I prayed a lot more about the housing issue than I did for Nathan's heart to be open to Jesus—but for God to answer my prayers about us living with Nathan would have been just as monumental in my mind.

Nathan was shocked to see us when we arrived on his doorstep. We had decided not to send word ahead that we were coming, but just to show up and see what would happen. I got the cold (*freezing* would be a more appropriate adjective!) treatment, while Rachel and the kids managed to get what you might call a semi-hug out of him. Thankfully, he did invite us in and we shared our dilemma with him during the next few minutes. After a few sarcastic "I-told-you-so" remarks, a chastisement for leaving the God of Abraham, Isaac and Jacob and a smug declaration that this was simply our punishment for making such a poor choice of religions, Nathan told us that we could stay for two weeks, but then we would need to find our own place.

By this point, our kids were old enough to understand what the real issues were in their grandfather's heart, and that it was nothing against them personally. And boy did that ever help, because they were freed up to love him like never before. And he couldn't help but love them in return. I was extremely grateful for the two-week reprieve, holding out some hope that either we'd be set up for success on our own by then, one of the other people in the church would find additional space for us or Nathan would turn two weeks into four. And he did.

A Long Four Weeks

Those were probably the hardest four weeks of my life when it came to turning the other cheek and staying strong in my commitment to overcome evil with good. Nathan was so incredibly mean to me. It was obvious he had decided to single me out and, in his mind, help me to realize that I was the main problem in this whole family crisis. I can't tell you how many times I wanted to fight back and chastise him—he claimed to be a man of God and a believer in the Almighty, but he continued to treat me so poorly. And it wasn't just me who wanted to go after him. By this time, Rachel wasn't all that warm and fuzzy in her feelings for her father, and Joseph and Miriam knew enough scripture to be able to set him straight as well. But we determined to let our lives do the talking, not our mouths. We decided we would trust that the righteous path David had taken while King Saul tried to kill him—the path of letting God be the judge and avenger—was much more effective and noble.

After those four weeks had passed, we knew it was time to leave. I had secured work with a carpentry business in town, and Joseph, now 16, had also found part-time employment. Our combined income put us in a position to be able to rent a place about a mile away from Nathan's. By this time, Nathan was even asking us if we would like to stay for another few weeks, but we all knew it was time to go. Though it looked like he was softening up a bit, as the verbal attacks were dwindling in number, we all felt like we just couldn't submit ourselves to that discouraging environment any longer, and we all knew we would be better off living away from him. And that was the advice we had been getting from so many people in the church, although they were always quick to say that we should do what we believed was best in the eyes of God.

We moved out a week later and into our own place. Although he would never admit it then, I think I caught a tiny tear in the corner of Nathan's eye as we said our farewells. Over the next number of weeks, all five of us stopped by his house at least twice a week, just to say hello and to let him know how much we loved him. I even got the courage up a few times to go visit him by myself. Nathan didn't attack me as he had while I was staying with him, but the temperature in the room didn't warm a great deal, either. But God used those visits and our fervent prayers to at least give him a chance to see that our love for him was genuine, and that our lives as disciples of Jesus were nothing to fear. And he even got to meet a few other members of the Brotherhood and discover that they, too, weren't a bunch of weird losers from the spiritual abyss who couldn't find anything else to do with their lives other than become Christians.

Coming Home

About eighteen months later, we got word that things had settled down quite a bit in Jerusalem and that it was now safe to come back and pick up where we had left off. Of course, the Jerusalem church would no doubt be smaller, we thought, and who knew what other changes we might face if we did decide to go back. By this time, the church in Caesarea had grown considerably. To leave Caesarea and the church at that juncture was going to be difficult, but they were in very capable hands, and we felt pulled in our hearts to return to the city we loved.

Saying goodbye to the church was extremely hard, but we always knew we had a second home should we ever visit in the future, or should God call us back there again. Saying goodbye to Nathan, however, was downright horrible. He was in rare form, you might say. He accused us of treating him like a puppet on an emotional string, and said we never should have come back into his life if we were only going to break his heart again. The root of bitterness was still there, it had just been disguised when he began receiving love from the people he had sorely missed. Only now that we were leaving him again, he felt abandoned. When we went to his house to say good-bye, he asked us to leave and even refused to show us any physical affection.

What was it going to take for Nathan to get his heart healthy enough to see his lack of love? What would God have to do to soften him to the point that he would deal with all of his anger, bitterness and resentment? And were we actually making things more difficult on him and his chances for salvation by leaving Caesarea? We knew we had come with the express purpose of trying to help him get saved, but would our departure now erase all the good we thought had been done during the past year-and-a-half? But we quickly concluded that only God could break Nathan down and bring him to the point of repentance. Our presence in Caesarea was really inconsequential—this was between Nathan and God..

We returned to Jerusalem to see a smaller but still spiritually thriving Brotherhood of Believers. And although the church was smaller in number, we were encouraged by the news that the overall Brotherhood was busting at the seams in its growth. Samaria was experiencing a revival of sorts, thanks to the preaching of Philip and the amazing response to his message and miracles. We even heard that Simon the Sorcerer (the David Copperfield of our day) had been baptized, but sadly his faith had been short-lived and he was now contributing to the persecution that still lingered in various parts of Israel.

Many of our friends from the early days had also returned to Jerusalem, but our closest friends had not. Yet it didn't take long for us to develop some new and amazing friendships in the church. And it wasn't long before my carpentry business was back up and running. My children were growing up fast, and Joseph and Miriam were praying for God to bring them helpmates of their own. My youngest, Benjamin, was turning fourteen, and he was so excited about helping me out at the shop, even expressing how much he wanted to be like me and become a carpenter as well. It was amazing to see how different his heart was than mine had been when I was a young man. He actually *wanted* to follow in his father's footsteps, and I was so thankful to hear him say that, although I never wanted him to feel pressured into doing so. But he was a big help to me in many ways.

By this time, there were churches all around Jerusalem and Judea, as well as in the northernmost parts of Israel, many of those the result of the dispersion of disciples after the persecution brought on by Saul and the Jewish leaders. God had turned a tragedy into a triumph, a bad situation into a big winner. And we continued to learn that nothing was an obstacle for God in building his church, if only people were willing to talk about him and his Son wherever they went—whether that was in Bethsaida, Joppa, Caesarea or all points in between.

Three months later, when we heard the most amazing news of all—news that made us fall to the floor in shock and praise—we knew that there was nothing our God couldn't and wouldn't do. His greatest desire truly was to give all men and women the best chance of being a part of the Brotherhood of Believers and a home one day in the heavenly realms.

Chapter Sixteen:
I Don't Believe What I Just Heard

The rumors had been circulating for a few days, and all of them were causing a great deal of anxiety and excitement among the members of the Brotherhood. Saul of Tarsus, the arch-enemy of the church, had been converted. Some were saying it was the most amazing thing to ever happen and that God was far more loving and forgiving than they had ever imagined. Some were saying it was a hoax, or just bad information. Others thought that the news really was true—but whether his conversion was sincere was another question altogether. Others believed it, but had a hard time figuring out how they would deal with their hearts in regard to how Saul had brutally treated them and other members of their family. Others refused to believe it until they heard it straight from the horse's mouth—and if he had been baptized, they wanted to put him through a number of tests to make sure he was legitimate. Others stated that it was all a part of his master plan to bring us down once again. Was Saul up to his old tricks? Would he again attack the Brotherhood in Jerusalem now that many of us had returned? Was he infiltrating our ranks to plot strategy for the biggest and boldest effort yet to snuff out the Brotherhood altogether?

The Truth About Saul

Those were some of the feelings in our hearts when we gathered for our time of worship that Sunday. What was the real truth? And how would we respond to whatever the real truth turned out to be? We were all quite nervous, as any of the above possibilities presented every last one of us with stiff challenges. But no matter what, we knew we needed to respond in a godly way.

Then Peter took the podium and shared the truth about Saul. He really had been baptized. It had been a true conversion. He really was no longer a problem for the church, but a powerful witness for our Lord. We were told he had been testifying to the truth for a few weeks since his conversion, and he had been highly successful in those outreach efforts. And Peter also said the apostles felt it best for Saul to plan a trip to Jerusalem to meet the church here. No doubt they wanted to give him a chance to offer his sincere apologies for all the trouble he had caused, and the opportunity to offer his assistance in building up what he was once so determined to destroy.

All I could do was think about how awesome and abundantly gracious God was to save someone like Saul. And then I quickly realized that I was actually a lot like Saul, and I thanked God for his amazing love in saving me and everyone else in the Brotherhood of Believers who were equally unworthy. And then I wondered about how Saul's conversion came about in the first place. Who had met him? Who had studied the Scriptures with him? Who had baptized him? And were there bodyguards during all three of those activities just in case things went south in a hurry?

Peter shared that it was Jesus who had met Saul. And I couldn't help but feel a connection with Saul when I heard that, as I too had been met by Jesus during my conversion process. Then I heard that Ananias had actually gone to meet him and explain the Scriptures to him, giving him the same information I had received about how to obtain salvation and be added to the Brotherhood. But we also heard how tentative Ananias had been at the beginning—and we all agreed that he reacted the same way we would have reacted had God commissioned us to spend a little "alone time" with the person we considered to be the meanest man on the planet with the least likely chance of being saved.

When Peter sat down, Barnabas was next to share. He had spent some time with Saul and said that none of us should ever doubt the sincerity of his conversion. He understood our hesitancy about the matter because of all the pain we had suffered at his hands, but he also called us to love Saul and embrace him as we would anybody else who had been baptized into Christ. He was vouching for Saul, and that was certainly something a number of people needed. After all, if Barnabas felt good about him, who were we to think otherwise? But Barnabas was also sensitive to those who still doubted. He offered to spend time with those people, and even said he would arrange for them to meet with him and Saul together to work through any unresolved issues of the heart. And Barnabas said that the idea for those meetings had been Saul's, not his.

Hearing that sure helped a ton! But it was all still a bit much to digest, especially since we had to let this sink into our hearts by word of mouth and hadn't had the chance to meet the new Saul ourselves. But we would have plenty of other opportunities to do so, and I would love to tell you about the first of those for the Jerusalem church.

A Humble and Changed Man

It was so incredible meeting Saul for the first time. He had spent a few days in Jerusalem before he got the chance to speak to the entire church, and he had been quite bold—both in his sharing about Jesus and in battling the church's critics. Barnabas had been by his side for most of that time, and the two of them were now debating the same group of men with whom Saul once sided.

When Saul was finally asked to share a few of his thoughts with the church, we were all on pins and needles, wondering what he might say to those of us whom he once considered to be the scum of the earth. He was now our fellow scum, you might say. He was now the persecuted, not the persecutor. And we were now related in Christ, family in every sense of the word. He shared his conversion story for a few minutes and gave absolute honor to the God who had saved him, the worst of sinners. He then spent the bulk of his time sharing apologies and shedding tears over the people he had hurt in the church and all the grief he had caused.

Though I hadn't been a direct victim of Saul's violent rage, my life had been deeply affected by his misguided wrath when I was forced to move my family to Caesarea. But I had already concluded that God had allowed that to happen, and I could readily give a lengthy list of positives about the good that had come from that terrible persecution. So I wasn't really personally upset with Saul. After all, I had been a persecutor just a decade earlier, and I had been given an equal amount of grace when I got the opportunity to right those wrongs.

Saul apologized profusely to those in the audience, knowing he had been used by Satan to both imprison and kill family members and friends of the very people he was addressing. And his apologies weren't insincere. I never sensed that he wanted to just get the apologies over with and move forward in the grace of God. I never felt like he simply wanted to claim, "Well, the past is the past so you have to forgive me." He was willing to meet with people on a personal level to make things right. He welcomed the idea of proving his repentance by his deeds—the very message he was commanded to preach by the risen Lord he had met on the road to Damascus.

After he was finished, he received a standing ovation for about three minutes. It was quite apparent that he was feeling incredibly uncomfortable with that applause, but it was the very thing he needed. It reassured him that not only was God on his side, but the Brotherhood of Believers—even in the very city he once terrorized—was behind him as well. He wept throughout the ovation, and afterward, one by one, people approached him to give him the warm embrace of fellowship and tell him how grateful they were to have him as their brother in Christ. And while Saul was always quick to point out how much the grace of God motivated him to be the man he was, he also said he would never forget the grace supplied to him by the brothers and sisters on that day, and in many similar meeting in the weeks ahead. That grace served as God's tool in modeling true forgiveness for Saul. And he said he felt deeply thankful to be a part of a group in which forgiveness was actually practiced, not just preached.

A few people hung toward the back of the gathering, still a bit unsure as to how to respond to Saul, while others were just hurting and uncertain about how to get things resolved in their hearts with their new brother in Christ. But all those issues and relationships got worked out over the next few weeks, as Saul had a number of appointments just to get things totally squared away with everybody who needed it. He spent his remaining time in Jerusalem trying to help the lost get things squared away with God. And wow, was he ever successful at doing that!

Some of Saul's success was simply due to the amazing conversion story he had to share, and some of it was that people found it difficult to argue with a man who had made such a radical transformation. He had been so evil and hateful, but now he was showing himself to be both kind and understanding toward those who opposed him. And Paul could definitely preach. Sure, he wasn't quite as eloquent as brothers like Apollos and the apostle John. But he didn't have any difficulty laying out the truth in an understandable and exciting fashion, and I always loved to hear him speak to the church—an experience I enjoyed four or five times.

More Exciting Times

For some unknown reason, the church was blessed to enjoy a time of peace during the few years after Saul's conversion. The apostles continued to do their outstanding work of leadership, and more amazing miracles were done by God through their hands. A high-ranking government official from Ethiopia had gotten baptized a short time before Saul joined our ranks, and word of the church growing like wildfire in Africa upon his return was being heralded in the Jerusalem Brotherhood. Churches throughout Judea, Galilee and Samaria enjoyed much growth and encouragement, and churches that had begun during the dispersion were continuing to spread the word as well. And we would soon come to find out that many others were hearing the word of God all around our nation, and that something truly amazing had just happened in Caesarea—an event that would shock the Brotherhood of Believers and pave the way for hundreds of thousands to be added to the church in the years ahead.

Chapter Seventeen:
The Missing Piece

While the reality of Saul's conversion rocked the Jerusalem Church, nothing could quite compare to the startling news that came our way from the apostle Peter a few years later. Peter announced that the first true Gentile had been baptized and had become a full-fledged member of the Brotherhood of Believers. Cornelius was his name, a lover of God in every sense of the term and a military leader who was respected by Jews and Gentiles alike. He was the first of dozens of Gentiles to be granted salvation in Christ at Caesarea, and most of those who had been baptized were either his relatives or closest friends. Sure, through the years the Brotherhood had witnessed a number of Gentile converts to Judaism becoming disciples of Christ. But to have true, uncircumcised Gentiles included in our number was revolutionary, and both exciting and troubling to many. I suppose you could say that we were wrong to be troubled, and you'd be right in that assessment. But it wasn't so easy to come to that realization in my day. And no doubt our problems back then have a few parallels in your day as well.

A Shocking Revelation

As a movement of God, we were growing in numbers. We were growing in our faith. We were growing in our convictions. We were growing in our desire to bring the gospel to as many as possible. And we had plenty of work left to do in converting Jews living in cities all around the Roman Empire. So we had virtually no idea that we were so far removed from where we needed to be in our evangelistic outlook, and we were so ashamed when we came to that understanding a short time after Cornelius and the other Gentiles had been baptized.

Of course the Gentiles always should have had equal access to the Brotherhood of Believers. Of course the Gentiles were loved by God just as much as the Jews were. Of course they didn't need to first be circumcised and converted to Judaism and our way of life before they could be baptized into Christ. Of course we were arrogant to believe they were a lesser people than we were as holders of the Jewish faith.

Of course we should have naturally shared with them just as much as we did with the Jews. But the sad truth is that we didn't.

Oh sure, when Peter told us the amazing news, and how God had thoroughly convinced him of his own error in steering clear of the Gentile population, many of us were convinced that we had been ignorant and slow to come to the same realization. After all, that message was scattered throughout the Old Testament Scriptures, and it was spoken straight from the mouth of Jesus on a number of occasions as well, most notably during one of the meetings he had with the apostles after his resurrection and before ascending into heaven. But we just didn't see it! We were so busy enjoying our salvation and so busy sharing that truth and joy with our lost Jewish brethren that we were completely clueless that something was missing. But thank God we were given much grace during that time, and thank God we eventually got it right.

Boy, did we ever get it right! We got more exited about the Gentile mission work than anything we had ever done, and God used so many of my Jewish brothers and sisters to both plant and progress his work in cities where the church membership was predominantly Gentile. But our transformation didn't come about without a lot of study, a lot of talks to keep our people unified and a lot of ongoing repentance whenever biases against one another entered our hearts and minds.

There were many high-tension meetings to help all of us understand how God felt about the Gentiles. There were plenty of apologies we Jews had to offer up to our Gentile brothers and sisters, and plenty of "help-me-better-understand-how-you-think" conversations that got us unified and kept us unified. But we did it. And I'm so thankful we did, because I gained so many amazing friends in the days ahead, friends who were Gentiles through and through, people who I can't believe I ever disdained or disliked.

The other great thing about Cornelius being converted was that he lived in Caesarea, a city that was still very much on my heart. Perhaps God would use this latest surge of excitement in the church there to move my father-in-law closer to the point of interest in the Brotherhood. Unfortunately, I also must admit that I felt a little uncertainty as well, as I feared that Nathan would especially not want anything to do with the church now that Gentiles were a part of the mainstream population. But mostly, I was just hoping that God could somehow use it to make a difference in his heart.

Missing Anything?

I think you can probably relate to the things I'm sharing. And at this point in my story, I would like to ask you a number of questions about the direction you and your church are currently taking. Is it possible that you, too, are moving in a mostly positive direction, yet quite oblivious to some crucial points along the way?

Have you busied yourself with so many *good* things that you can't possibly see the *great* thing you're missing out on at the moment?

Have you excluded a main point from the plan of God, while still clinging to most of his plan? And would you be willing to return to the Scriptures another time and search for the possible culprit?

Are you completely in the dark about some aspect of your spiritual life, and are you willing to allow someone to shine the light of truth in your direction?

Is there something your church could be completely overlooking at this very instant? If so, would you be willing to start a movement toward repentance should you locate it before anyone else?

To be more specific, is your church really into helping the poor but not really into teaching them the truths about Jesus? Has your church concluded that filling people's stomachs is of greater importance than feeding their souls? Or is your church really into helping the lost but not nearly as focused on visiting the sick, feeding the hungry and clothing the naked?

Is your church really into evangelism and saving people's souls but not equally concerned about their spiritual condition thereafter? Are they primarily concerned with getting people to respond to truth for the first time, rather than also making sure those same individuals remain committed to it for a lifetime?

Is your church so engrossed in international missions that you've forgotten the people in your own backyard? Is Africa in greater need of the gospel than America? Are the ghettos of Capetown, South Africa crying out to your church in greater ways than the ghettos of Columbia, South Carolina? And how do you determine which one has a greater need at any given time?

Is your church so into teaching the truths of the Bible that they've forgotten to set up a plan to help people obey them?

Then we should spend a little time discussing the general make-up of your congregation of believers. While we in the first century were definitely on the right track in many ways, and while there was some diversity among the Jewish members of the Brotherhood in my day, we fell woefully short of the multicolored, multiracial, multinational group God had expected us to be. Consequently, we all pretty much remained comfortable with one another. We were rarely challenged on dealing with those parts of our character or culture that made others uncomfortable or, even worse, uninterested in hearing the message of truth from our mouths. And while we were definitely used by God to build a solid and safe foundation of obedience for the church, God wanted to use a variety of characters and cultures to construct the walls and the ceiling in his amazing building. And as more Gentiles became grafted into our fellowship, and as I had the occasional opportunity to visit the predominantly Gentile churches, I was convicted all over again about what we had been missing all these years.

What does your church look like? How diverse is that group? How much of a melting pot of society is it?

If you live in a large city, does your church's population represent your city's population?

Is there a certain group of people in your city that your church is overlooking in their evangelistic efforts?

Even more importantly, is there a certain group in your city that your church is overlooking on purpose because most of the members feel uncomfortable around them? Or has your congregation justified those decisions by saying that those "different" people will probably do much better worshiping with their own kind than they ever would with the make-up of your church's membership?

Does your church consist of all white people? If so, then you'd better make sure there are no other races in your community.

Is your church an all African-American membership? Again, that's fine if there aren't Asians, Caucasians and Latin Americans to bump into on a regular basis.

Is your church all Hispanic, all Asian or all European? If sports teams, big businesses and major universities can figure out ways to get all races of people together to form a winning combination, why can't churches?

But it's not just race or color that we need to address, although that's probably at the top of the list. While racism is still an issue in many people's hearts and an issue in countless churches (one that must be dealt with decisively), what about the overall demographics of your church?

Does your church have members who are wealthy and members

who are poor? Or does your church think it's best that these categories of people be separated because the two groups don't relate well—and that way, everyone will feel more comfortable fellowshipping with only those of their kind on Sunday mornings?

Is your church made up of an almost equal amount of blue-collar and white-collar workers? Does the garbage collector have an equal shot of leadership in your congregation as the hospital administrator? Does the CEO of a major corporation find favored treatment above the restaurant dishwasher? Would the two of them be able to find sweet fellowship in your congregation, or would their chances of ever meeting, let alone forging a friendship, be slim?

And if your church does happen to be multiracial and multicultural (and I think you realize by now that you should be in that kind of church, no excuses), that doesn't automatically mean they're doing what God expects them to do. Every member must be personally involved in building relationships with different kinds of people. Who among us, regardless of our race, color or background, doesn't need people from other races, colors and backgrounds in our lives? These people can help to balance out our lack of understanding or lack of love in certain areas of our lives. Do you really think you can do just fine by spending the majority of your time with people just like you, and that God will overlook that in the end?

These were convictions that we Jews came to deeply understand and appreciate in the days and years after Cornelius was welcomed into the Brotherhood of Believers. And although God had remained patient with us during all those years while we remained in the dark, we also knew that once we had been confronted with the truth, we needed to address the situation and change it as quickly as possible in order to please him. And that's exactly what I'm encouraging you to do as well.

Making the Necessary Changes

I want to remind you that it's not enough to feel bad about some of the answers you've given to these questions. What *will* be bad is if you don't display repentance, and still carry on as if nothing had ever happened. That's what a few of the Jewish brothers wanted to do in the church. But the rest of us wouldn't let them get away with it! As a group, we wouldn't allow one another to maintain that kind of sinful separation, and neither should you. Make a decision today to analyze your personal walk with God and your church's overall state. Make sure you're committed to following *all* of God's plans for your life and your religious community. This commitment may mean that you decide to humbly confront your congregation's leadership, or it might even mean that you remove yourself from a certain fellowship of believers. But your first step is to do a self-analysis, not a church analysis.

However, I've been told that segregation is a serious problem among religious groups today and that a vast majority of churches have succumbed to the standards of the world, refusing to make the necessary changes to follow the Scriptures. Don't let that be said of you or your church family. It took some serious guts and hard work for us to get the Brotherhood in line with God's plans and expectations for unity and diversity, but we were much better off in the long run for taking those strong stands.

While you're thinking about the church you're a member of at the moment, I hope you're also taking the time to seriously examine yourself in light of these thoughts and questions. For you, that might mean examining what the Bible says about how to become a Christian and then obeying it—regardless of whether or not that decision contradicts what you've always believed or been taught to believe.

It might mean ending a special relationship that you know is taking you farther away from God, not closer to him.

It might mean finding a different church—one that teaches the Bible and holds people to its standards.

It might mean busting out of your comfort zone and working toward developing a friendship with someone of a different age, race or background.

It might mean devoting more of your time to helping the poor, or more of your time to reaching out to the lost. Or perhaps you need to do more of both!

It might mean deciding to give more of your time, money and attention to missions so that more and more people can get the opportunity to come to Jesus.

It might mean confronting a sin you see in someone's life, or it might mean going to someone with an apology about how you've been holding something against them.

I'm not sure exactly what all of this means for you, but I do know that it means something. Remember, I'm not privy to the details of your personal life, but I have spoken to the one who will judge your life in the end. And he has given me permission to call you to fully examine the ways of your life and the ways of your church, and to encourage you to make sure you're following his plan for your life.

The Gospel Goes Global

Things began to move fast after Cornelius' conversion. Churches were being planted everywhere and the excitement had never been greater in the Brotherhood. Miriam got married a few months after Cornelius was baptized, and two years later, she and her husband Zerah ventured north to Antioch to help strengthen the new disciples there (a desperate need in a church full of so many new converts). I felt that Miriam was in good hands, as Saul (now known as Paul) and Barnabas spent considerable amounts of time in Antioch, and I trusted that they would do all they could to keep a close eye on how she and Zerah were doing.

Later, Paul and Barnabas took off for missionary work in the open and ripe Gentile fields. Despite constant threats, persecution and physical attacks on their lives, they helped the gospel take root and thrive in places like Iconium, Lystra, Derbe, Pisidia, Perga and Attalia. Later, Paul teamed up with Silas, and they and their traveling companions bore great fruit for God in places like Philippi, Thessalonica, Athens, Corinth and Ephesus. Remembering these exciting times of Brotherhood expansion leads me to the next major topic of discussion in my story—the importance of spreading the good news to your world and how vital it is that you take an active role in that effort.

Chapter Eighteen:
The Fields Are Ripe

"Always remember that God is the one who opens hearts, moves hearts and changes hearts. We are simply called to plant seeds in those hearts and water them."

I heard words similar to those on so many occasions during my time in the Brotherhood of Believers. And those words were such an integral part of our mind-set about evangelism that God later chose to include them in the Scriptures via the inspiration of the apostle Paul in his letter to the Corinthian church. And did we ever need to be reminded of those words of truth on a regular basis!

Whether by feeling at times like absolutely no one was interested in our gospel presentations, or by thinking that we were God's gift to personal sharing and that we could rush to put people on the fast track toward baptism, we often got off-track in our understanding of our role in evangelism. We needed constant reminders that it was God who saved people! It was God who opened people up to even listen to the gospel message in the first place! Sure, our role was vital, as God had always looked for people willing to work alongside him to save as many as possible. But we were always sobered by the reality that we were nothing but damaged vessels of clay, imperfect and incapable of rescuing a single lost soul from hell. Only God had enough fire-fighting equipment for that!

For us, it came down to simply doing our best. It came down to constantly staying aware of the opportunities God was placing in our paths to witness to the lost. It was about setting an example in life and speech to the very best of our abilities, allowing love and patience to tear away at any resistance mechanisms in the hearts of those with whom we shared the truth. It was about having an understanding that we were working as the heralds of truth, not the hallmark of truth! It was about being couriers of sorts to those around us, delivering the greatest of all invitations—come to God's eternal party!

Whenever we digressed in one of these crucial areas, we repented and recommitted ourselves to the task of testifying to the gospel of grace. And like almost everything else in our discipleship efforts, we were constantly tweaking our strategy and mind-set to find the right balance between faith and fervor, between reliance upon God and readiness to preach on all occasions.

Staying Focused and Fervent

At times, it even became a bit too easy to overly enjoy our salvation and security in the Brotherhood. And whenever that happened, our tendency was to forget the pain and suffering going on in the lives of the lost we came in contact with every day. And especially during strong periods of persecution, we had to stay sharp and resist the temptation to retreat and hibernate until the cold months of cruel treatment subsided. But for the most part, we stayed on target with our goal of giving every single person a great opportunity to respond to the truths of the gospel. And whenever I kept my heart in the right place in this area of concern, I enjoyed my Christianity a great deal. So allow me to spend a few moments sharing with you a few of the things that helped me the most in my efforts to win as many as possible—mind-sets and behaviors that God used to turn us from a small and insignificant group into a movement that turned the world upside down.

First and foremost, I had to stay humble. I had to constantly remind myself that I was simply one beggar telling another beggar where they could find bread. I didn't find God due to my righteousness and really fine heart. I was found by God in the middle of a sinful mess. And even though my life of sin had changed in so many ways, and although I was no longer enslaved to the sins that still ensnared so many others, I had to remember that I had once been in the same boat as every other sinner. And if not for the amazing grace that provided the perfect set-up for me to find God, I never would have discovered the salvation I came to treasure.

No, I didn't have all the answers for lost souls. I just knew where they could find them. I didn't have life figured out completely. I just knew I was around a group of people who were committed to helping me stay headed in the right direction. I wasn't better than the lost people I encountered. As a matter of fact, I met so many people with more sincere, open hearts than I'd had when I was first introduced to Jesus. And I came to realize that the more humble I was in my heart and in my conversations with the lost, the better my chances of successfully turning someone toward the Lord, and the more likely it was that God would be willing to use me for his purposes.

I also came to understand the importance of never taking credit for being used by God to help guide someone into the Brotherhood of Believers. I deserved no credit—whether someone's life changed in part because of my initial invitation or because of my ability to open up the Scriptures with them and explain a difficult point. It was God who deserved the credit for the entire salvation process. He alone deserved all the praise and accolades for what occurred in the life of a soul who was coming to him. After all, it was his plan of salvation to begin with, not mine. It was his Son's death on the cross that opened the door for people, not my retelling the story about it. It was God's wisdom and timing that drew people to him, not my wisdom that led me to realize my need to share about him. And you, too, will do well to make sure humility rules the day while you roam the streets in search of a wayward soul. Besides, nobody is all that interested in spending time with someone who comes across as a know-it-all. I found that being gut-level open and honest about my weaknesses while sharing my faith was the absolute best way to increase my chances of having a good initial conversation with someone. Such vulnerability on my part produced a greater hope of finding a person willing to schedule a follow-up conversation with me.

I would also come to greatly appreciate accountability in this crucial area of my discipleship. I usually wasn't in great need of many reminders, because I tried to keep my purpose on my heart as often as possible. But there were definitely a few episodes in my Christian life when I was being downright lethargic (sinful would be an appropriate word as well) with my evangelism. And whether it was overcoming a day-long diversion from seizing the opportunities God had given me to share my faith, resisting the temptation to go on a "well-deserved" week-long vacation from keeping the lost on my heart or wanting to anounce that I'd be taking a month-long sabbatical from teaching the Scriptures to anybody who might be interested, I needed the brothers and sisters to keep me as "sharing sharp" as possible. Actually, evangelism was a topic of conversation almost every time we met together, whether that was in a large-group setting, a small-group meeting or a one-on-one encounter. We were so excited about reaching out to people that we couldn't help but talk about it with one another.

Thank God for the reminders and encouragements to evangelize that I received in the Brotherhood, most of which included some, most or all of the following questions: How have your efforts in evangelism been going? Did you meet any open people today? Who are you spending time developing a relationship with these days? Would you like to meet together tomorrow and spend a few hours reaching out to people? Who can I be praying for that you're trying to influence for God right now? Are you having any problems with fear or lack of faith in your evangelism?

While defensiveness did crop up from time to time during these conversations, most of the time I was so grateful to be reminded about something I really wanted to do in the first place, something that typically brought me greater joy than anything else I ever did as a disciple of Christ.

An Endless List of Candidates

One of the greatest things I discovered about evangelism was that there was never a shortage of work or opportunities. Everywhere I went in Jerusalem and outside of Jerusalem, I was surrounded by people, and the vast majority of them weren't saved. Most of those who did business at my carpentry shop weren't disciples. Almost all of my neighbors needed to know the truth, and much of my extended family was lost as well. So I always had the opportunity to make a difference, and it made life a whole lot more exciting.

And whether it was a friendly hello, a one-minute conversation or an extended study with someone, I always tried to keep it simple—put in a good word for Jesus! I wanted to turn the conversation as quickly as I could to Jesus and let people know a little something about him that they might not know, or else disprove their wrong impressions of him. Sure, I invited people to attend our regular worship services and other church gatherings quite a bit, but even then, I tried to make sure that I gave people more than just an invitation. I tried to also leave them with something to think about, information that I had learned from the apostles about the life and teachings of Jesus

In my opinion, it was always best whenever I went out with another disciple to do what you would call cold-contact evangelism— that is, meeting new people and telling them about Christ. It seemed to take the pressure off in many ways. And whether I barely knew the other disciple or we were best of friends, we always seemed to work well together and could easily play off one another's sharing. And it sure helped me to overcome any fear I might have of sharing with a particular individual, and it also kept me from stereotyping my way out of a potential conversation—those times I was tempted to automatically conclude that a person wouldn't be open to hearing what I had to say. Besides, Jesus often employed this same partnership strategy in his ministry, and who was I to think that I could figure out a more constructive approach to saving souls? And going out two-by-two was the absolute best way to keep us from quitting too early or getting discouraged whenever people persecuted us or passed us off as misguided fools. When that happened, we often got even more determined and went after it with even greater zeal. Usually, we had to take a short break and get away for some prayer to refocus our minds on God and our mission. And then we would be ready to get back out there again.

One day, after a brother named James and I had shared with about fifteen people who, one by one, told us we were about as useless as the dirt we were walking on, we were both feeling like we needed a well-deserved break from our efforts that afternoon. But we looked at each other and knew we needed to keep going, even if it was for just one more minute with just one more person. So we went to a private place, got down on our knees and asked God to give us the strength to keep on persevering. We asked him to help us find at least one individual who would listen to the truth. We both went quite long in our individual prayers, perhaps still trying to put off the inevitable. But after about ten minutes or so, we got up, looked at each other and decided to seek out five more targets of God's grace. We were determined to meet five more people before calling it a day.

Those first four people were probably the meanest, nastiest, most spiteful people I had ever encountered. I got called names I had never heard before that day. And it was all so discouraging. But James and I had made a commitment to God and to each other that we would meet five people before we stopped sharing. But the very next person we saw wasn't alone. He was with a group of four other men, and it was all we could both do to keep from bypassing what we thought would surely be a humiliating experience. We were both thinking that if we waited to share with the next person who was walking alone, we would probably encounter a much tamer tongue-lashing.

But I wasn't about to wimp out and wait for James to begin the conversation. So I stopped the entire group, told them I had something amazing to share with them, and spent the next fifteen minutes telling them about God's plans for their lives and about Jesus being the ultimate solution for everything. It turned out that they were a family of five brothers. Four of them were from out of town and were visiting their brother, Joel, who had recently moved to Jerusalem. The four brothers from out of town had heard about Jesus, and Joel said he had even wanted to check things out in the Brotherhood, but hadn't possessed the courage. But now that his brothers were there with him and expressing some interest, he too gave us his undivided attention, and they all agreed to come to my home the following evening for a more thorough discussion. Amazingly, all five men were baptized in less than a week. I can't tell you how many times I was asked to share that story with people. It gave them hope that keeping the faith and keeping the fires of evangelism stoked in the middle of great discouragement was well worth it.

Interruptions

I guess you could say we were interrupters! We believed that God was using us to interrupt people's lives and get them thinking about him. Most people back in my day had God in the back of their minds, not the front. Most people were just too busy. Most people, even the most religious ones, were blinded by greed, lust and the short-term pleasures of sin. So we felt it was our job to jog their brains a bit and get them thinking about eternal matters. And we didn't apologize for doing this. Whether it was in a busy marketplace, at work, on a quiet street or in the neighborhood, we felt it was essential to stop people in their tracks and get them to think about things they never would have thought about otherwise.

Sure, we were always told to do everything within our means to be as polite as possible. We made sure to show great respect to people even if they had no interest in listening to our presentation. And we always wished people a good day when we were done, though at times it came with a warning as well. But we knew we often had just one shot with people, and we wanted to make sure we didn't pass it up. With people in our neighborhoods and others who we saw more often, we tried to find ways to use our regular interactions to bring them to belief. But even so, we still needed to be bold with them and say what needed to be said whenever the opportunity arose. After all, we didn't know whether they would be alive the next day or not, and to lack urgency on their behalf, presuming they would be around for years to come, was both arrogant and outside of the truths we found in the Scriptures.

Balancing all of these issues wasn't always easy. But again, we had each other, and we were constantly helping one another to be our best in the area of evangelism— whether it was with strangers we just happened to meet, people we had a few opportunities to talk to or people who would be involved in our lives on a regular basis. We just knew that they all needed to be saved, and that they deserved as much of a chance to know about Jesus as we did, if not more! I certainly felt less worthy of salvation than most of the people with whom I shared the gospel. At least they hadn't been there to call out for Jesus' crucifixion. At least they hadn't given in to the maddening crowds and been a part of the worst jury judgment of all time.

Some Hints for Effective Evangelism

A few other things are important to consider in your evangelism, the same things I was taught and trained to keep in my heart. First, your outreach will be quite powerful when people see you remaining joyful amid your challenging circumstances. Second, even though what you're sharing is great news, not everybody will see it that way, and that's okay. Third, do everything you can to be as relatable to people as possible; try to understand where they might be coming from and why they may be responding negatively. Keep in mind that God is working on people's hearts and that he wants them to be saved a whole lot more than you do. Remember that you are an ambassador of Christ—people must see Jesus in your life before they will believe it from your lips. If you share your faith with someone but then grumble and complain to them about everything going on in your life, what will they think about your religion and the power of your God? And sharing your faith isn't about feeling good about yourself or being able to pat yourself on the back for your efforts. It's about being used to point people to God. Great evangelism involves being in step with the Spirit as he nudges and pushes you toward someone in your path (Philip knew all about that after his unlikely encounter with the Ethiopian eunuch in the middle of the desert), trusting that he'll give you the right words once you follow his urging and open your mouth.

I could go on and on, but I suppose you get the point by now. Evangelism wasn't just a part of my life, it was my life. I was so fortunate and privileged to be in the Brotherhood of Believers, and I wanted nothing more than to give others the same chance I had been given of experiencing salvation in Christ. We were all doing it. And we were doing it daily. That's why the church grew so much in those early days—everybody wanted to bring someone else to Christ. And we were in an environment where people were constantly being added to the faith, so it was hard to escape the fact that God was using us for his glory. We were given regular charges about evangelism and our role in the salvation process. We heard numerous sermons about the love of

God and how his greatest desire was to welcome people to heaven. We heard tons of lessons about the practical aspects of evangelism, prayer in evangelism and purpose in evangelism. The desire that was already deep in our hearts just kept growing, in part because of our leaders' encouragement to make sure we were being the people God had created us to be—soul-winners and salt for a bland and decaying world.

A Soul-Winning Check-up

If all of this sounds strange to you, that would concern me greatly, and it would be a clear sign that you've either never been on the right path or you've strayed from it significantly. While your evangelism strategies might not be exactly like ours, the spirit and the productivity should be quite similar. So to help you to come to the needed conviction about this topic, allow me to ask you some more probing questions.

How often do you share your faith with the lost? Is anybody holding you accountable for you efforts in this crucial area?

When was the last time you talked with a stranger about Jesus or invited them to study the Bible with you or attend your church?

How committed are you to sharing the truths of the gospel with your friends and family? Do they know where you stand on important matters of eternity and where you believe they stand with God?

Do you ever partner up with another person and go out for the sole purpose of meeting people? Do you ever organize group activities in which evangelism is the primary focus of your time together?

When was the last time you brought a visitor with you to church? When was the last time you opened up the Bible with someone and taught them about Jesus?

What kind of example are you setting for the unbelievers you're in contact with regularly, and do they see Jesus in your daily life?

Do you *look for* opportunities to share your faith on a daily basis? Do you *make* opportunities to share your faith on a daily basis?

Have you helped someone become a Christian recently? When was the last time you were used by God to meet a stranger, teach them the truths about Jesus and lead them to the point of baptism?

How about evangelism in your church? Is it something that every member feels compelled to do, or is it something relegated to a committee or a select group of people with the heart to do so?

Do you hear many sermons on evangelism and your purpose in life? Is your minister committed to the cause of evangelism and does he expect it out of himself and the rest of the congregation?

How much has your church grown in recent years with new converts? Is there any type of accountability for members in their efforts to help the church grow?

How much of your prayer life is committed to the lost and your desire to bring them to salvation?

Has persecution from past evangelistic efforts put out your spiritual fervor or added fuel to your evangelistic fire?

Do you know what to tell people when you meet them? Has anybody helped you with the practical aspects of how to be more effective in talking to strangers about Jesus?

Do you feel evangelism is optional, or is it an obligation in your Christianity? Do you just talk about it, or do you live it out?

What would the people who know you best say is the most important thing to you? Are there certain people you've totally avoided sharing with because you fear the possibility of ruining what you consider to be a good relationship?

Who do you need to share with today? What habits do you need to start developing to put yourself in a better position to live the way we did in the first century? What habits do you need to break in order to devote more of your time to teaching the gospel to others?

Are you using all the evangelistic avenues God has given you—your workplace, the restaurants, stores and shops you patron, the athletic teams you compete for, the school you attend and so on?

Are you willing to allow others to help you become an expert in this area? Are you willing to let God use you to bring about the greatest event known to man—the salvation of one soul?

Simply put, evangelism was the heart of the Brotherhood of Believers. We were committed to loving God and bringing honor and glory to him as often as we could, and we knew that nothing brought more joy to God than seeing a lost soul get baptized into Christ, thus affording him one more opportunity to extend the forgiveness of sins to another grateful recipient. We knew that God wanted the best for people's lives, but more than anything else, he wanted them to find salvation. So it was always seen as an honor and a pleasure to be involved in the soul-saving business. And one of the greatest pleasures I ever experienced in my outreach efforts happened near the end of my life—an amazing gift from God that will serve as a fitting end to my story.

Chapter Nineteen:
A Fitting Finish

Our move back to Jerusalem was totally blessed by God. In the few years following our return, Joseph, Miriam and Benjamin all were blessed to get married to other disciples, my business got back up and running and was doing better than ever, my sister Deborah and her family had also returned to Jerusalem, Rachel and I were greatly enjoying our empty-nest years and we were being used by God to help grow and strengthen the Brotherhood in our wonderful city. Miriam and Zerah eventually moved to Antioch, and although they had left the faith for a short time, they were now back in the fold and bringing glory to God once again. Benjamin was my partner in the carpentry business, and said he was quite content to stay in that role for the rest of his life. He and his wife, Julia, were doing well in their faith, helping to strengthen the churches in Judea and the surrounding areas as much as they could. Joseph and his wife, Sarah, had moved to Samaria and were a vital part of the spiritual explosion that continued in that location. Rachel and I were involved in a number of ministries in the Jerusalem Church, but closest to our hearts was our work overseeing the children's ministry and training the younger parents on how to best raise their children in the Brotherhood.

We were constantly encouraged by the news of rapid growth in the churches around the world. We were growing in our personal faith, and God continued to use us in greater ways to help the church grow and to maintain unity among the Jews and Gentiles. We were blessed to travel on a few occasions to visit other churches, and we were so blown away when we heard the news that every creature in the known world had been given an opportunity to hear the gospel, something Paul shared a short while later in his letter to the church at Colossae. While we were becoming even more educated in the Old Testament Scriptures and the teachings of Jesus passed on to us by the apostles, we were also at the beginning stages of getting access to the new Scriptures that were being written as well. Paul's letters and the very first Gospel had become essential reading material for all of us, and superb tools for our outreach efforts as well. There were now disciples all over the world, and we were always amazed that God had let us experience such a rich and fulfilling life in such a wonderful place as the Brotherhood of Believers.

More Work to Be Done

But not all was rosy and comfy-cozy! We still dealt with the sadness of seeing people walk away from God and leave the Brotherhood. We still attended funerals for our friends and loved ones and had to endure the grieving process each time. We still received fairly consistent persecution wherever we went. A few disciples, most notably the apostle James, had actually been put to death for their faith in Jerusalem, and a number had died as martyrs of the faith throughout the Roman Empire. And after Herod had James put to death, and when he saw how much that decision pleased the majority of the people in our city, he made similar efforts to put an end to Peter's life. But God pulled Peter out of yet another predicament by freeing him from Herod's clutches. He even ended up on the doorstep of the home where hundreds of disciples had been passionately praying for his release. I wasn't there, but it sure was hilarious hearing those disciples give an account of how shocked they were to see Peter show up a few hours later as a direct answer to their prayers. Of course, those "faithful" prayer warriors all had to be convinced that it really was him and not just his ghost they were talking to that night.

We were also constantly being challenged to take it deeper in our level of love and unity, and to learn from our brothers and sisters from different cultures. We dealt daily with the prejudices that constantly threatened the unity of the church—a unity that Jesus both prayed for and expected. But if Jews and Gentiles and Samaritans could figure out a way to get along and work side by side for the cause of Christ, I have to believe that anybody can! The only things our three groups had in common were that we were human beings and we were loved by God. But those two commonalities were enough to motivate us to figure out how we could work together and love one another, and the union of our three groups was an incredible testimony to the world that any and all prejudices could be overcome with a little bit of patience and perseverance.

We regularly put out small fires of racism and religious prejudice within the Brotherhood, because we were committed to dealing with problems rather than putting them under a rock or ignoring them altogether. Working to straighten things out and being committed to cutting out any and all bitter roots in our hearts were always difficult tasks. But I praise God that we did. I don't regret a single moment of fighting to keep my heart in good condition and striving to keep Satan from his ultimate goal of devouring me before my final breath could be taken.

And through all the joys and victories, and through all the efforts we were making to grow and strengthen the Brotherhood, we continued to deal with the sadness of our separation from Rachel's father and his continual outpouring of insensitivity and disapproval of our decision to live as followers of Christ.

An Unexpected Visitor

We had only seen Nathan a couple of times since our move away from Caesarea. He had decided to come to Jerusalem less and less often during those years, and although we had visited him on a few occasions, we felt that our times with him were ultimately hurting our hearts more than they were helping him. So we decided to simply let go of that relationship and wait for God to move in his heart, if that were even possible.

I was fifty-two years old by this time and Rachel had just turned fifty. All of our children had children of their own and we were enjoying our role as grandparents immensely. And it wouldn't be long before our oldest grandchild would be in a position to make a decision to become a disciple of Jesus. We were ecstatic that God was moving us closer to seeing a third generation of disciples in our family—the family of a man who at one time had been dead set against Jesus.

God had been so good to me. I was so excited to continue to honor him for many more years and to see the church continue to prosper all around the world, just as it had been doing in the more than two-and-a-half decades since I had been baptized into Christ. More than a quarter of a century following Jesus—what an amazing achievement, and what an incredible privilege I'd had to call myself a Christian for that length of time! It had been a wonderful twenty-six years, and I was primed and ready for much more action in the next twenty-six years—twenty-six years that I knew could be just as good as the first twenty-six, or even better.

I was busy working at the shop one Wednesday afternoon, when one of my employees came to find me in the back and told me I had a visitor who would like to talk with me. I asked who it was, but my employee said he wasn't sure and that the man hadn't offered his name.

I was curious as to who it might be, as I wasn't expecting anybody, and it was rare that someone would come by to talk unless they were a regular customer. When I reached the front portion of the shop, my heart stopped. I couldn't believe my eyes! It was Nathan. It had been four years since the last time we had seen each other, and I couldn't help but think that he had come to give me more grief. He asked if we could step out of the shop and talk for a few minutes. I agreed, and we walked about a hundred yards and sat down in a private area to talk.

Nathan began to speak, but it became difficult for him to finish as tears filled his eyes and soon he began to weep. He threw his arms around my shoulders and sobbed for about a minute; whenever he could catch his breath long enough to speak, he just said how sorry he was. I had no idea what had happened, but obviously he had come to the point of remorse about how he had handled our relationship and his interactions with the rest of my family—especially with Rachel, his one and only daughter. Finally, he was able to speak in a normal fashion and share more about what had been happening in his heart to bring him to this point of repentance. I must admit that I had no idea it had anything to do with Jesus. I was just thankful that in his old age he had come to see his erring ways and had apparently decided to set things right before he passed away, mostly for his own benefit. But at least it was a step in the right direction, I thought. Little did I know that he had actually taken a number of giant leaps toward God and toward accepting the truth we had so desperately wanted him to know!

Softening a Hard Heart

A woman by the name of Mary had been living in Caesarea for a number of years, and Nathan had met her and her husband at the local synagogue. They, too, were members of the upper crust of society, and Nathan had developed a good friendship with them through the years. Sadly, Mary's husband had passed away, and upon his death, she and Nathan began developing an interest in one another. This was a total shock to me, as Nathan had always said (since the days of his wife's death) that there was only one woman for him and that he had absolutely no interest in finding anyone to replace her. He had used his more flexible single lifestyle to work his way up the ranks of the shipping business, and had never seen the value of finding another lifelong partner. But things started changing in his heart as he aged into his mid-sixties and beyond. He became less and less involved in his business and began feeling more and more lonesome with the extra time he had on his hands.

He and Mary had spent a few private moments together, and both of them sensed a strong amount of need and attraction for one another. At fifty-eight years of age, Mary was ten years younger than Nathan, and he said he was looking for anyone or anything to keep him as young as possible. For the next few months, Mary and Nathan grew closer and began discussing the possibility of marriage. Mary needed to leave town for about two weeks to visit her three daughters in Tyre and share the news with them, and she and Nathan intended to make specific plans for their wedding once she returned. Little did Nathan know that, at the very same time, plans were afoot for his entrance into the Brotherhood! While in Tyre, Mary discovered that all three of her daughters, each of their husbands and ten of her grandchildren had all been baptized in the past three months. Those two weeks with her girls, her sons-in-law and her grandchildren moved Mary's heart in a tremendous fashion, and she made the decision to be baptized into Christ, even at the risk of ending the relationship she had with Nathan. But she concluded that if the relationship wasn't centered on the cross and Jesus, it was already headed for ruin.

On her way back to Caesarea, Mary rehearsed and rehearsed how she would break the news to Nathan. She knew all about his deep animosity toward the Brotherhood of Believers and how it had ultimately separated him from his immediate family. How would he respond to her? Would he treat her in the same way he had treated his own flesh and blood? Mary wanted more than anything to be a tool of God to speak the truth to him and bring him to Christ—regardless of whether or not that would result in marriage.

At first, Nathan responded in similar ways to Mary as he had to us. But when he left her and returned home to an empty and lonely environment, his heart began to stir with deep sadness. And he wondered what all of this could mean. Why had God taken his wife, his daughter and her family and now the only woman he had ever contemplated being with since his wife's passing? What was the common denominator? Was he the ultimate problem in the triple-terrible scenario? Had God been trying to get his attention for all these years and he just hadn't been listening? Should he talk to Mary and find out more about her faith? And would she even be open to getting with him after he had reacted so sharply to her?

Nathan took the risk and went by to see Mary. By this time, his heart had slowed a number of beats per minute, and he was open to hearing her story. Only this time, he wasn't only open to hearing her story, he was open to hearing the story of Christ. They spent three hours talking. Mary answered all of his questions to the best of her ability, then asked him if he'd be willing to get with some of the members of the Caesarea church for further discussions. He agreed. While he wasn't open to attending a function of the entire church right away, anticipating strong pressure from his Jewish friends, he was open to a private meeting with a few of the Brotherhood leaders.

One meeting turned into two, two turned to three, and after the tenth time together, Nathan agreed to attend his first worship time in the Brotherhood. And he couldn't believe what he saw and felt. Everything he had been missing in the Jewish faith for the past sixty-eight years of his life he now saw in living color in the Brotherhood of Believers. He saw love, he saw power and he saw people committed to being their best for God. In the two short hours he spent in their presence, it was obvious to him that this movement was of God. He was sold. God had used the death of his first wife, the division of our family, the decision of his fiancée to follow Jesus and the day-after-day discussions about the truths of Scripture to break Nathan's heart.

A Strong Show of Repentance

Nathan told the leaders he wanted to be baptized. By this point in time, he cared little that most of his closest friends and fellow synagogue members in Caesarea had ostracized him and were persecuting him for his soft stance on the Brotherhood. He wanted to be saved, and he wanted to begin living the life he had been missing out on ever since we had tried to convince him twenty-six years earlier. But he felt in his heart that it wouldn't be right to get baptized right then and there as his leaders had encouraged him to do. Nathan believed that he had so hurt his family and had so badly strayed from a God-honoring path that he owed it to God and to us to make a trip to Jerusalem, express his deepest level of remorse, prove his repentance and allow us to be a part of his salvation homecoming.

To my utter amazement, Nathan had come to Jerusalem to ask me to baptize him. He said he couldn't think of anyone else who he would want to do it, nor anyone else who was more deserving of his love. I was so humbled and moved by his response. I can honestly say that there wasn't any place in my heart that wanted him to spend a number of days proving to me that he had changed. And there was no place in my heart that felt like offering him a few "I-told-you-so" comments before baptizing him.

It was simply amazing. We finished our talk and hurried home to tell Rachel the wonderful news. Needless to say, there were a lot of tears and tight hugs in the next few hours. Word spread quickly through the Jerusalem Brotherhood about what was happening, and hundreds congregated at one of the regular baptism sites to witness the miracle. Nathan spent about ten minutes sharing his story and apologizing to the entire church for how difficult he had made things for us and for them. He pledged his complete devotion to God, voiced his undying loyalty to the lordship of Jesus Christ and we walked down into the water to finish the miracle. Before I baptized him, Nathan whispered these words in my ear: "Son, I love you very much and I am so very sorry. It will be wonderful to not only be your father-in-law again, but to be your brother in Christ." I hadn't been called "son" by him in twenty-six years. I began to cry. I thanked him, gave him one last hug and buried him in the waters of baptism. What a joyful celebration that was! We must have stayed there for about two hours after that, just talking and hugging everybody in sight.

Nathan told us more about his relationship with Mary and his plans for marriage. We were so excited for them. His plan was to remain with us for about three weeks, get a chance to get to know the brothers and sisters in Jerusalem and also take some time to get strengthened in his faith before the journey back. Then he and Mary would sell their homes and businesses in Caesarea and move to Jerusalem to be with us for the remainder of their lives. They would get married here as well, he told us. It was all about making up for lost time, he said. And we couldn't have been more excited about their plans.

Saying Goodbye

When Nathan and Mary finally returned to Jerusalem, I had been in bed for a few days and not feeling all that well. Benjamin had been doing the lion's share of the work at the carpentry shop, as I just couldn't seem to get rid of whatever had invaded my body. I did manage to get the energy to participate in Nathan and Mary's wedding, and what a beautiful and touching ceremony it was. And it was sure great to get to meet Mary's entire family during the week-long marriage celebration. But I was exhausted after the wedding was finally over, and I went right back to bed.

I suppose it would be more exciting to tell you that things got better, that I fought off the infection and kept on fighting for truth in the streets of Jerusalem. Perhaps you're hoping I'll tell you that Rachel and I enjoyed the next number of years growing old with each other and spending unforgettable time with our children, grandchildren and great-grandchildren. Perhaps you're expecting me to say that it was a blast being with Nathan and Mary for the next twenty years or so until their time on Earth was completed. Perhaps you're banking on the fact that God answered my prayers and the prayers of the church for restoration of my health. But none of that happened.

Despite the best efforts of the doctors and the faithful prayers of the saints, God took me to Paradise three weeks later. Initially, I was pretty discouraged about the inevitability of death. I begged God to give me an extension of life and that I would do my absolute best to honor him if he did. I didn't want to say goodbye to my family and friends yet. I wanted to live. I also have to admit that I was even a bit afraid of where I would go once I took my final breath. Had I done enough for God? Would I be rewarded for my efforts in serving him, or were my sins and struggles to stay faithful through the years just too many for him to overlook? Was the blood of Jesus really sufficient as I had believed for so many years, and as I had taught others to bank on as well?

Thankfully, I worked through all of those feelings and fears and surrendered to my fate. Knowing what I know now, I would have surrendered much faster and asked God to take me in two minutes instead of twenty-one days. But on the other hand, those twenty-one days were the most glorious days of my life. To spend that time with family and close friends, to be united in heart with my brother in Christ and father-in-law, Nathan, to have so many people come by and share with me how much I had been used by God to bless their lives, to be surrounded by people who cared so deeply for me, to be confident that my entire family would continue to get their needs met by those in the Brotherhood, to know that I had lived a faithful life for Jesus for twenty-six years, to know that I would soon be entering the wonderful place called Paradise and to know that I was about to secure my eternal reward in heaven—how could it be any better?

God even gave me the opportunity to witness one final time to my brother, Jonathan. He was living in Jericho at the time and had received a message from Deborah about my illness. He said he saw it as his duty to show me that my health issues were a direct result of my departure from the Jewish faith. He actually said that God was giving me one last opportunity to recant my position as a Christian. Jonathan didn't stay long, just a little more than a day. And although he never made the decision to follow in the footsteps of the greatest man to ever live, and although I must admit his words saddened me momentarily, I did see Jonathan's visit as one last chance for him to witness the peace in my heart, a peace which I knew he had never possessed.

I was also a bit disappointed in that I had always secretly hoped I'd be able to leave this world as a martyr for Christ. Nothing could be more worthwhile and God-honoring than that, I thought. But at the same time, I had always been somewhat concerned about the possibility of prolonged torture and whether or not I'd have the courage to stay strong in those final hours through the intense amount of pain I might have to endure. But even with that fear of suffering, for me to die what I called a "normal death" was something I had hoped to avoid. But all of those thoughts became quite irrelevant once I took the time to really think about the ultimate goal of my Christianity—dieing faithful to the Lord. So whether I went as a martyr or via the mainstream route, it really didn't matter.

Thankfully, I was able to remain coherent until my final hours, and I got to spend much of that time with my family. The other brothers and sisters were doing everything they could to meet all of our needs, and they were extremely sensitive in allowing us time alone, although a number of them did manage to peek their heads into the room to tell me goodbye as well. And a few of the brothers came by just to make sure my heart was staying in good spiritual condition. And why not! They knew the devil would be fighting against my faith to the bitter end, and they weren't about to let him cut in on me and steal a victory in the waning moments of my life.

I spent those last few days reliving the journey and thanking my family for the love they had offered me along the way. We laughed a little bit, although it was hard for me to do that in my condition. We shed a lot of tears as well, and talked of future times together in Paradise that would bring all of this pain into perspective. I can't tell you how many times in the last few hours of my life that I looked into Rachel's eyes and expressed to her how much she meant to me and how she had been used by God to keep me on the straight and narrow path so many times. I thanked Nathan for his courage to give his life to God, and Mary for being bold enough to put their relationship on the line. I expressed my heartfelt gratitude to Joseph, Miriam and Benjamin for the amazing joy they had brought into my life, all while doing my best to wrap my arms around my six grandchildren.

Last Words

My final words weren't spoken to my family, but to God. During the early evening of my last day on Earth, I mentioned to them that I was getting very tired and that I wanted to end the day with some personal prayer time to the one who had made these amazing memories possible. Here are the words I spoke to God that evening. These are the words that were leaping from my heart at my hour of death—words that will once again serve as my closing testimony.

"God, how can I ever thank you enough for what you've done for me? I am far from deserving of all the love I've received from you or worthy of all the love I've received from the people surrounding me at this hour. I simply want to thank you for introducing me to the most amazing man who ever lived and the most amazing group of people to call family. It has been an absolute privilege serving you, and I can't wait to see what Paradise is really like. God, may you continue to work in each of the hearts represented here today, and may you continue to bless the men and women in the Brotherhood of Believers around the world so that their faith can remain strong and they can help preserve this great and awesome institution. Thank you for blessing me far more than I ever deserved, and thank you for the promise of something greater than the life I am now living.

I look forward to meeting you, Jesus. It will be an honor to meet the esteemed leader of the Brotherhood and to personally let you know how much you've meant to me. I know I saw you on the day you were crucified, and I know how disappointed you must have been with my decisions at that time. I hope you're proud of me at this moment. It will be so wonderful to see you on the other side and to hear you say, 'Well done, good and faith servant, enter the joy of your master.' Good night, Lord!"

No more than five minutes later, I passed from this life and was given a hero's welcome into Paradise. And I would like nothing more than to be a part of the jubilant throng of men and women from the Brotherhood of Believers throughout the centuries who participate in your "Welcome Home" parade.

Epilogue

I suppose I could have told you a whole lot more about the Brotherhood of Believers and all that took place in the first century. And I suppose you're wondering why I didn't include certain elements in my story that perhaps you've deemed to be important or essential to the faith.

Granted, I spent very little time talking about matters of opinion. As a legalistic Jew by nature (though often off-target in that legalism), I was always working on separating truth from tradition and allowing people the right to express their freedoms in Christ. But I hope that I left you enough information that will lead you to practice great patience and restraint with one another when discussing matters that aren't black and white by virtue of a specific command of God. And I hope you're well aware that you should never trample on another man's faith while you enjoy your freedom in Christ—and should even give up that freedom altogether if it causes even one soul to struggle. Possessing this kind of attitude is very important to God. After all, he is the one who set up the multiracial, multinational, mixed-bag church in the first place.

And I didn't talk much about things like holidays, special days, order and style of worship and the best plans for integrating the church into your community. But I did remind you to make sure that whatever you set out to do—do it with all of your heart and do it to the glory of God.

I didn't talk at great length about a number of doctrinal matters, aside from the essentials of who Christ really is and what one must do to come to him and stay faithful to him. I spent more time talking about matters of life and putting what you believe into practice, because I was always so convicted about the lukewarm tendencies that had dominated my life as a religious person in the early stages of adulthood, and the way they hindered me from being the man God wanted me to be. It's not that doctrine isn't vitally important, because it is! But in the quest for doctrinal purity and the desire to shame the opposition with eloquent presentations of truth, many people miss the mark. Just as I once did, most of those people lack a drive for daily righteousness, and thereby miss out on the real chance of changing the mind of a mis-led soul.

Nor did I talk about church buildings (we never had any), how to properly view the entertainment industry, what to watch or not to watch, what to listen to or not listen to, what to wear or not to wear, what to buy or not to buy, where to work or not to work, how to raise your kids to love the Lord outside of setting a good example for them, how to best help a ten-year-old, a teenager, a thirty-something or some-one transitioning into their golden years to be their best for God, how to deal with a marriage crisis, a mid-life crisis or a family management crisis, how to interpret the complicated apocalyptic literature found in the book of Revelation, how to view the second coming of Christ and a plethora of other subjects you may have wished I had discussed. But I have left you with more than enough information to get started in your efforts to please God, and enough to give you a pretty good idea as to how you should tackle these and other important issues you're faced with in the twenty-first century.

I did, however, give you the information you need to cover the three most important components of the human experience—getting saved by the blood of Jesus, staying saved in the blood of Jesus and helping others experience those same two blessings along the way! Ev-erything outside of those three emphases along your spiritual journey is most likely a matter of opinion about what is good, what might be con-sidered better or what the absolute best decision would be for building upon the right foundation of faith—the faith found in the Brotherhood of Believers which I've shared with you in my story.

Time also didn't allow me to tell you about the many amazing miracles that were wrought in the first century. But if you get too hung up on the miraculous side of things, you will likely miss out (as many Christians in Corinth did at one point in their early history) on the weightier matters of faith, hope and love.

I could have told you about how our worship times were organized from beginning to end, but you might begin to think that publicly worshiping God and having a great collective experience as Christians involved a specific formula, instead of appreciating what it really should be in all generations and for all people—a free and grateful expression of the faith you possess, done in an orderly manner and within the proper cultural boundaries in which you live. And you might be tempted to think that the majority of your focus should center on Sunday and thereby fail to remember that every day is equally important in worshiping God, whether it's done publicly or privately. While we did enjoy our share of fantastic times of public worship, there were also long periods (sometimes for months in a row) when the threat of serious persecution kept us from meeting together in any other way than a few families gathering together at someone's home.

I could have told you more about the Ethiopian eunuch, Lydia the seller of purple fabric from Thyatira, the jailer from the town of Philippi and all the other amazing men and women whose conversions were recorded in the book of Acts. But one conversion was never considered better than another in the Brotherhood. All of them were rightly recognized to be amazing—the working of the Almighty God who was incredibly generous in bestowing his gift of grace.

Time did not allow me to go into detail about the incredible blessing it was to meet people like the Samaritan woman; Mary and Martha of sibling rivalry fame; the Gethsemane gardener who was privileged to overhear a few of the Lord's prayers during his many visits to the area; the numerous lepers who became spot-free and fired up about their new lease on life and new definition of love; the adulterous woman who was rescued from the rocks of condemnation as a result of the brilliant question Jesus posed to those holding stones nearby; and hundreds of others like Nicodemus, Joseph of Arimathea and Bartimaeus; all of whom were touched by Jesus' love while he lived on Earth. I can testify that they, in turn, touched many others with that same love for the remainder of their lives. Few people I met during my days in the Brotherhood were as grateful as those whom Jesus had personally met, as they always remarked that they felt as though they had been treated to an extra helping of blessings by being in position to cross paths with the Lord.

I could have told you about the amazing Jerusalem Conference and how God worked through the leaders to diffuse a potentially explosive argument and possible long-term division between the Jews and the Gentiles. But I did give you the basic building blocks for staying tight, together in heart and totally free of prejudice, and you can use those truths whenever Satan launches his next "let's separate" attack.

I could have told you more about the death of the apostle James, the first apostle to die for his faith. But James made sure I wasn't going to present him as having a better "end of life" story than anybody else who died during my days in the Brotherhood— whether from natural causes, a disease, an accident or martyrdom. According to James and the other apostles, everybody who died faithful to Jesus was considered a hero of the faith.

I could have told you more about the successful missionary journeys and how God used Paul and many others to saturate the world with the gospel. But I did give you enough information to let you know that the same type of dynamic growth is possible in your religious community if you simply choose to be used by God in the simple, day-to-day duties of loving him with all of your heart, soul, mind and strength and loving your neighbor as yourself.

I could have told you more about the apostles and their amazing lives and leadership in the first-century church. But they, too, refused to be elevated in stature or importance above others while they were alive—whether in their dress or their daily responsibilities—and now that they're here in Paradise, they definitely don't want to be singled out as unusually great men of God.

I could have told you more about my many experiences in the Brotherhood of Believers and how God used each of them, the wonderful and challenging alike, to make me the man of God I became in my lifetime. But I have offered you enough of my story to enable you to grasp how a common and sinful man like me could ever stay faithful to God for his entire life and end up in a place like Paradise.

But I chose to tell you what I did because, in doing so, I wanted to give you the basics for the best possible Christian life. I wanted you to find out the whole truth about God's plan of salvation so you can really be a Christian. I wanted to make sure you realized the importance of having people in your life who can help you work through any and all of your sins, weaknesses and challenges. And I wanted you to grasp how important it is to allow yourself to be used by God to bring others the truths of the gospel along the way. These priorities defined life in the Brotherhood of Believers in my day, and they must be the same activities that describe your life as a Christian in the twenty-first century. Anything beyond that is merely icing on the Christian cake.

My fervent hope for you is that I will see you one day in Paradise, and that ultimately we will be together in heaven in our resurrected state. And I hope that you will take to heart the words of my testimony and allow them to be used by God to get you here when your days on Earth have passed.

As for me, it's time to get back to my glorious routine. I miss my normal time spent in the various fellowship centers of Paradise, and I think the first place I'll head to is the Jesus Center to spend a few hours talking with the Lord about how I'm still so blown away that he had the heart to forgive me for what I did to him nearly two thousand years ago. After that, I'll spend some time in the many other centers and enjoy meeting some new residents along the way. It's been a little while since I've been out and about, and I'm pretty sure there are at least a few more souls who are experiencing that first incredible rush of emotion from being here.

As for you, since you're now leaving the Testimony Center, it seems appropriate to ask you a few final questions about your testimony: Do you have one? Is it one that can be backed up by the Scriptures? Is it one that is consistent with what you've heard in mine? Is it one you gladly share with others in hopes of helping them to arrive here someday? Is it one you protect with all your heart and soul? And do you allow others to monitor it to help you make sure it lasts a lifetime?

It's been a privilege spending time with you. I'll be greatly anticipating your arrival to Paradise in the days, weeks, months and years ahead.

Index of Scriptures

Chapter 1:
Luke 16:19-31; Hebrews 1:14; Hebrews 13:2; John 20:26-29; 1 Peter 2:17; Philippians 2:1-11; Hebrews 2:14-18; Hebrews 4:14-16; Mark 9:42-49; John 3:16-17; John 12:47-48; Hebrews 11:6; Matthew 28:18-20; Hebrews 3:12-14; Hebrews 12:15-16; 1 Corinthians 15:12-58; Philippians 3:20-21; Hebrews 9:27-28; John 11:1-44; 2 Corinthians 12:1-7; 2 Peter 3:8-13; Acts 2:40-41

Chapter 2:
Genesis 3:8-9; Genesis 4:6; Genesis 18:13-14; 1 Samuel 15:13-14; 1 Kings 18:20-21; Job 38:4; Job 38:37; Job 41:11; Psalm 119:9; Psalm 121:1; Proverbs 6:27; Micah 6:8; Haggai 1:3-4; Matthew 6:26-27; Matthew 12:11-12; Matthew 14:31; Matthew 16:8-11; Matthew 16:13-15; Mark 2:8; Matthew 21:16; Matthew 21:24-25; Mark 9:33; Luke 10:26; Luke 11:11-12; John 13:12; John 21:15-17; Acts 16:29-30; Romans 2:21-23; Romans 6:1; Romans 8:31; 1 Corinthians 1:13; 1 Corinthians 6:7; 1 Corinthians 12:27-31

Chapter 3:
Matthew 26:47-27:56; Mark 14:43-15:39; Luke 22:47-23:49; John 18:1-19:37; John 2:44; John 5:16-18; Matthew 9:9-13; John 2:13-18; Luke 12:13-21; 2 Timothy 2:14-15; Acts 17:10-12; Acts 18:24-26; 2 Peter 2:1-22; Romans 16:17-19; Genesis 6:1-9:17; Numbers 13:1-14:45; Jeremiah 6:13-15; Jeremiah 7:1-11; Jeremiah 8:8-12; Ezekiel 13:8-12; 2 Timothy 1:6-14; Acts 4:32-37; Romans 6:11-23; James 5:13-16; 1 John 1:5-10; Joshua 7:1-26; Ephesians 6:10-19; 1 Peter 5:9-10; Galatians 2:11-14

Chapter 4:
Ephesians 5:22-33; 1 Peter 3:1-7; Hebrews 13:4; Genesis 2:18-25; Malachi 2:13-16; Matthew 22:23-33; Ecclesiastes 12:13-14; John 14:15-27; John 16:5-15; Galatians 5:22-25; Exodus 12:1-28; Exodus 13:1-16; Genesis 6:1-8; 2 Kings 28:1-22; Ephesians 5:18-20; Colossians 3:16; Matthew 28:11-15; 1 Corinthians 15:12-58

Chapter 5:
Exodus 23:14-17; Exodus 34:22-24; Deuteronomy 16:9-12; Acts 2:1-41; Proverbs 13:12; Matthew 27:11-26; Matthew 3:1-6; Romans 10:9-10; 1 Timothy 6:11-16

Chapter 6:
Matthew 10:17-20; John 16:12-15; 1 Peter 3:15-16; Acts 17:24-28; 2 Timothy 2:24-26; Exodus 3:1-4:17; 1 Samuel 17:1-58; Esther 4:1-17; 1 Corinthians 2:1-5; John 20:19-29; John 16:33; Luke 14:25-35; Luke 9:23-26; Luke 9:57-62; Matthew 10:32-39; Luke 3:7-14; John 8:2-11; Matthew 12:30; Acts 2:42-47; Matthew 28:18-20; 2 Corinthians 8:1-9:15; 1 Peter 1:3-9; James 1:3-4; Psalm 139:13-16

Chapter 7:
1 Thessalonians 2:15; Matthew 28:18-20; 1 Thessalonians 3:10; 1 Corinthians 14:26-40; Luke 5:1-11; Matthew 16:21-28; Matthew 20:20-28; Hebrews 3:12-14; Hebrews 4:12-13; Luke 19:1-10; Acts 2:44-45; Acts 4:32-37; Luke 21:1-4; Colossians 4:1; 1 John 2:1-2

Chapter 8:
Genesis 14:17-20; Genesis 28:20-22; Deuteronomy 26:1-15; Malachi 3:6-12; 1 Timothy 6:3-10; Luke 16:1-14; Proverbs 3:9-10; Genesis 4:1-7; Hebrews 13:5; Acts 2:43; Acts 3:1-10; Acts 4:33; Acts 5:1-11; 1 Chronicles 29:1-20; 2 Kings 7:1-11; Exodus 35:4-36:7; 2 Chronicles 31:2-10; 2 Corinthians 9:7; Matthew 6:25-34; Mark 4:1-20; 1 Timothy 6:6-11

Chapter 9:
2 Peter 1:5-11; Romans 5:6-11; John 8:42-44; Galatians 6:7-10; John 3:16-17; Ephesians 3:14-19; 1 John 3:16; 1 John 4:7-16; 1 Corinthians 15:33-34; Proverbs 13:20; Matthew 7:13-23; Galatians 1:6-9; 1 Timothy 6:3-5; Matthew 10:34-39; Matthew 7:7-11; Luke 18:1-8; Philippians 4:4-7; Colossians 4:2-4; Ephesians 6:10-19; Romans 13:1-7; Titus 3:1-2; Matthew 5:38-42; 1 Peter 2:13-17; John 16:33; John 15:18-21; 1 Corinthians 3:5-9; Romans 2:5-11; Luke 16:19-31; James 4:7

Chapter 10:
Acts 4:4; Acts 5:14; Acts 6:7; Acts 20:13-16; Matthew 16:17-18

Chapter 11:
1 Timothy 4:15-16; John 3:16; Luke 8:13; John 8:31-32; Hebrews 11:6;

1 Peter 2:4-8; James 2:14-19; Luke 3:1-14; Luke 18:18-25; Matthew 18:1-4; Luke 9:57-62; Acts 17:30; Acts 26:19-20; 2 Corinthians 7:8-11; Romans 6:1-4; Acts 2:37-41; Acts 22:1-16; Galatians 3:26-29; 1 Corinthians 12:12-13; 2 Thessalonians 1:5-10; Hebrews 10:19-22; Acts 8:26-39; Acts 16:13-15; Acts 16:25-34; Acts 18:7-8; Titus 3:3-8; Acts 8:14-19; Romans 8:5-11; 1 Corinthians 13:8-14:25; Matthew 3:13-17; John 3:22-23; Acts 18:24-28

Chapter 12:
2 Corinthians 4:7-12; 2 Corinthians 4:16-18; Romans 8:28-39; Hebrews 12:7-12; Colossians 1:28-2:5; Proverbs 27:17; Hebrews 10:32-39; Romans 12:9-21; Romans 12:1-2; Matthew 5:43-48; Acts 4:1-22; Acts 5:17-42; 1 Corinthians 4:9-13; John 15:18-25; Galatians 2:4; Hebrews 6:1-8; 1 Corinthians 15:1-2; 2 Peter 2:17-22; Numbers 14:1-25; 2 Chronicles 36:15-21; Ezekiel 13:1-12; Obadiah 1-4; John 6:60-66; Luke 15:11-32; Matthew 19:16-26; Deuteronomy 4:9; Deuteronomy 6:4-25; Hebrews 10:26-39; 1 Peter 2:1-3; 2 Peter 1:19-21; Proverbs 19:2; Proverbs 11:14; Proverbs 12:15; Proverbs 19:20; Proverbs 20:18; 1 Thessalonians 5:12-22; 1 Peter 5:5-7; Ephesians 4:17-32; Matthew 5:27-30; Matthew 7:1-5

Chapter 13:
Acts 5:1-11; Acts 4:32-37; Isaiah 48:17; Isaiah 55:6-13; 2 Samuel 6:1-7; Jeremiah 7:21-27; Acts 5:11; Proverbs 1:7; Psalm 111:10; Genesis 18:16-19:29; Exodus 32:1-35; Numbers 21:4-9; 1 Samuel 15:1-26; 2 Samuel 11:1-12:14; 2 Chronicles 36:15-21; Deuteronomy 8:1-5; Hebrews 12:25-29; Philippians 1:27; 1 Timothy 3:14-15; Matthew 18:15-20; Titus 3:9-11; 2 Thessalonians 3:6-15; Hebrews 12:14-17; Colossians 1:28-29; 2 Timothy 4:1-5; Matthew 5:23-26; Romans 12:18; Acts 5:12-14; Acts 5:17-42; Acts 6:1-7

Chapter 14:
Acts 6:8-8:3; Acts 9:1-2; Acts 22:2-5; Acts 26:9-11; John 15:18-25; Luke 22:32-34; John 8:42-47; Matthew 5:38-42; 2 Timothy 3:10-13; Psalm 22:1-24; 1 Timothy 1:18-20; 1 Timothy 4:14; 2 Timothy 1:6-2:7

Chapter 15:
Acts 8:4; Acts 11:19-21; Hebrews 10:32-34; Genesis 19:16-26; Hebrews 11:8-19; Romans 14:1-23; Hebrews 5:11-6:3; Mark 10:29-31; Acts 8:4-13; Acts 8:26-39

Chapter 16:
Acts 9:1-30; Acts 22:1-21; Acts 26:1-21; 1 Corinthians 4:9-13; 1 Timothy 1:12-17; 1 Corinthians 15:9-10; 1 Corinthians 2:1-5; Acts 9:31

Chapter 17:
Acts 10:1-48; Acts 11:1-11; Hosea 2:23; Romans 9:22-26; Acts 1:1-8; Acts 11:19-26; Acts 14:1-28; Acts 16:11-34; Acts 17:10-12; Acts 17:16-34; Acts 18:1-11; Acts 15:1-35; Acts 13:1-3; Galatians 3:26-29; Ephesians 2:11-3:13; Acts 19:1-10

Chapter 18:
1 Corinthians 3:5-13; Acts 17:24-28; Acts 16:13-15; Acts 16:25-34; 1 Timothy 2:1-7; Luke 14:15-24; John 1:14; Romans 3:9-20; 2 Peter 3:8-9; Luke 10:1-24; Acts 17:16-17; 1 Peter 3;14-16; Ephesians 4:15; 2 Corinthians 5:11-6:2; Colossians 4:2-6

Chapter 19:
Acts 8:5-25; Acts 11:19-26; Titus 2:3-5; 1 Timothy 1:18-20; 2 Timothy 4:8-18; Galatians 3:1-5; Galatians 4:8-20; Galatians 5:7-10; Hebrews 12:15-16; 1 Peter 5:8-9; Revelation 7:13-17

Epilogue:
Romans 14:1-23; Philippians 3:12-16; 1 Corinthians 8:1-13; 1 Corinthians 10:23-33; Colossians 3:17; Colossians 3:23-24; 1 Corinthians 12;12-13:13; Acts 8:26-39; Acts 16:25-34; John 4:4-42; Luke 10:38-42; John 11:1-44; John 18:1-2; Mark 1:40-45; Luke 17:11-19; John 8:2-11; Acts 15:1-35; Acts 12:1-2; Acts 13:1-21:38

Books from the Teaching Ministry of Curt Simmons

Curt Simmons is a native of Washington and earned a degree in Journalism from Western Washington University in Bellingham. Curt has served in the full-time ministry since 1982, working in eight states and leading churches in Lincoln, Nebraska, Cincinnati, Ohio and St. Louis, Missouri. Curt and his family live in Chicago, where he works as a writer and speaker. Curt's website is www.curtsbooks.com.

You can email Curt at: **csimmons@chnts.net**

Small-Town Heroes. Mike Krzyzewski, head basketball coach, Duke University, says of *Small-Town Heroes:* "A son's love for his father and a solid formula for success are told extremely well in *Small-Town Heroes.* Curt does an amazing job of using the book to send out these and other important messages that all of us should hear." Much more than a story about basketball, *Small-Town Heroes* is focused on the game of life, full of valuable information on the real definition of success and the right direction to travel to find it on every front.

DETAILS - $14.00
ISBN: 0-9776954-1-7. 208 pages. Paperback

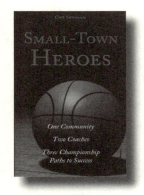

The Unveiling: Exploring the Nature of God. Written in a unique and refreshing style, *The Unveiling* will be hard to put down. Author Curt Simmons blends insights into contemporary culture with an invigorating look at biblical wisdom to show us the real God of the Bible and how he impacts lives.

DETAILS - $12.00
ISBN: 1-577882-0-0. 203 pages. Paperback

The Revealer: The Man, The Majesty, The Model. This book will take you on a trip back to the first century where you'll discover the one who claimed that he alone was the Word made flesh, the way to the Father and the only flawless example when it comes to victorious living! *The Revealer* will help you to understand the Son of God in new ways, to see his humanity, to understand his divinity and to realize how he is the perfect model for our lives.

DETAILS - $14.00
ISBN: 0-9745342-5-0. 264 pages. Paperback

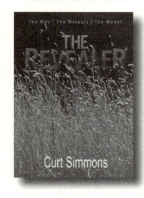